GANGSTERS

AND

GOODFELLAS

THE MOB, WITNESS PROTECTION, AND LIFE ON THE RUN

HENRY HILL

AS TOLD TO GUS RUSSO

M. Evans
Lanham • New York • Boulder • Toronto • Plymouth, UK

Published by M. Evans
An imprint of The Rowman & Littlefield Publishing Group, Inc.
4501 Forbes Boulevard, Suite 200, Lanham, Maryland 20706
www.rlpgtrade.com

Estover Road, Plymouth PL6 7PY, United Kingdom

Distributed by NATIONAL BOOK NETWORK

The hardback edition of this book was previously cataloged by the Library of Congress
as follows:

Hill, Henry, 1943–
    Gangsters and goodfellas : the mob, witness protection, and life on the run / Henry
    Hill as told to Gus Russo.
        p. cm.
    1. Hill, Henry, 1943– 2. Criminals—United States—Biography. 3. Witnesses—
Protection—United States. I. Russo, Gus. II. Title.
    HV6248.H453A3 2004
    364.1'092—dc22
                                                                                    2004001731

ISBN-13: 978-1-59077-029-0 (cloth : alk. paper)
ISBN-10: 1-59077-029-3 (cloth : alk. paper)
ISBN-13: 978-1-59077-129-7 (pbk. : alk. paper)
ISBN-10: 1-59077-129-X (pbk. : alk. paper)

⊗™ The paper used in this publication meets the minimum requirements of American
National Standard for Information Sciences—Permanence of Paper for Printed Library
Materials, ANSI/NISO Z39.48-1992.

Manufactured in the United States of America.

To Kelly and Justin
For your love, patience, and tolerance.
Please forgive me.

ACKNOWLEDGEMENTS

Henry Hill would like to thank: Kelly and Justin; my ex-wife Karen and my daughter, Gina, and her special husband, Greg, and his family; Joe Hill; my sisters; Donald Brown, Bob Pick, Linda Murdock, Stephanie Pick, Mike Mycon, and Cheri DeShaw, for keeping me sober most of the time and for their patience in putting up with me; Bryon Schreckengost, Peter Doyle, and Priscilla Davis; Dawn and Shawn Waters and their three little girls; Darlene Zimel, Scott Murray, Asa, Dr. Canata, Craig Wells and family, Justin Smulison, Jeff Stone, Shannon and Rachel (my two special daughters); Todd Plesco, Boyd Grafmyre and Somer, Ken Bucci, Madeline and Commander Hue; Howard Stern, Robin, and the crew from the shows. All my friends in Washington State, Redmond, Lake Wenatchee, and Leavenworth; special thanks to "Star Spankle Manor" Big Red and all the fine help. Ed McDonald, Al McNeil, John Capp, Ed Guevara, judges

Barker and Warner. The Cold Case Squad of the NYPD, Gus Russo and the excellent ways he has of interpreting the second half of this life so far.

Special thanks to my spiritual advisor, Rabbi Mark Borowitz, and his wife, Harriet, and all the special people in my life I failed to mention—you know who you are.

Gus Russo would like to thank: Noah Lukeman, an indefatigable literary agent who just happens to be a great writing talent in his own right and a tireless protector of his clients' interests. Likewise, my entertainment attorney, Jeffrey Silberman, has gone above and beyond to keep me from being eaten alive by the sharks of Hollywood. At M. Evans, P.J. Dempsey, Matt Harper, and the gang all made useful contributions and suggestions in a spirit of congeniality, encouragement, and mutual respect. Thanks also go to Ed Guevara, Kelly Hill, Nick Pileggi, and Sherry Anders, for taking time to share their memories with me. For me, 2003 was a busy year, and there is no doubt this book would never have been delivered on time without the help of Justin Smulison who, with great attention to detail, transcribed dozens of taped conversations between myself and Henry. Towson University should be proud. And especially, thanks go to Henry Hill, for his trust and friendship. Receiving the call from Henry was particularly meaningful since the film about his early years, *GoodFellas*, just happens to be my favorite mob movie. Getting to know the real Henry has been a great ride with never a dull moment.

CAST OF CHARACTERS

SHERRY ANDERS
Henry's second wife.

BILL ARICO
Rockville Centre, Long Island, enforcer and international hit-man. Bill bought guns from Henry, which he subsequently used to kill Italian bank liquidator Giorgio Ambrosoli during the aftermath of the Vatican Bank scandal.

RABBI MARK BOROVITZ
Coordinator and spiritual leader of Beit T'Shuvah, Rabbi Mark is a convict-turned-rabbi who helped Henry sober up.

JIMMY "THE GENT" BURKE
Henry's mentor growing up and the mastermind behind the Lufthansa Heist, in which $6 million was stolen. After Henry

turned state's evidence, Jimmy set his sights on killing him. Henry's testimony put Burke in prison for life; he died behind bars in April 1996 at the age of 64.

TOMMY "TWO-GUN TOMMY" DeSIMONE
Burke's protégé and one-time Lucchese family hopeful. He was known for his temper, and his nickname came from the matched set of pearl-handled pistols he carried. Tommy was killed (presumably by John Gotti) for his part in the murder of wiseguy Billy Batts and a Gotti associate named Foxy.

JOHNNY "DIO" DIOGUARDI
Old school wiseguy who did time with Henry and Paulie, Sr., while in Lewisburg.

PARNELL STEVEN "STACKS" EDWARDS
A "gofer" and wannabe member of the Burke gang. Presumably killed by Burke's crew after leaving his finger-prints on the wheel of the getaway vehicle used for the Lufthansa Heist.

BOBBY GERMAINE
One of Henry's drug crew, Germaine was a stickup man whose son turned out to be a confidential informant for the FBI.

JOHN "THE DAPPER DON/ THE TEFLON DON" GOTTI
One of the most famous mobsters of the 20th century, he was an up and coming Gambino wiseguy in the '60s and '70s. Gotti died while serving a life sentence on June 10, 2002.

ED GUEVARA
FBI agent who dealt with Henry during the early stages of

turning state's evidence. Ed is currently the head of the Federal Transportation Bureau in Florida.

KAREN FRIEDMAN HILL

Henry's first wife and mother of his children Gina and Greg. After a long separation, they officially divorced in 2002.

KELLY ALOR HILL

Henry's third and current wife, and the mother of his son Justin.

MARTY KRUGMAN

Owner of a wig shop next door to Henry's bar, The Suite. Marty helped plan the Lufthansa heist, but did not take part in the actual robbery. When his demands for his cut of the loot became too much for Jimmy Burke, he was whacked.

RICK KUHN

During the 1978–79 Boston College basketball season, Kuhn was willing to shave points for kickbacks. Henry testified against him in what was known as the Boston College Fix.

GAETANO "TOMMY" LUCCHESE

Namesake of Paulie Vario's Mafia family, the Sicilian-born Lucchese started out as a bootlegging underboss in the 1920s, then graduated to full boss in 1953. From his headquarters in the Bronx, Lucchese oversaw a powerful, if low-key, operation that specialized in gambling, truck hijackings, and labor racketeering, and encompassed not just New York City, but much of Long Island. He died of brain cancer in 1967 (age unknown), but his organization continued to prosper for another decade under Vario.

AL "MARSHAL AL" MCNEIL
Kentucky Witness Protection Program Head Marshal Al McNeil, who was Henry's nemesis during his Kentucky stay.

PAUL MAZZEI
Henry's dope connection in Lewisburg and, eventually, Pittsburgh. Henry's testimony helped get Mazzei seven years on drug charges.

ED McDONALD
Assistant U.S. Attorney for New York who served as Henry's unofficial handler during his time in Witness Protection and eventually became one of Henry's closest friends.

ROBERT "FRENCHY" McMAHON
Numbers runner from Hell's Kitchen who, as an employee at the Air France cargo terminal, helped devise heists with Henry and Burke that brought them millions of dollars in the '60s and '70s. Frenchy was another of Burke's Lufthansa victims.

CP MIDDLETON
Elderly man in Washington who employed Karen as his twenty-four-hour-a-day caregiver. He would live with the Hills for a few days at a time and quickly became a family fixture.

BOB PICK
Henry's friend and business associate, whom he met while in a Malibu Alcoholics Anonymous program. Pick runs PickHill Productions, Henry's movie production company.

NICHOLAS PILEGGI

Famed mob journalist who wrote *Wiseguy* with Henry in 1985, which became the basis for the 1990 film, *GoodFellas*.

LINDA ROTONDI

Henry's most famous *goomah*; Linda and Henry had an ongoing affair that lasted10 for years, even during some of his time in Witness Protection. She died of cancer on February 28, 2003.

JACK VANCE

Kentucky acquaintance who talked Henry into opening a horse-drawn carriage business, and later double-crossed Henry out of a sum of money.

LENNY VARIO

Paulie Vario's "favorite" son, who was Henry's best man at his first wedding. He was burned to death while torching a union job.

PAUL VARIO, JR.

Paulie's son, who introduced Henry to his first wife, Karen.

PAUL "PAULIE" VARIO, SR.

Boss of the Lucchese family, Paul made much of his fortune from bootlegging and expanded to numbers, truck hijackings, and, indirectly, drugs. Henry's testimony in the KENRAC trial put Vario in a Ft. Worth prison, where he died in 1988 at the age of 73.

PETER VARIO

Paul, Sr.'s other son.

TUDDY VARIO
Brother of Paulie Vario, Sr., Tuddy ran the cabstand and pizza joint where Henry spent most of his childhood. He helped run Paul's day-to-day operations and was typically the go-to guy for anyone requesting his brother's help or protection.

INTRODUCTION

*"There's no action. I'm an average nobody.
I get to live the rest of my life like a schnook."*

With those words, spoken first in 1980 then re-enacted and delivered at the end of the 1990 film *GoodFellas*, former mafia associate Henry Hill left the public consciousness and entered the invisible world of the Federal Witness Protection Program. Hill assumed his new life would play out in white-bread, lawn-mowing boredom. He could not have been more mistaken. As Hill now says, "The last twenty-three years on the legit makes my life as a wiseguy seem tame."

Indeed, life for the mob turncoat and his family, saddled with new identities and cut off from everyone they knew and loved, was about to spin out of control in ways unimaginable. Henry's experience is a classic story of survival, redemption, and continuing struggles with personal demons. His adventures since that closing scene in Martin Scorsese's film include tales of quick getaways in the night, landmark court decisions, the occasional fall off the straight wagon—not to mention the effect of it all on Hill's loved ones.

This book affords Henry the chance to finally fill in many of the blanks left largely unresolved in *Wiseguy* (and *GoodFellas*), such as how his family coped with the realization of what Henry had become, what happened to all the cash, and who really whacked whom. This is also an inside story of day-to-day life in "the Program" and the unlikely close bonds formed between captor and captive—that endure to the present day. Laced with Henry Hill's unique sense of humor, the continuing Hill saga begins with his version of the early years with the New York mob, then picks up in 1980 with his family being whisked away for a brief stay in a small guest cottage in the Hamptons, then to Nebraska, where the wide-eyed, Brooklyn-bred hood encounters Big Sky country for the first time. With no notice, the Feds, tipped that Hill's mob enemies are zeroing in, move the family to Kentucky, where Hill gravitates to the world of horseracing. From there the family runs to Redmond, Washington, with Microsoft their next-door neighbor. Throughout, Hill's outgoing personality attracts a range of colorful friends—one could say angels—who take turns staking his attempts to find legitimate success.

In the Northwest, Henry's internal enemies (read *substance abuse*) emerge again. He is sent to prison after his minor role is disclosed in a drug-dealing operation. In federal prison, Hill becomes a target of some fellow inmates who happen to be associated with Paulie Vario and Jimmy

Burke—the bosses Henry had ratted out. After two murder attempts in stir, Henry is sent to another facility.

Eventually, Henry lands squarely in the capital of reinvented lives, Los Angeles, where his lifelong serendipity places him in league with his newest fan, a pillar of the community worth many millions, who sets Henry up in any endeavor he desires. Henry's comparisons of the underworld hoods from his former life to the studio honchos with whom he now deals are revealing.

Henry insists that the story is not merely a succession of gangster tales and eventual success in Hollywood, but, more importantly, one of encouragement for others caught in the throes of drug addiction. During the last twenty-three years of his amazing journey, Henry has struggled to overcome a lifelong addiction to both alcohol and narcotics. Only in the last six years has he seen long stretches of being clean.

In his efforts to give something back, Henry now spends countless hours at prisons counseling young hoods, and at alcohol halfway houses and hospitals giving comfort to the afflicted; he also advises federal and local prosecutors in their ongoing casework—all free of charge. "Between my producing work and all the volunteering, I'm never home," Henry says. "My wife thinks I must be having an affair. It's ironic—when I used to cheat, everything was cool. Now that I'm faithful, I get the third degree. Go figure."

From a personal standpoint, I have to say that Henry Hill is one of the top-ten "characters"—out of thousands over the past few decades—I have ever interviewed. The fast-tongued, quick-witted, hyperactive hood from *GoodFellas* is about as accurate an interpretation of the screen character as I have ever seen. During my first meeting with him, it quickly became apparent how his childhood issues rendered him a virtual lamb waiting to be slaughtered by the world of the gangsters: Henry suffers from dyslexia and attention deficit hyperactivity disorder (ADHD)—both undiagnosed until recently—and genetically inherited alcoholism. The acceptance and status offered by the wiseguys living it up right outside his bedroom window when he was a child seemed the only palliative for the abuse he took in school and at home.

Throughout our association on this project, my role as a prompter and chronicler of Henry's past has been made easy by Henry's gregarious personality. Although I was flattered when Henry called and asked me to help him resurrect his past, one shouldn't conclude that this is a love song to Henry Hill. Henry is the first to admit that for much of his life he was a bad guy who made only weak attempts to break away from the world of crime. But he wants readers to know that even lifelong hoods are capable of change. I believe Henry has made numerous personal improvements since his mob days. Hey, he only threatened to clip me two or three times—just kidding.

So perhaps Henry's story will help others win their own battles with crime or drugs. But I doubt that anyone will do it with more flair than Henry Hill.

—Gus Russo

HENRY HILL: For a guy who has spent less time reading books than Paulie Vario spent on a treadmill, I am the last person from our crew who anyone would guess would eventually write a book. But, hey, a guy's got to make a living. Besides, a lot of people want to know what happened to that character from the movie. I get asked about it constantly: "Hey, Henry, did Paulie's guys ever track you down?" or "What really happened to Tommy?" or "Where's the Lufthansa cash?" or "What about you and Karen?" And that's just for starters.

The fact is that twenty-three years ago I went into the

Federal Witness Protection Program. I was supposed to disappear. I was supposed to change. I had to. I didn't. I honestly thought my life was over and I had to live like a schmuck. I accepted it. I really did, but only for a little while. That revelation didn't last. It was like trying to stop a train, an out-of-control train. I was so used to this lifestyle; I mean, I couldn't sit still. They (the Feds) expected me just to accept my role. Well, when you did what I did for so long, you are conditioned to hustle, to find the loopholes and scores, the excitement and danger. I just couldn't shake that—not even close.

To make matters worse, my wife Karen and the kids were endangered more than ever. Before, they were protected, while I was always in danger. Now they were the ones in the crossfire. They were even targets. The Sicilian Rule was to punish one, if they had slipped away, by killing their family members. It was one of those things to keep everyone in line, to scare you from squealing. I mean, for as dangerous a line of work we chose, we sure didn't let it affect us popping out the kids with our wives and sometimes others. They did away with the rule in the late '80s, but back in the early '80s it was still there. So I had that hanging there. Still, I couldn't quit—too many vices.

I hope by now you get the idea that when it came right down to it, I was anything but a goodfella. To us, a goodfella was a guy who did the time and kept his mouth shut. Once I started talking, I didn't shut up for eight years. They tell me I was directly responsible for sending over fifty of my old friends to the joint, both here and overseas. Some goodfella.

After I sang to the Feds, I really tried to be normal—believe me. But normalcy to a gangster is like another planet, another world. I guess I was gradually going through the process of adjusting to Americana. But the Feds didn't want gradual, they wanted now: "This is who you are, this is what you do, now shut up and do it." Thirty years of the life, and I'm supposed to mow the lawn and wave to my neighbor with a smile, and eat fast food? Right. Thirty years told me every morning, "You are a loser, Henry."

I've had more lives than a cat: second chances, third, and so on. These Feds, for as much shit as they get, sure took care of me in the end. And just because I left New York didn't mean I couldn't find hustlers with the same zest for scores. I met them all: sophisticated coke whores, drug dealers, murderers, stunt men, and the media. They were all just as bad, if not worse, than the old crews in the city. It wasn't all apple pie and happy times out in the country. The whole world is nuts.

So this book is meant to fill in some things that had be left out in *Wiseguy* and *GoodFellas*, and to finally show you some photos of me, my family, and my old crew. We couldn't include them in the first book because I was supposed to be in hiding. As you'll see, those days are long gone. But maybe the biggest reason for this book is to let all of you who stop me in airports, restaurants, and betting windows know what the hell I've been doing with my life. I guarantee you, I haven't just been mowing the lawn.

—Henry Hill

CHAPTER ONE

A HOOD IN THE HAMPTONS

In 1980, my life as a stand-up gangster, a goodfella, came to an end when I entered the Federal Witness Protection Program. I was Witness Number 4427, meaning I was the four thousand, four hundred, and twenty-seventh guy taken in. Today there are probably God knows how many. The Feds took me into the Program on Memorial Day weekend, 1980. My wiseguy days were over. I traded my Brioni and Armani for Levi and Pendelton, and I became a normal citizen. I became Joe Shmoe.

A couple weeks earlier I had been busted for narcotics trafficking, and I was willing to face the six-to-ten-year rap. It was the smallest part of what I had been involved in for the last twenty years, working for the crime families of Queens Irish boss Jimmy "The Gent" Burke and that same borough's Mafia capo, Paulie Vario, of the legendary Tommy Lucchese family. I would have been a goodfella still, until I learned that they were going to whack me, just as they had my boyhood hoodlum pal Tommy DeSimone and countless others. I decided that if I was expendable, then so were they. Fuck 'em.

Because of my mob connections, the Feds were informed of my arrest and immediately took over. When I was pinched on that spring day by Nassau County cops for drugs, the Feds couldn't have cared less about those charges. They didn't want to hear about drugs, even though I knew all about the biggest heroin network in the United States at the time, the so-called Pizza Connection. Honestly, I had to force that on them. When the Pizza Connection trial came up, they never used me. They had a million informants, and I was just one little guy.

But the Feds knew I could open another Pandora's box because the informant who gave me up said I was part of Jimmy Burke's crew. Everyone, even the Feds, knew that Burke had overseen the biggest heist in U.S. history, a six-million-dollar theft from the Lufthansa Cargo Terminal at JFK Airport in 1978. Over a year had gone by, and still no one from the crew had been nabbed. Assistant U.S. Attorney Ed McDonald, who had been in charge of that case, was getting desperate, so when I fell into his lap, it was like a gift from heaven. Except that I wasn't going to give that story up so easy. Before I was accepted into the Program, I danced around with him, giving him other tales, until I felt I had the best deal I was going to get.

■ ■ ■

After my first night in the Manhattan Correctional Center (MCC), I spent the next day in McDonald's office. The in-laws, the kids, Karen—they were all there at the FBI office, tucked away from me in a private conference room.

For weeks prior to this, I had been visited at my home by the Feds, who tried to scare me into flipping by showing me and Karen crime-scene photos. They were graphic scenes that showed the bullet-riddled bodies of the rest of Burke's Lufthansa gang, guys that he ordered whacked. Now I'm in Ed's office, and—surprise—Ed showed me the crime scene photos *again*. By now I had every wound memorized. "Do the math—you're next," he said. "All we want is the Lufthansa shit, but you got to be totally honest. Otherwise, you got no deal."

Then he explained the Witness Protection Program. I would be given transactional immunity for everything I ever did wrong; I could never be charged for anything I had done to this point. In return, I'd have to tell about Lufthansa, then change my name and move thousands of miles away, with no promise of ever being able to contact anyone I ever knew or loved. Karen immediately said she didn't want to go into the Program. So I said to Ed, "We got no deal. I won't leave her behind." But she changed her mind when Ed told her he had her on tape as a co-conspirator. The fact was, she knew a lot. She was there when a contact named Marty Krugman gave me the tip on the Lufthansa transfer, she ran messages to Paulie for me, she helped disguise one of the crew for a heist we pulled at Estee Lauder's East Side apartment. And her parents knew the score, too.

From fifty yards away I could hear her my mother-in-law yelling and screaming at the agents and the U.S. attorneys. She made a scene, carrying on like a banshee in the police station, but she was no idiot. She and her husband knew all along where the money had been coming from, and they'd spent it well all those years. They spent that dirty money for fifteen years. When I was on vacation and I would take them all with me, I'd pick up the tab. And they weren't just innocent bystanders, believe me. In fact, in some of my capers, the in-laws made more profit than me. But that's the way it was. It was normal for me. I lost about one hundred thousand dollars on one deal, but my mother-in-law and her brother made about two hundred thousand each. All her friends made out well. I told them, "Don't tell nobody." They all scored, and I didn't. I felt stupid, but I was doing so many other things that I didn't need the money. So, my mother-in-law knew what was going on. But I got to give it to her, she put on a good show for everyone, screaming at the top of her lungs until I told the cops, "Get her the hell out of here."

So I just flat-out told Ed that we had no deal, and I would not leave my wife and children behind. It was not selfishness on my part. I wish I could have left them behind, but I knew what would happen if I didn't show at the first trial. I had been with my wife for over fifteen years, was with her every day. Once it was done, there would be nothing. At that point I was willing to just go to prison. My co-defendant, Bobby Germaine, wound up doing six years. I heard them telling me twenty years, but I thought that was bullshit. I knew what was going on. First of all, they had nothing on me. They had some tapes—big deal.

So I said, "Hey, Ed, the only way I'll cooperate is if my family goes with me." He told me "absolutely." He totally agreed with me. He knew what the wiseguys were capable of. They had killed two women up to that point. But Karen was still holding out, crying one minute, then calm—the entire range. She was not leaving her family. I made the decision and now the ball was in Ed's court, if he could convince Karen. By that time Karen had gotten indicted by Nassau County, and not just on his tapes; they also had watched her delivering packages to Jimmy for me. She was a co-conspirator. She was half a wiseguy in those days, often running messages to Paulie. (I think she was screwing Paulie.) She was there when my contact tipped me to the Lufthansa stash, so she could've done twenty years herself. She knew about everything, and they knew it.

So now Ed played bad cop and threatened Karen. "If you both stay, you'll both go to prison," he said, "Today. You're not going to see your family anyway. You're a co-conspirator." Which she was, in reality. She could either be missing her family in prison, or in a paid-for house thousands of miles away. Ed said, "Listen, we'll take your in-laws, too. We'll put your whole family in." But Karen's parents decided not to go. Ed told them the possibilities. But they took the risk.

■ ■ ■

Karen finally agreed, and we had to get my mother-in-law out of there so they could take the kids. They agreed to put a car at her house for a couple of months, twenty-four hours a day. Late that afternoon they took us to an airport hotel about a half-hour out of the city, and I got to talk to my attorney on a speakerphone. I hadn't been formally approved yet, but I knew I was unofficially in the Program. We stayed in the hotel for two or three days before they made the arrangement for the safe house. I never went back to my house—never saw it again, even though I had money and diamonds stashed there. I had all kinds of stuff. I tried to hold onto the drugs in the house, too. I had ludes and a couple kilos of heroin in the basement. When I started redoing the house, I had put in special compartments; that's why they never found the drugs on those first visits. I had jewels that I had stolen from the cosmetics tycoon Estee Lauder—about a quarter-million dollars worth of diamonds. I told them where all the diamonds were, knowing that if I wasn't on the up-and-up, they could take away the deal. There still might be stuff stashed to this day, because when I used to get high, I'd stash stuff and then I could never find it. I told Ed Guevara's guys from the FBI what I wanted out of the house, like pots and pans. I gave them a list.

I still own that house in a beautiful area in Rockville Centre, but it's in my sister-in-law's name and she told me to go screw myself. She's still living there, having converted it into three apartments, and she kept one. It's up to about $700,000 in value. She did kick back some money to me, and it paid for my son's college and law school.

From that point on the Feds were always with me. There was a squad that was made up of six-man teams. There was always a team with us in the next two rooms.

FORMER FBI AGENT ED GUEVARA: At the FBI office in Queens, the place was a madhouse. There were four agents, Henry's wife, kids, his in-laws, his sisters-in-law. They had come because they had no idea when they'd see the Hill family again. And we couldn't tell them because we had no idea, either. There were tears and recriminations. Karen's mother in particular was screaming at Henry about how all this was his fault. . . . We had no idea what to tell them to pack—we were young agents with surprisingly little input from our superiors. All the while Henry was bouncing off the walls—literally. He couldn't sit still—probably something to do with all the drugs he was on. All Henry cared about was getting his huge collection of big old cooking pots out of his house in Rockville Centre. We took as many as we could and, by the end of the week, we were glad we did—when Henry was relocated, he cooked feasts for us.

I signed the Witness Protection contract after reading that thing over and over and over. The bottom line: new names, new location, no contact with family or friends, and $1,500 per month walkaround money. Al McNeil, the head marshal of the Program, played tough guy with me. "This ain't going to be a free lunch," he said. If they caught me in one lie, they could revoke my agreement. The initial Witness Protection agreement read, "just the Lufthansa robbery." To tell the whole story, I had to go into all this other shit; they soon realized that they had hit the jackpot, and they were going to learn about twenty years of Lucchese madness. When I signed on I wasn't sure about my future, but I knew that their careers were made.

When they put me in the Program, they offered it to everyone in my family and everyone in my wife's family. But none of them wanted to go along. It was their decision not to go. Paulie and Jimmy loved my mother and my little brother, so I knew I didn't have too much to worry about there. They were all going to my sister's. And my big brother, Joe, was in California. So that was it. It was just me, Karen, and the kids.

Al McNeil read us this whole book of rules—rules about letters, phone calls, travel—you name it. They would arrange for me to call my family from time to time. But they would want me to go to the marshal's office and use their secure phones. They would go and get my family, or send a message to my family or to my in-laws, and tell them to go to a certain phone booth and make sure they weren't followed. I suppose some guys could live this way. I knew I couldn't, but I didn't tell Ed that. I knew it was only a matter of time before I cracked and the whole thing fell apart. I don't know if the marshals could tell what was coming. I never asked for counseling, but they would've gotten me anything I wanted. We're talking twenty-three years ago. Counseling wasn't as common then. They didn't have shit set up. I'm sure today they have a whole regimen for someone going into witness protection, but not then.

The first night after I flipped, my family stayed in a motel with federal agents. The next morning we drove out to the Hamptons, to an abandoned rental cottage that was owned by an agent. It was part of a big estate, located right on the beach. When we got there it wasn't in good shape, but Ed McDonald and his guys bought mattresses and stuff. Actually, the place was a moldy dump, but the Feds did everything they could to make us comfortable. Any requests we had they tried to grant. The sky was the limit as far as what we spent on food or other life necessities. They paid for everything, which was fine by me. We ate like kings, and I cooked for everyone—not just my wife, Karen, and the kids, but all the marshals and agents who were around. I'd plan the night's menu in the car while they moved us from one town to another, and the minute we arrived, I'd get two Feds to push shopping carts at the supermarket. We loaded up on lobster and filet mignon. These guys never ate like this before.

My talent in the kitchen goes hand-in-hand with my former profession, since a big part of the whole wiseguy experience was eating. It might still be, for all I know. Food was the center of a wiseguy's day. When you've got a belly full of lasagna or fresh sausage and peppers, you're in a better mood. You're nourished, and your mind is clear and ready to start making decisions about how to skin the potatoes for dinner, who to bribe, who to rough up, or who to whack. You'll never see a stick figure for a mobster—even on television. A mobster may be thin, but only in comparison to the blimp he's sharing a cannoli with. A wiseguy's daily life revolves around food for logical reasons, because he eats wherever he goes. His agenda is to start with his colleagues over breakfast, then he sips some coffee with another friend, and then he's off to his place of business, which is usually a restaurant, where he hangs out with *paisans* until he goes out for another meeting over a light meal and drinks. Then he returns home to join in the family's dinner. The best way to get on a wiseguy's good side is through his stomach.

I was thirteen years old when the 1957 Apalachin Raid went down.* That's when I heard on the radio how important food was to all the nation's wiseguys. There was a special newsbreak coming from the radio that my mother had left on in the kitchen. Federal agents had raided the meeting of all the top mobsters from California to Kansas to New York and everywhere in between. And while the dons and wiseguys dashed into the nearby woods, a bunch of the agents sat down and ate the leftovers on the tables. There was radicchio and top-notch prosciutto. (Back in 1957, grade-A imported prosciutto was all the evidence the government needed to prove there was a Mafia in the U.S.)

It dawned on me that being handy with pots and pans was just as important as being able to shake a guy down. There was the next big meeting of the Mob's top guys a few years later in Sicily. They figured the old country was a safer place to convene than upstate New York. My stomach growled, thinking what those guys were having for dinner halfway across the world. Paul Castellano, the godfather of the Gambino family, was rubbed out en route to Sparks Steak

---

*The Apalachin gangland convention raid by U.S. Treasury agents, and local and state police, at an outdoor cookout in Apalachin, New York, where a who's-who of organized crime had gathered.

House in New York City 1985. History repeats itself in the Mob, usually when godfathers get whacked, they are either going into a restaurant, eating in one, or leaving one. The movie *The Godfather* was pretty accurate in the assassination attempt of Vito Corleone at the vegetable stand outside his office. I can say from personal observation that good, hearty Italian food was the wiseguy's Achilles heel.

As for me, I was something of a Mob mutant. Early on I developed a taste for higher cuisine. I couldn't just load up on any swill that was drenched in tomato sauce. Maybe that was one of the reasons dons packed it on after they hit forty—they ate anything that was Italian, especially the most fattening dishes. Sometimes people will ask me how I stayed so thin if I was eating so much. One reason is that I eat well. I shop well. I could be a nutritionist. In fact, I later studied that in jail. I used to watch my mother, who was a great cook and taught me all those authentic Italian recipes. Simple. My metabolism was in overdrive from nervous energy, and I was constantly on the move. Some guys just don't get heavy. All my sisters are huge. I'm the smallest one in the family, five-ten in heels. Twenty years later I got up to almost 200 pounds, but by then I was heavy into coke, so I'd go on the actors' diet—less food, more coke. Who needed that low-carb garbage? I don't like to be fat. I had a twenty-nine-inch waist until I was almost forty years old. But when I finally did put on weight it was because I had gotten crazy with coke.

■ ■ ■

In no time, I became friendly with all the agents. We'd get drunk every night and had a ball. They gave me a white tennis cap so they could spot me when I walked on the beach. Maybe this wasn't going to be so bad after all. I mean, who doesn't like the Hamptons?

The first day in the Hamptons was nice. I really had a sense that I was about to enter a new chapter of my life—hell, it was a whole new book. We were living with ten officers; five FBI at all times, on shifts. I cooked, they debriefed.

My kids, Greg and Gina, were unbelievable. They thought it was all real cool with the agents coming and going with machine guns. The kids took it in stride and never really voiced an opinion about my past. But Karen was miserable. All she talked about was her mother.

I was not in fear when I was with the Feds. Never. I was never even in fear when I eventually got into the courtroom with my former Mob bosses. But I felt like a piece of shit sometimes, so I had a doctor give me valium. I was off drugs, but drinking a little and sometimes eating too many valium pills.

I got to know the Feds real fast, and I have to admit they weren't the schmucks we had convinced ourselves they were for all those years. Steve Carbone was the head of the Lucchese squad at the time. He later had problems because his brother was a wiseguy. He never got indicted, but he got demoted and retired. Now, he's half a wiseguy himself. Seriously. And *he* would threaten *me*. I'd say, "Get the hell out of my face."

Edmondo Guevara, who looks like a movie actor, is now head of the Federal Transportation Bureau in Florida; he dresses in Armani suits and four-hundred-dollar shoes. I guess if you're working undercover you can afford nice clothes. He was a kind of short guy, but he was a Latino G-man during the affirmative action thing, so he moved up the chain fast—not because he was Hispanic, but because he was given a chance to show how sharp he was. He went to Washington as a suit, and he became a boss of the FBI—one of the main bosses. I think part of his success is because of my arrest, which was definitely a career-maker. He pole-vaulted right up the corporate ladder with the government, all off my case.

Now, another guy on squad was Tom Sweeney. This guy is a character, and the nicest human being you could ever meet. But, he is Mister Book. Every move he made he cleared through Washington and through his office, but he became one of my mentors and my best friends. They all did: Ed McDonald, Tom Sweeney, Ed Guevara, and John Capp, head the Brooklyn-Queens office of the Lucchese squad. He was second-in-command under Carbone. We used to call him Barney Rubble.

■ ■ ■

Most mornings I'd be driven back to the city, where the debriefs took place. They had a special building in Manhattan—I don't remember exactly where it was, but that's probably a good thing. I'm sure that the wiseguys know where it is today. It looks like a normal office building, but you can't get in from the street level. You pull into this underground garage, the garage doors open, shut, and then another door opens, and then you go into another sub-basement and it looks like you've walked into a hotel lobby, even down to the murals on the walls. Each room has a different setting, and each office door is wired with a ton of monitors.

There were a half-dozen FBI agents in there most times; probably three during the night. During the early morning hours, they would be transporting guys like me. At any given time there might have been a dozen rooms with informants coming and going, but we didn't have contact with each other. Although they tried to keep us as separate as possible, we did occasionally make eye contact. I saw Jimmy "The Weasel" Fratianno there one day.

So I would go there most every morning, and I'd be

there just as everyone else would be punching in. On some days we'd go to the U.S. Attorney's office in the court building. It was another very, very secure place. Real secure. It had a big library, big conference room, and maybe three dozen offices all manned with U.S. attorneys. If they were going to debrief me, most of the time we would go into the library if it wasn't being used, which was nice and comfortable.

There was a parade of other law enforcement agencies always wanting to see me: the Brooklyn District Attorney's office, the Manhattan District Attorney's office, the FBI Lucchese squad, the ATF—you name it. The usual routine was that two or three agents would interview me at the same time, just firing questions at me constantly: "One more question, one more question." It was terribly draining.

■　■　■

There was always a difference between what they knew and what they thought they knew. One of the funny things that happened during the debriefs had to do with something they had overheard from one of my wiretapped conversations, something about "the Big Irishman." Nassau County's district attorney would come to me at Ed McDonald's office every day when I was there, and say, "Hey, prick, you've got to give up Carey, the Big Irishman." See, on these two months of wiretaps that Nassau County had on us, there were constant references to "the Big Irishman." Now, the district attorney's office thought we were talking about New York Governor Hugh Carey, since Paulie's next-door neighbor at his waterfront property in Island Park was the governor's brother.

"What are you, fucking crazy?" I said. "You're gonna put words in my mouth. Get the hell out of here." It was the funniest thing, because the Irishman was, of course, Jimmy Burke. But they had put one district attorney away—we were in prison with the guy—and they were juiced for another big headline-making collar. I'll bet to this day they still believe Governor Carey was in bed with Vario and the Luccheses.

Anyway, this kind of thing would go on until I'd tell them I had to stop. Then I'd take a smoke break, or get some coffee. Sometimes I stayed over, and the facility that we lived in at night had menus for just about every restaurant in the area. If I wanted to eat *scungilli*, if I wanted to eat Chinese, or Japanese, or whatever, they took care of it. If I had to stay overnight, they put me up in a secure building where they housed informants. My room was set up just like a hotel room, except that it had a camera on the ceiling. I was monitored 24/7 even in the bathroom.

During the course of all the interviews, I learned a lot from Ed about what life was like working for Uncle Sam. Truth is, these Feds weren't half as bad as I had been led to believe. In fact, guys like Ed were downright terrific, and I quickly learned that I could trust him. So I decided to tell him what it was like to work for my "uncles," Jimmy Burke and Paulie Vario.

CHAPTER TWO

THE WISEGUYS AND THEIR WORLD

I was born on June 11, 1943, the son of Henry and Carmella Hill, and one of eight kids. Not long after I was born we moved to the Brownsville section of Brooklyn. I often wonder what my life would have been like if I hadn't grown up in a kingdom overseen by powerful hoods like Paulie Vario and Jimmy "The Gent" Burke—the very neighborhood that spawned the legendary gang known as Murder, Incorporated.

Growing up, I lived in a happy home. It really was. There were eight kids who all got along pretty well. My mother was always the loving, wonderful Italian mother. She had dinner on the table every night, and we had to sit down and say our prayers. It was a fun childhood, but from the start I was consumed by rebelliousness. I don't make excuses for what I did during those years. Most of it was my fault, but there were other contributing factors to my behavior that I can no longer ignore. The real problems were my father's alcoholism and my own learning disabilities.

My father was a heavy drinker, whiskey mostly. Today I can relate to it so much, since it's obvious I inherited his booze gene. He would start drinking in the morning. I'd awake sometimes when he'd get up and I'd see him stop at the liquor store first, pick up a fifth of Fleischman's, and drink half that fifth in the morning; he'd save the rest. It was his version of a wake-up call. Honest to God, this guy— I don't know how he drank so much. When he got home from work at four o'clock, he'd go straight to the liquor store again, pick up a fifth and some wine—he loved wine—a gallon of Gallo. He used to keep it at the foot of his chair at the head of the table. He'd bring the two bottles home, shower, change, have a few drinks in the house, and then he'd walk down to the corner to the bar. And it was quiet for a while, until about six or six-thirty, when my mother would say, "Henry, boy, go get Daddy at the bar." Sometimes he'd make me sit next to him and introduce me to his friends. I'd have a Coke.

My father would stagger by the schoolyard when I was hanging out with my friends, and my classmates would laugh while he stumbled from one telephone pole to the next. How embarrassing that was for me? It alienated me from him. I don't know if he got this way because of his genes, or what. I guess we made him crazy in the house with eight kids. I think he was just overwhelmed by the size of his family and the pressure of having to feed and clothe all of us. It's interesting, but the booze problem rubbed off only on me—eight kids, and I was the one who inherited that.

My parents didn't want me hanging out in the schoolyard because it was a regular, Jewish-Italian, blue-collar neighborhood, and there were a lot of gangs that used dope. I now realize that my folks were trying to protect me, but I didn't know it then. I was a kid.

In the schoolyard, while the Jewish guys played basketball, the Italian kids would be on on those big long steps of the school, the landings, playing cards, with another gang on the corner smoking pot. My father saw what was going on there and didn't like it—just like he didn't want me hanging out at the cabstand where the wiseguys were. He realized what was happening there. He said, "Those are fucking bums." I said, sarcastically, "Yeah, they're bums, with the diamond rings and the woman and all that. Dad, we ain't even got a car."

I was a good little kid going to school, but I was a bad student because I was dyslexic and had attention deficit hyperactive disorder (ADHD). I didn't realize it, of course. Nobody did. I just thought I was stupid. None of those things were diagnosed in those days. So I spent most of my school days outside the classroom. I stopped going to school in junior high—eighth grade, I guess. I went to about twenty-six days of high school, and I didn't even go on those days—I cut most of them after I got there.

Around that time, I was introduced to the world of the wiseguys. The bedroom window that I shared with my brother was diagonally across from the cabstand where the flashy wiseguys congregated. We spent many nights just watching them out the window. To me, anyway, it looked like a better life: to see the excitement that went on there, the gaiety, the

Cadillacs pulling up, the guys outside in suits—we didn't see people in suits except in church on Sundays. These were the role models for me: these women and these guys getting ready to go to the Copa every night. Then they would sit outside all night long and play cards, laughing and drinking with a bottle of J&B on the table. In my neighborhood, who had a Cadillac? Who wore silk suits? Who had a beautiful woman on each arm?

I just couldn't stay away—I'd start cutting school or go there right after school. When I first went across the street, it looked like a nice, clean operation. They had limousines and cabs outside. The first job I got was washing their cars with my friend Clemy, who lived a couple of houses down. His father owned a plumbing company. I thought we were poor schmucks. In my eyes, at that age, that's what I considered myself.

I didn't meet Paulie Vario, the boss of all the local wiseguys, right away. First I met his brothers, Lenny and Tuddy. Lenny was a union delegate and Tuddy, the youngest, had a wooden leg and walked with a limp. Me and Tuddy became real friendly, and soon the Varios gave me a job washing cars—I was also hired to clean Paulie's boat. That's where I learned to drive and park cars, because across from the cabstand was a parking lot for the subway station. I was twelve years old and driving Cadillacs. Paulie used to pull up there in his Cadillac. It all happened so naturally; I became a wiseguy before I knew what hit me.

Funny, but the truant officers never came after me. The cops, who used to walk their beat there, with their sticks, would bother me occasionally. But they never really did anything to me because they knew I was affiliated with the cabstand.

At first my parents thought I was going to school every

day, but they eventually caught on. By the time I was fifteen years old, I had a union card. I was in the Laborer's Union, Lenny's union. I actually attempted to work there a couple times. The foreman used to pick me up in the mornings and drive me to the job sites. The first day they tried to make me push a freaking wheelbarrow. I couldn't; I weighed eighty pounds and couldn't move the thing. They tried to show me how to push it with my thumbs, how to balance a thing full of concrete. And then you had to run it up a ramp to the elevator. So Paulie said, "You know what you do? You walk around the building and pick up the papers between each glazed brick. And then at nine o'clock you go for coffee; at nine fifteen you take numbers; at eleven you take the horses . . ." When they finally got to like me, this became my real job—collecting bets for the gang. Basically, they knew I could keep my mouth shut, so I got involved with the numbers.

And I still got a union paycheck at the end of the week: $114 a week. Good money. My father was bringing home maybe a deuce a week. That was big money, too. He paid $6,700 for a house.

I didn't know how important those guys were. How could I know? But my eyes used to light up like a Christmas tree. And the money! The guys from Murder, Incorporated used to hang out there during the daytime and drop a bundle on me. I'd get a five-dollar bill for parking their car for them. You know how much that was in them days?

■ ■ ■

It's real simple what made Paulie rise to boss—violence. Not only was he smart and tough, he had five brothers for extra muscle. But most important, he was tight with Tommy Lucchese, who was old-world Mafia, royalty among criminals. Paulie and his brother Tuddy were made at a real young

33

age by the Luccheses—that was enough by itself to guarantee respect on the street. In the bootlegging days the Luccheses made a lot of money, and Paulie followed in their paths. He had a huge stash of cash because he didn't have any bad habits—except screwing and drinking. He wasn't a gambler. He was a tightwad. Well, not a tightwad, but frugal. When he used to go out, he'd have $10,000 in his pocket and he'd ask me, "Go get a credit card. You got a credit card? You got a muldoon [stolen credit card] with ya?" But it didn't matter anyway, because anywhere we went, the owners would be too scared to charge Paulie and his crew for anything. If he didn't want to pay, he didn't have to pay.

If you crossed him, then that was it. You were fucking dead. God knows how many people he whacked for Lucchese. I saw Paulie beat a woman with a baseball bat. This was probably in the '60s—maybe '65 or '66. At the time, Paulie was doing one of his barmaids, who also managed one of his joints. For some reason, this broad ratted him out to his wife, and Paulie hit the roof. He took me over to the barmaid's apartment. I couldn't believe what happened. First of all, I thought he was going to send me up there. "I ain't gonna hit a fucking woman," I said. I didn't have to; Paulie clocked her himself, and I thought he was going to kill her. We went right in the house and up the stairs of her apartment. He broke her arm, her shoulder, and her collarbone. It was disgusting. And she never turned him in.

The bosses also practiced tradition. Looking back, it seems so immature now, like a bunch of overgrown children with their little clubs. But it also worked. See, the old bosses were made guys already. They had their own families and crews. They owned the city; they were princes of the city. It all came about because of prohibition in the 1920s. Without prohibition, these guys would have been nothing. But those temperance idiots made guys like Vario and Lucchese rich and powerful through bootlegging. And because of their tradition, they always took care of the old lenders back in Italy. Today it's not so important to be a made guy. It's all about money, not about the tradition anymore. The tradition went when Mustache Petes died, and the drugs took over. It got so ass-backwards. The mob changed so much from the '60s and '70s when I was running the streets. Now it's all turned into shit. Everybody's an informant, or half an informant. It's crazy.

Guys like Paulie and Jimmy did it all for the respect. The power. The ego. It wasn't about the money. For some guys like me, it was about the money. I needed money to cover my ass. And we paid cash for everything. This way, there were no records or credit card receipts.

But the old-timers screwed up. They didn't pay taxes. They were morons in some ways. They wanted all this power, and yet they never planned what to do with the money they were making. That was the hardest part; hiding the money, not making the hit. So a lot of those guys, they'd have a secret stash somewhere. Paulie used to keep a million, a million-and-a-half, in his mother's house in a safe. It's funny, but in a lot of ways, Paulie never really knew how to live. I mean those guys didn't know how to enjoy themselves. Some of those guys, they didn't go off their blocks. They wouldn't go out of their own neighborhoods—I'm talking for fifty years.

But Paulie did have a beautiful boat, a forty-four-foot Chris Craft with no name on it licensed in his cousin Steven Otto's name. The dock was at Paulie's house in Island Park, on the water. For you non–New Yorkers, this area, Paulie's kingdom, was a strip of beachfront communities on the southern flank of Brooklyn. All the towns are connected by

the Belt Parkway, which I was soon able to drive with my
eyes closed. The Belt led all the way to Idlewyld Airport—
later renamed JFK International—which just happened to
be Paulie's personal golden goose and free one-stop shopping center. For a while he kept the boat in Johnson's
Boatyard in Brooklyn, a big place in nearby Sheepshead Bay.
All the wiseguys had their big boats, and there was another
country club, a beach club in another coastal town,
Canarsie, where we all used to keep our boats. They used to
use those boats to dump guys with cement shoes. I took my
boat out one year about three times, just barely took it out
of the bay to use it like a hotel room.

■ ■ ■

Anyway, I fit in real smooth with Paulie's style. Paulie, of
course was a made mafioso, meaning he was one of the elite
few Italian wiseguys invited to go through an elaborate ini-
tiation ritual that bound him not only to a life of crime, but
to keeping his mouth shut. In Paulie's world, this was the
greatest honor, and it brought with it immense respect, not
only from other hoods, but from a huge part of the community. See, the Mafia always knew how to work the mass-
es, always giving away money and jobs like water. It was
brilliant, and it's exactly how they reeled me in. Since I was
only half-Italian (actually Sicilian, on my mother's side), I
could never really be made, but I could care less. I would
never be able to rise to the level of boss, or even underboss,
but I didn't care—I just wanted the action. In 1955, Vario
landed me a "no-show" union bricklayer job. But I was
actually a runner for bookies and fencemen who peddled
hot merchandise. I was first arrested in 1959 for stolen
credit cards, and it "broke my cherry."

It's a fact that after you do time you gain the respect
of your crew, and after I was pinched that's exactly what

happened to me. Now every day I'd go to sit-downs with Paulie. He used to introduce me as his nephew. And he'd let me sit there; I'd get up to leave the table and he'd say, "Nah. Nah. Sit down. This is my nephew." If you remember the movie *The Godfather*, I was like the kid that they adopted, Tom Hagen—Robert Duvall's character. I knew all the bosses, every boss in the city, and they thought I was Paulie's nephew. They didn't even know my last name; they thought it was an alias. The cops used to bust my balls. "What's your name?" "Henry Hill." Ba-boom. "What's your real name?" "Henry Hill." Ba-boom. They didn't like that I was lying. "Okay, you cocksucker." After about the third time I got hit with their billy clubs, I'd give them my mother's maiden name. "Okay, I'm Henry Costa." So somewhere in Brooklyn, there's a file for Henry Costa written by some dumb copper in the 1950s.

As a young guy, I used to see Tommy Lucchese every day. And I didn't pay attention, really. I didn't give a fuck. Since I knew I wasn't going to be made as a young kid, it gave me the latitude to talk to any boss in New York without going through my boss, without getting an okay. I didn't have to go through the chain of command. I should have been expendable, not being a made guy, but all the bosses thought I was Paulie's nephew. They used to call me the Mayor of Queens Boulevard. I was still just a kid.

Johnny Dio (Dioguardi) was the legendary union controller who had come up in New York's legendary Murder, Inc. gang of the '30s. He was a hell of an earner and one of the first true stylish hoods. He had more style than even John Gotti. And Paulie was the same way. When these guys became bosses of their families, they became gods in their own minds. On the other hand, this front they put up didn't hide the fact that these guys were also capable of being complete idiots. Most of the new guys like Paulie were the biggest suckers in the world for schemes; they'd go for a scheme in a New York minute. They'd put up hundreds of thousands in a heartbeat, and I'd look at them like they were nuts. They'd lose two-hundred large in a scheme, and yet at the same time they wouldn't bet two dollars on a horse. Someone comes up to them with a fish story and they'd go along hook, line and sinker—but they'd also make sure they got repaid.

There were always a lot of young guys trying to get to the bosses with get-rich-quick ideas. Constantly. So they would have to go through the underbosses, and then the real bosses would have their enforcers steal the scheme— some of the big bosses were greedy bastards. They wanted a piece of everything. If you had a hot dog stand, they wanted their nickel.

A classic old-world boss like Carlo Gambino understood how to go low profile. The new breed acted like they were invincible. Big mistake. The New York crews used to like seeing their names in the papers, even back then. It was like we never heard of Al Capone and Lucky Luciano, and where all that ink landed them. We didn't get it. I remember the first time I saw my name in the paper, after I got pinched with ten or fifteen bosses. My name was in the papers a few other times, too, but I remember this one time it was the headline. It was a feeling of power. And Paulie couldn't get pissed since the headline was there because of stuff I was doing for him.

Paulie never yelled at me. I used to break his balls constantly—his buttons were so easy to push—but he never unloaded on me for it. Me, this guy Brooksy—another guy who wasn't Italian—and Jimmy used to take Paulie's wife Phyllis out. She was young and beautiful. We'd be somewhere and she'd say, "Let's go rolling." That's what we used to call it. And we'd hit the Copa, the Latin Quarter, or the Blue Angel. Paulie would only go out Saturday nights; even after I got married in 1965, I'd always go with him, usually with my wife and his wife. Sometimes Jimmy used to go also. When Paulie walked into a nightclub, people started kissing his ring. It was unbelievable. At the Copa, each family had their own table. If we didn't want to sit ringside, which I didn't like unless someone like Sammy Davis, Jr., was there, we'd sit up by the balcony where we could look down on the Gambinos at their tables, this other crew at their tables, and the black mafia at their tables.

At that time, if Paulie had three beers, he'd be shitfaced. But I remember back in the early days he could drink a bottle of Chivas in a night. He either drank that or beer. Paulie wouldn't drink before dark, even till the end (whereas Jimmy Burke drank constantly—it didn't matter).

I socialized with Paulie all the time. Every Saturday night we went out. We'd go to dinner and then we'd go to the Copa or the Latin Quarter. This went on for many years. In the '70s, I even talked Paulie into seeing the great Scorsese movie *Mean Streets*. That was one of my favorite movies at the time. Me and Bobby Brooks—"Brooksy"—took him to see it one day. I had to talk him into it. If it wasn't a cowboy movie, he didn't like it. He loved the shoot-'em-ups. And he loved *Mean Streets*.

While I'm on mob movies, I remember going to see *The Godfather* with my girlfriend when it came out in 1972. We had heard a lot about it, and everybody had said that they didn't use the word *Mafia* once—they had reached an "arrangement" with Joe Columbo, the New Jersey boss. Everybody's waiting for it to come out opening night. They didn't have valet movies at this joint, so we parked the car.

I watched that movie, and I don't think I got up once. And that's not like me. I'm always up and down, up and down, what with my attention deficit disorder. We came out of that movie and got into my new Riviera and I reached down under my seat and pulled out my pistol and placed it behind the small of my back. I just felt powerful. It was such a great feeling.

And Paulie's guys loved it. It made them feel big-time, too. I mean, they were big-time before that, don't get me wrong. It just gave them a sense of empowerment. The fact that it wasn't realistic didn't matter. It was an ego trip. Some stuff was made up for *The Godfather*, and the real gangsters started using those words. You go anywhere, and somebody's going to use some line from that movie. I get it 24/7, especially now. That's why I don't want to stay around one place too much. But I still watch it when it's on television. I don't watch *GoodFellas*, but I'll watch *The Godfather* for the eighty-seventh time it's on.

And there were constantly women who were gangster groupies. Unbelievable. And the actresses! They see you—the nice, fun part of you; they wouldn't see you digging holes and burying motherfuckers, or hitting people with bats. They just see the party and booze. Burke and Vario probably had women after them all the time. Jimmy's girlfriend was Tommy DeSimone's sister—a beautiful girl, Phyllis. He went out with her when she was sixteen years old—and she was best friends with his wife. We had one cardinal rule: "Don't mess around with the boss' wife." You did, and you'd get whacked. There was so much insanity going on. It was all bullshit.

CHAPTER THREE:

A FULL-TIME
WISE GUY

My life at the time was one big contradiction. On the one hand, I was seduced by Paulie's lifestyle, but at the same time I was nagged by my Catholic upbringing. This wouldn't last much longer, as I would eventually give in completely to the pull of the underworld. But in 1960 I was still struggling with the last vestiges of a conscience, so I joined up and became an army paratrooper, a half-hearted attempt to escape the life. Typical for me, I lied about my age—I told them I was eighteen, when I was actually just seventeen.

The army was a trip and a half. Fort Bragg, North Carolina, where I was stationed, was like the planet Mars to a young street hood. I was a kid who hadn't gotten his Italian loafers scuffed in years. Hell, I had no idea what the term camping out even meant. There were no woods in Brooklyn. And campfires? The only fires I ever saw lit were when the hoods torched some joint in an insurance scam. But guess what? I loved it. Military life introduced me to the world of the great outdoors, an appreciation that would come full circle forty years later. And it was no surprise when I easily qualified on the shooting range. I'm sure I was the only guy in my platoon who knew firsthand how to shoot a guy to death *before* joining the army. Of course, those lousy M-16s with all their recoil were no match for the handguns I was used to. But I adapted.

I was also able to exploit my love of cooking when I got myself assigned to the kitchen. It was this assignment that also convinced me I was a hood at heart. See, I couldn't resist the temptation to fence all the leftover food from the mess; I saw right away that the amount of food that was discarded was not only obscene, but could fetch a king's ransom. So I started selling off stuff, mostly coffee, butter, and condiments at the bars and restaurants we'd frequent across the state line in South Carolina on the weekends. Often, it just covered our bar tab, but it was a score nonetheless and it gave me a rush.

It was a hell of a time to be in the military. The Cold War was at its height, and it made the mob wars in New York seem like child's play. We were always on alert if things would flare up in Berlin or Cuba. I was sent to Florida twice, during the Bay of Pigs invasion and the Cuban missile crisis. We thought we were going in for sure both times.

We were on alert so much that it got me into AWOL trouble a couple times when I'd arrive back late from leave only to find that my troop had left base, sent out on more alert bullshit. So I got two court marshals for going AWOL; no big deal, but I served an extra two months to make up my away time and the time I served in the brig. I could have gotten out two months earlier than I did, but I didn't want to be a wimp. It's a damn good thing I got on the Army's good side since I ended up with an honorable discharge, and those GI benefits, especially the health insurance, have been a lifesaver a hundred times over.

■ ■ ■

Not long after I got "pardoned" by the Army, I went into the untaxed cigarette business after I met Jimmy "The Gent" Burke, the tough Irish boss of Brooklyn, Queens, and the best parts of Long Island. He was actually a Columbo first, but he had an Irish crew. He was a legend. In fact, cigarettes were the reason for me getting hooked up with Burke. Cigarettes were his gig. I had met him earlier at crap games. Paulie's brother, Tuddy, took me down to meet him one day at the dress shop they owned on Lefferts Boulevard in South Ozone Park, next to Robert's Lounge, which Jimmy Burke owned. Burke gave me his address and told me to show up at his house the next day, where he loaded my trunk with cigarettes. I think we were paying a buck and a quarter a carton at the time and he says you could get a deuce a carton. That was my first real "going-to-work" job.

There were guys who hated Jimmy but were afraid to make a move on him. Jimmy was even more violent than Paulie. Fuhgeddaboutit. Years later I saw him strangle columnist Jimmy Breslin one day in my joint, The Suite, a restaurant I had purchased by then. It was in '69 or '70. Breslin, who lived in Rockville Centre in Nassau County, was a syndicated columnist for the *Daily News*, and was known for his mob stories. He used to stop in my joint every day on the way home (from Manhattan, east through Brooklyn, then to Rockville) to milk his sources and kick a few back. Anyway, Breslin, who liked to show an Irish tough-guy image, wrote something that Jimmy didn't like. He wrote about Paulie and some black numbers guy. Jimmy grabbed him by his tie and almost killed him. Jimmy was so powerful. He just tightened the tie and had Breslin begging for his life—and there were fifty people in the place at the time. Jimmy didn't give a fuck. Jimmy had the hugest fore-arms I had ever seen. If he grabbed a hold of you, you weren't getting away. I guess Jimmy felt he needed to show Breslin what it really meant to be a tough Irishman. Hysterical. We laughed about that one all night. In 1971, Breslin wrote a goofy book parody of the Brooklyn crews called *The Gang That Couldn't Shoot Straight*. Everybody thought it was all such a joke. But all I remember is that Breslin wasn't doing much laughing that night at The Suite. (Ironically, when that stupid book was made into a movie, a young Bobby DeNiro played an Italian bicyclist who gets in trouble with this inept New York mob. Years later, Bobby played the real Jimmy Burke in the movie *GoodFellas*.)

But Burke was like a split personality. At times he had a heart of gold. Come Mother's Day, Christmas, Easter, he'd buy twenty-dozen roses, and he'd go to the houses of the mothers and wives of everybody who was in the can and drop off envelopes. He'd be stoned on blow, and he'd go borrow $10,000. A lot of kids' hospital bills were comp'd by Jimmy. There was that nice, good Jimmy Burke. After Huey Mulligan died, Jimmy was like a kindly Irish godfather. That's why the Westies Irish gang in Manhattan and all their guys loved him. He'd take care of everybody. If the guy could have been made in New York, he could've been president of the United States. His charming personality and way he could work a room reminds me of former President Clinton.

The trick to staying on top was to have the toughest, most crazed crew in town. That lunatic Tommy DeSimone, the guy they called Tommy "Two Guns," was a prime example of this kind of hood, who would shoot a guy for looking at him sideways, or just because he felt like trying out a new gun. And there were a dozen guys like Tommy in our crew. See, our crew was the most powerful crew because we were the most violent crew. That's why no one would mess with us. And Paulie didn't care. He'd go to sit-downs with Carlo Gambino and tell Carlo, "Go fuck yourself." He was a little *umbats* (crazy).

I took care of Paulie even though he never got into the cigarette scam. I kicked some back to him out of respect. I also took care of his brothers Lenny and Tuddy. So I was like their cigarette guy. Nobody from our crew was in the cigarette business until I got into it. We were paying a dollar-fifty a carton and you could sell them for about four bucks a carton. In the first day I made about one hundred dollars, and in a couple of weeks I was making four grand a week.

When I met Jimmy Burke in 1964, he practically owned New York's Kennedy Airport. If you ask me, they named the place after the wrong Irishman. Occasionally there were dustups with unions there that refused to pay up, so Jimmy would have us waltz over and shake the place up. In February 1964, I was doing some routine shit at JFK. We were having union problems with the TWA terminal employees. It seemed that the bartenders, waiters, and waitresses weren't in the union, which we were bilking, and we had to convince them to join. Those catering people were just a pain in the ass. At the time, Casey Rosado was the president of the union, and we owned Casey lock, stock, and barrel. So me and a few other guys started to make our way onto a few of the parked TWA planes at the terminal to throw stink bombs on them. Even though we pretty much owned the airport, we couldn't be out in the open.

So while we're standing around trying to figure out the fastest way to get in and out, there was a huge commotion coming from a couple hundred yards away. It was loud. I mean, it sounded like a riot. Then we looked out on the tarmac at the international terminal. It turned out that was the day that the Beatles landed in the U.S. There were thousands of high-pitched screaming girls across the way at the Pan Am terminal, with hundreds of New York's finest busy keeping them behind the posts. With this diversion, we jumped into the planes and threw nasty stink bombs under the carpets to get our point across to the TWA people. You couldn't get that smell out. They got the message and joined up. It's the funniest thing; the Fab Four were our accomplices that day.

■ ■ ■

At the airport, unions were important, but not as important as the swag we were walking away with from the cargo terminals. For over a decade we did a lot of robberies and hijacking out of the local airports. We would get loads constantly: furs, suits, silks. There was a lot of stuff from Italy— watches, gold lighters. High-value stuff. We didn't walk around with garbage. If they imported it, we got it. The airlines had these guys that were in charge of the cargo, loading and unloading it on the plane. Hoods used to kill for these bags. That's where the traveler's checks were carried— I mean, hundreds and thousands of dollars in traveler's checks on their way to the banks. Back then traveler's checks were big business and everybody used them, since it was the only way you could protect your money when you were traveling. Today we don't think of this because everyone has credit cards or uses cash machines to avoid carrying cash.

Sometimes we only got fifteen minutes notice of a shipment coming in. We always had a crew—ours, not theirs—ready to go. It was like an army of predators, ready to strike anywhere and anytime. We had a network of insiders that was just as good as our unloading crew. If there was a load that was coming off a plane, usually they had the bill of lading before it even came in, a couple of hours before. Like on the money scores, we knew when it was coming in. The money used to come in a couple times a day at certain times; we knew what times Wells Fargo or Brinks would pick it up. We had that down to a pretty good science.

Since it was all insured, everybody got their money back. And I mean, fifteen minutes after we'd nail a load, the Feds would be right on Robert's Lounge or Geffken's Bar, or John Gotti's club, which was right up the street. Between the Gambinos and the Luccheses, the mob had the airport locked up really good. The cops knew it was us. We used to laugh in their faces an hour after a score. We'd go back to the bar and celebrate, and they'd be watching us from outside. They knew, but what could they do? The drivers would never identify anybody.

We were selling Rolex watches all over Queens Boulevard. They never caught us, and if they saw you with one or two watches, you'd say, "I bought it from this nigger on the corner." If you had a half-dozen on your arm, they wouldn't go near you. They wouldn't even attempt to bust you because they wanted the whole load or nothing. They wanted Burke or they wanted Paulie, they didn't want little guys like me.

The real trick was to break the load down real fast. And that's what we did. Sometimes we wouldn't even use a drop. We would just line up a couple of fourteen-footers back to back to each other in the neighborhood or certain streets that we used and unload part of the stash there. Some of it Jimmy would take to his basement, some of it would go to my mother-in-law's basement, some of it would go to Paulie's mother's house. We had different places for different things. Sometimes it would go right to whoever we were selling to. I mean, it would go so quick. We had it down to a science; it was unbelievable. And Jimmy Burke used to love to unload. He loved to work up a sweat. To him that was heaven. We had power-lifters and forklifters, and could strip a forty-foot trailer clean in seven minutes, quicker than ten union people could do it. Depending on how broke we were, we'd do two or three loads a day.

There were so many heists. The most valuable were probably the U.S. mail trucks—those forty-foot trucks. We used to destroy them. FedEx wasn't the way it was today. The brown trucks [UPS] had just started, also. So the U.S. mail was the main thing back in our day. A lot of foreign governments used to ship money by U.S. mail, and there were millions in cash. There were also negotiable things—jewelry, stocks and bonds. We would never know exactly what was in the trucks. We referred to these trucks as grab bags: "Come on, we got a grab bag." And we had to go through every parcel and every bag.

The postals were mostly stickups. They didn't have the computers like they do today, and everything was hand-delivered. It had to go through a whole chain to get to the bonding warehouse, or the customs warehouses, passing through a dozen or so hands. But we had it covered. The whole place was infiltrated by our people. It wasn't just guys, either—it could have been a woman clerk who somebody was banging. And it wasn't like it is today. It was wide-open, no security at all. You could drive into the cargo area just like you were driving into a McDonald's.

You might guess that there was a temptation to keep some of the swag from Burke, since there was no way he could know exactly how much our crew had scored. It's true that we could have cheated him, but we didn't. Burke was the head of our crew. Now Paulie was another story. If we could get away with just taking care of Paulie, then we would take as much as we could without letting him know the total take. Sometimes he found out and he'd come back and start screaming at me, "You fucking cocksucker," and we'd laugh about it. We could put three furs in the trunk and he'd never know about it. He didn't really care though, as long as he got his cut and as long as we took care of his girlfriends and his wife and gave him his envelope. He knew he was getting robbed every day. But it was a joke. He used to get so pissed at me, because I used to do things without Burke and without those other guys. And somebody might snitch on me: "Hey, I heard Henry made a $200,000 score over here." And if Paulie didn't see me for two or three days, he'd send for me. He'd be in front of my house, honking the horn and screaming, "You little cocksucker, get down here!"

It's funny, but even with all the airport security they have now, a Sopranos-type crew could pull it off today—just grab the trucks coming out of the airport. You stay on the outside of the airport. A truck has got to get on the freeway, and on a freeway it's got to make a turn. It's got to slow way down. They use two cars today—a lot of valuable loads come out of the airport with tail cars. You got two armed guys in a tail car. So first you take the tail car. You put a car in front and a car in back; the car in front stops, and you walk up—they are not expecting it, and ninety percent of the time it's the element of surprise. And if they don't have a tail car, it's a piece of cake. Because normally the truck is going to get on the freeway; if the driver stays on the service roads, it's a joke because you can nail him at any corner. You put a car in front of the truck, you put the car in park, two guys get out—if you got a driver and a helper—and they walk up to the driver. Most of the time they got just one driver. I mean, you walk up with a pistol in a bag. There could be a hundred people watching, and no one knows what's going on.

The only wrinkle today is now they got this Lojack tracking device that sends out a silent beacon so the car can be tracked by cops. But in our day, all they had were these combinations on the trucks, devices where you have like six buttons under the dashboard, and you'd have to have the combination to move that truck. If you didn't hit the right combination, an alarm would go off. That was the beginning of the Lojack concept, I think, but nowhere near as effective because if the drivers give up that combination, then you're home free. And you're a worthless hood if you can't even persuade a minimum-wage driver to give up the numbers.

■ ■ ■

Without a doubt our biggest airport score in the '60s was the heist from the Air France cargo terminal in April 1967. That job came because of a tip from Bobby "Frenchy" McMahon. Frenchy was the foreman on Air France's cargo dock, hence his nickname, and a regular customer on my cigarette route. For years we received tips from Frenchy about merchandise just sitting on the docks waiting to be lifted. One day he told me about the bags of untraceable cash that were shipped from Europe, headed for the U.S. Treasury so the money could be converted into foreign currency and credited back to the European banks. I guess the money had been spent by U.S. tourists overseas.

The actual heist took a few months to plan, but when it came down, it was so simple that it was anticlimactic. Initially, the idea was to grab the moneybags during a period where they just sat on the dock while a new vault was under construction. After casing the place a few times, me and Tommy DeSimone both decided there were too many workers hanging around to stick the place up. So we decided to wait until the vault was finished, and then get a copy of the guard's key. But how could we get the key away from him long enough to make a copy, and without him knowing?

The answer came when Frenchy learned that this guard was into porn and hookers big-time. Piece of cake. The oldest trick in the book. We started setting him up with a gorgeous call girl at a motel near the airport. After a few dry runs, we made our move when Frenchy alerted us to a huge cash shipment coming through the terminal. We had the broad take our mark off to the motel's private steam room, and while they were there for over an hour, we went to his room and made off with his key chain—all eighteen keys. Then we raced over to a locksmith, but he only had blanks for about eighty percent of the keys. We had them cut, and crossed our fingers that the key we needed was copied. Then we returned the keys to the guard's room while he was still getting his rocks off. Frenchy took the copies and reported back that we had hit the jackpot. Bingo!

A few nights later, on Saturday, April 8, Tommy and I showed up at the terminal with our key, walked into the vault, and loaded the cash bags into a suitcase. Nobody harmed, no witnesses—it was perfect. Air France didn't even realize they were hit for two more days. We were ecstatic when we counted the loot: $480,000. After we gave tribute to the various bosses who shared the airport, Tommy and I bought new cars and then flew to Vegas. Now that I think about it, we should have bought a car for the hooker, too. The rest was given to Jimmy to set up a "bank" for our crew. For years thereafter, whenever we needed cash, we got it from our bank, the Henry Hill Savings & Loan.

■ ■ ■

We fenced our booty in different ways. If we had a load of pharmaceuticals, then we had a wholesale pharmaceutical guy. If it was a load of watches or lighters, we would usually get rid of that ourselves. We went a lot after cash, too, because then we didn't have to get jerked around by the fences, who always low-balled you. Just because we were thieves didn't mean we wanted to get taken by another bunch of thieves. Jimmy, John Suvino, and this ex-cop, Jimmy Santos, were like our distributors. In other words, we would hijack a load and then turn it right over to them. They controlled all the distributors—whether it was cosmetics or clothes—and they had the guys to handle it.

Because I moved around so much I had a lot of my own fence guys, which is why I became so valuable. I found a guy with these wholesale drugstores, so that was my guy. Half of the time I didn't have to go on a hijacking, because I had the guy as a distributor. I would get my piece just for setting up the fence. They would pay those guys a third of wholesale. Say the load was worth $100,000—that was the bill of lading, the wholesale price. We would get maybe $30,000 to knock it over, and it took three guys to do it. So for a $100,000 load, you'd get ten grand to hijack it. But those fence guys drove a bitch of a bargain. They used to fuck us constantly. Sometimes they'd give us ten percent of the loads. We would bicker with them constantly, but sometimes we had no choice.

As far as fencing goes, nothing's changed. Especially in depressed cities, in urban areas. If there wasn't black-market underground commerce, a lot of people would have no income at all. I just came from Erie, Pennsylvania—I shot a movie there—and we were filming in the town a little bit. We were staying in town, too, and could see what was going on. There were a lot of drugs, but I mean guys were also selling cigarettes and shit out of the trunks of their cars, just like the old days. The same thing goes on. It hasn't changed much.

■ ■ ■

The bottom line is that we had everything. It was constant. If the airport was slow, we always had our gambling shit. We would have our work done in time to make the daily double, which used to go off in the winter at 12:30 P.M. and in the summer at 1:30 P.M. Our day was finished.

In those days we were practically immune from prosecution. So many officials were on the take it was a big joke. See, the local politicians needed the rank and file of our unions—the bricklayers union, the labor unions, and the rest. And we hardly had to worry about the courts, since Paulie made judges. We always had a judge who was on the take. In fact, Senator Alphonse D'Amato was in bed with us—him and his brother, an assemblyman in Island Park, just a few miles east of JFK Airport. His brother was partners with both Long Island boss Phil Basile and Paulie Vario. When Phil was in court for getting me a no-show job years later, Alphonse testified on his behalf. It later came out that D'Amato had accepted campaign contributions from Basile's wife. There were also some restaurants and land deals out there, and I'm sure some of that money would get kicked back to the good senator. We also had the district attorney. What did we need the mayor for? We had the district attorney in Queens; he retired before he ever got nailed. The Feds were never on the take, but the locals were always on the payroll, a lot of guys from a squad out of the Brooklyn-Queens office. They were always around, also. Most of those guys were on the take. Now occasionally they would nail us. They'd follow one of us guys to a drop—we had a bunch of different drops, which were usually just warehouses. But if some square cop pinched us, we just took care of it on the other end with the judge.

That's what made Burke so damn powerful—he owned not only Long Island politicians, but also the Queens D.A.'s office, Mackel and the squad. He owned Thomas Mackel and that's why he got away, literally, with murder. So Paulie had Brooklyn, and with the Gambinos, he had Manhattan, Staten Island, and the Bronx all locked up. The capper was that Jimmy had Queens and Long Island. So it was easy to think we were invincible. Some political corruption goes on today, but nothing like it used to.

CHAPTER FOUR

SETTLING DOWN
MOB STYLE

Before I signed on to the Program, I first considered what it would do to my teenage kids, Greg and Gina. It didn't take a genius to know they would be fine. They were strong kids, and they seemed less bothered by the all the hysteria than anyone of us, especially the in-laws. In fact, there were times when I believed they were actually enjoying the adventure of it all. Maybe they thought it was some kind of *Spy Kids* adventure, and they didn't realize how dangerous it really was. Who knows?

Now Karen was a different story. Our marriage, strange as it was, seemed to work. She tolerated my lifestyle, and I tolerated her shopping sprees, gay-boy pals, and her parents. In truth, she was and is a great woman, and we both had a love for each other. But as any grownup knows, love is no guarantee that two people can stay together forever. Now I worried if our new life on the run would strain what we had past the breaking point.

■ ■ ■

I met Karen Friedman in 1965 at the Villa Capra on Cedarhurst Avenue in Brooklyn. This was one of the most exclusive restaurants in Cedarhurst and a wiseguy joint. I mean, they even had a big Apalachin-type meeting there, that was in all the papers. There was nothing but big noses and Cadillacs at the Capra. Tony Ducks used to hang out there so did Carmine Gribbs, Paulie, Frank the Wop, Tommy Lucchese, and me; Lenny used to go there every day. And we used to drink there for nothing. We didn't have to pay a cent because it was Paulie's joint. Paulie and Frank the Wop owned it. Frank was a boss, also. I had a bunch of arrests there for loansharking. No problem. Paulie always took care of it.

At that time, Karen worked as a dental hygienist a few blocks away, and she and her girlfriend Dana Shapiro used to go to the Capra after work for drinks. I had seen her there a few times. Karen knew the score. She had to know who hung out there. Christ, everybody knew. Now Paulie, Jr., who was the bartender at the Capra, had the hots for Karen's girlfriend, who was doing one of the guys there, a guy who owned a beauty parlor in town. He thought he was half a wiseguy. Anyway, Dana didn't want to go out with Paulie, Jr., who was married. While Paulie was making his moves on Dana, my job was to keep her girlfriend Karen occupied. Frankly, I was bored stiff, and that first night I couldn't wait to get away from her—I had business to do that same night. But even though I was preoccupied with business, I couldn't help but notice that she was cute and had a sense of humor. So I got her number and we started dating, and one thing led to another.

There I was, a twenty-three-year-old with a brand new car—all the money, diamonds up the gazoo on my hand. The first or second date I told her I was a business agent or some other nonsense, but she had to suspect something because she knew all about the Capra. After just four months we eloped and drove all the way to North Carolina. We drove through Maryland first but we couldn't get married there because we couldn't get a blood test right away. So we had to drive to North Carolina.

We lived in her mother's house when we first got married. I got my friend Artie Fisher and some other carpenters to come in and redo the upstairs. They only had one bedroom and one small bathroom up there. So I called a whole damn crew in, and in four days—a weekend and a couple of days— they banged out the other side of the dormer. We put in a huge bedroom suite and extended the bathroom.

As far as the wiseguy business went, Karen knew everything that was going on. At the beginning I told her I had an office job. That lasted for about fifteen minutes after we got married. I used to actually make like I was going to work in the morning. That lasted about two weeks. I would actually go and get these little brown envelopes. That's how they paid you back in the day. The bank would give me these small little manila envelopes, and I'd put $180 in there. And I would hand it to my wife and say, "Here." I remember we bought our first bedroom set on layaway, just for appearances. My mother-in-law actually wanted to stake us some money. What a joke. Believe it or not, Karen's still got that gorgeous bedroom set.

Like I said, that lasted about fifteen minutes. Pretty soon, every Saturday, Karen and her mother were shopping in the best stores, spending my money as fast as I could make it. But I could care less. It didn't matter how much cash I had. If I ever needed $25,000 by noon, by eleven o'clock, I'd have it. The point is, Karen knew what the deal was when she married me.

Immediately after we got married I converted to Judaism. I started the process immediately because her parents wanted us remarried in a Jewish ceremony. Surprisingly, my Catholic parents were supportive of Karen and my conversion because they thought I would calm down—they saw the direction I was headed. They were so supportive and so happy and loved her. I thought that they would be against it, but I was becoming bad then; I had gotten arrested one time, and they thought maybe I would start to settle down. My sisters were also supportive, in spite of the fact that one was a nun.

The craziest part of the whole thing was the fact that I had to get circumcised—in my twenties. The actual circumcision was like an operation, not like it is with babies, where they just do it. I had to go to a hospital and they put me to sleep. But the rabbi had to be right in there. It was a whole deal. I was in the hospital for a day. That was an experience. Then I had to go through three months of school to learn the religion. I had a private tutor, and I was kind of serious because I knew how much it meant to Karen's mother and her grandmother. I wanted to please everybody. I wanted to be kind of right. And I took the Jewish religion seriously after that. I started to do all that stuff. I am still practicing. To me, Judaism is the most understandable religion there is. I get more spirituality from it than anything else.

Our honeymoon lasted about a minute and a half because the IRS finally nailed me in 1965 for the cigarettes I was smuggling. I swear it was just weeks after Karen and I tied the knot. I still think I owe the taxman like a million-and-a-half dollars, so it must have gotten swept under the carpet when I flipped in 1980. Anyway, I had to do the time on Riker's Island, which was so corrupt back then. Hell, it still is. As I'm writing this book I see where they're investigating the guards there for letting the inmates smuggle in drugs in exchange for sex with their girlfriends. Those guards are a horny bunch, for sure.

That was the first time I ever did time—thirty days. I was the first guy to go to jail in New York for the untaxed cigarettes scam—and I just had seven cases. Before me they used to give a fifty-dollar fine. I got out the day before Christmas Eve, thanks to Jimmy pulling some strings.

■ ■ ■

In 1966 I decided to complete the picture of domestic bliss and go semi-legit and own my own business. Of course, it would have to involve my passion for cooking. About this time, our crew invested in a discotheque, Tempo Dance City. I'd go down there every Friday and Saturday night and pick up a paycheck. We'd hang around there half-an-hour, and then every two months they'd rack up a profit. We'd get a couple of grand. See, me, Jimmy, and Tommy pooled our money. Before the disco, Paulie had first told me to take my money and go buy a McDonald's. I actually looked at a McDonald's franchise in Howard Beach back in 1967. And then I spent about half the money. I had opened up a pizza joint with the rest. And Jimmy used to keep a record book at the disco and every Friday if I needed $500 or $1,000, I'd get it. I mean, half the time I didn't need it, but I'd take it anyway. He'd say "You need anything?" I'd say, "Yeah, gimme a grand. Give me five hundred." We gambled. But that money was in, like, a savings account. Then they opened up a shylock business out of it. But I never kept track.

I pulled all my money out and bought my own restaurant, The Suite, on Queens Boulevard. Paulie got all pissed at me, too. I had about $7,500 in the disco, but I needed the money for The Suite. The Suite's owners were going to lose the license because someone had been killed on the premises—there's a shocker. They yanked the license, and that was it. And then maybe three months later the discotheque was torched. I never heard the end of that one. I don't know what happened, why it even went up.

The Suite was in a perfect location, right on the way from Manhattan to Queens, Brooklyn, and the Island. All you had to do was take the 59th Street Bridge to Queens Boulevard. So people going to the city or coming back would stop, have a drink, and say hello. Before you could say *goombah*, the top wiseguys were calling The Suite their second home—guys like Joey Gallo and Tommy Agro, from the Gambinos, were always there. And with the barbershop that was next door, a lot of guys enjoyed the convenience and opportunity to spruce up before getting loaded.

A lot of business got settled in The Suite. It was known to a lot of people. Jimmy Burke set up Manny Gambino with the Irish guys and their crew. Manny was Carlo's nephew, a big shylock, and got smashed in my club. He used to meet Joey Gallo there. But they snatched him out of my club because they knew he used to stop there every afternoon, then took him out and whacked him.

But the craziest thing that ever happened there was the Billy Batts hit. Batts liked to see how far he could push the fact that he was a made guy in the Gambino crew, who liked to think they were invincible. Anyway, not long after he got out of the joint, they had a coming-out party for him. Plenty of booze, music, and hookers—just like always.

Billy was from the same neighborhood as me but he was

in a different family. He was the Gambinos. It was his neighborhood for shylocking. He owned a bar in Queens and was one of the major made guys around when he got put away for ten years. So when he came home six years later, Jimmy had taken all his customers. Jimmy was king of the neighborhood. But now Billy wanted his business back, so he started to beef every place he went. "I own this," he'd whine. So Jimmy was just as nervous about him as Tommy was. A lot of people think that what happened next was because of the way Batts played with Tommy. But it was more about the shylocking, bookmaking, and who was controlling the airport. That's why we knew we had no problem taking action against him. The airport was vital, so we weren't about to give it up; I'm sure Jimmy would have discussed the Batts problem with Paulie prior to taking action.

Not long after he got out, Batts saw Tommy, who was still only about twenty years old, at The Suite. He started busting Tommy's balls, asking him if he still shined shoes like he had when he was a kid. What Billy didn't know was that by now Tommy was an up-and-comer in the Lucchese family, but not a made man. Tommy, who was drunk as shit, saw it as an insult and was ready to pop, but he couldn't make a move because if he so much as slapped Billy, he'd be killed for touching a made man. So Tommy went home and got madder by the second.

A couple of weeks later, Billy was at The Suite again with me and Jimmy. He and "Bonesey"—Alex Corcione—had been drinking and coked up all night. Then Tommy came back from the Copa with his girlfriend, Rosie, while Batts was squawking to Joey Gallo about getting back his airport and loan sharking business from us—he didn't care, he was a made guy. We knew what was coming, so we had to clear the bar out fast while Tommy took Rosie home. It was about two in the morning. When Tommy got back, we had cleaned the whole joint out, emptied the place. By now Jimmy had Billy so drunk he couldn't have fought off an old lady. So Tommy walked over and while Jimmy had Batts in a headlock, smashed him over the head with his .38. He beat him till the gun fell apart. We thought he was dead. So I pulled my car around and we threw him in the trunk, and away we went.

On the way out, the drunk Tommy hit a car on the Van Wyck Expressway. And just as Jimmy started screaming at Tommy, Batts came to and started banging on the trunk. I was sitting in the backseat, Tommy was driving, and I heard "BA-BOOM. BA-BOOM." Tommy almost got into another accident. It was funny. They realized Batts was still alive in the trunk, so then we drove to Tommy's mother's house to get the knife, shovel, and lime. Then we drove up to Ralph Atlas's property in Connecticut. We called him "Ralphie." This guy was a big, tall, handsome, strappy guy. He was older than Jimmy, with silver hair; a real high-liner, a classy guy. Ralph raised German shepherds on a farm up there. When we got to the property, we opened the trunk and this time they made sure Batts was dead. Tommy beat him with the shovel while Jimmy clocked him with a tire iron. We buried him, poured on the lime, and came home.

A few months later, Jimmy was sitting around bullshitting with Atlas when Atlas told him that some company was going to build a condo out there—right where we buried the body. Turned out Ralph's girlfriend had sold a piece of the property and they started bulldozing it. Of course if the body came up then two and two—we're in trouble. So that night, Jimmy and I sat Ralph down and we told him, "Hey Ralph, we buried Batts up there." He practically had a heart attack. He wasn't involved and we never bothered to tell him we planted a body on his property. So we had to go up there the next morning, me, Jimmy, and Tommy. Ralph had company that day—his girlfriend, mother, and father. Jimmy took them to a kennel, saying he wanted to check out shepherds there. He took them to a kennel while we dug Billy up.

CHAPTER FIVE

LINDA AND BROADWAY JOE

O ur crew was always busy with numbers, bookies, and moving airport swag, but still not a whole lot of money got saved. We lived out of our pockets or our drawers most of the time because we spent it as fast as we made it—hard to believe since I didn't even have a drug habit yet. But if we made a big score, we'd throw a huge party, then take a ton of people on a rolling party to Vegas or somewhere. The only time I started to make serious money—I mean, real serious—was around 1969 or '70. It all seemed to start around the time I met the New York Jets' star quarterback Joe Namath. And the Joe connection would probably never have happened if I hadn't been constantly on the make—it was a couple of girls who brought us together.

Like any respectable hood, I had my wife at home and my girlfriends on the side. It's just the way it was with our crowd. The wives knew it, and for the most part they went along with it. They say it goes with the European heritage or some such bullshit. I don't know about that, but I do know that as long as the wives got to spend us blind at the boutiques and country clubs, they were happy to look the other way—just so long as we didn't rub their noses in it. For the most part my girlfriends were like a cup of coffee, nothing more. But it was different with Linda Rotondi. The first night I met her, I was in love. Christ, was she beautiful—like a California blonde, but she was from New York. She was different. She was refreshing compared to the other chicks I was bedding at the time. I fell hard and fast.

We met in Michael's Steakhouse, a club out on the North Shore. My partner at the time, Ray, had a brother who was the owner and manager of this joint. Michael's had a piano man named Val Anthony, who was sort of like Billy Joel—quite similar to him and his style. I don't know why we went out to that joint. I think it was because the manager was tight with Paulie. Whatever the reason was, we'd go out the North Shore to this place, and they didn't charge us. Everything was taken care of: what else is new?

One Friday night, I was there with Paulie's kid, Peter; Linda and her roommate, Veralynn, were sitting at the next table over. We brought them over and bought them dinner. Linda had just gotten back to New York from California, where she had worked at Disneyland. She was some kind of executive. Smart girl. Really smart girl. She went to college for a year or so, but never finished. She had no sugar daddy at this time. I met her on a Friday night. Peter was trying to score with Linda, while I was focusing on her friend Veralynn, another hot young thing who drove a white Thunderbird convertible. This was 1969. About ten minutes before we left I danced with Linda. And I looked in her eyes, she looked in my eyes, and we switched. I said, "Peter, you're taking Veralynn and I got Linda." This was Paulie's son, a made guy. He said, "Okay, I don't give a fuck." So Peter left in his car with Veralynn while me and Linda start heating up.

The Holiday Inn in Rockville Centre was our joint, so we drove there to be alone and still eat and drink for free. It was a top-line place with a big, beautiful piano bar. And the food was the best, the linen, tables, captains, waiters—the whole nine yards. Holiday Inns were nice joints back then. They had a restaurant upstairs and a restaurant downstairs, Michael's. That was the meeting place for the whole Lucchese family. Tommy Lucchese used to hang out there with Tony Ducks, "Gribbs," and other guys from his crew. Johnny Dio owned the joint, so the Feds were watching it constantly.

On the way there we're talking, and man, I was in love—in love big-time. She was so refreshing and so different from all the bimbos I knew. So we went downstairs to the piano bar at the Holiday Inn, got a couple of drinks, and that's it. I was a perfect gentleman. Linda didn't have a clue who we were. She was Ms. Pollyanna. But she saw the way people were waiting on me, and blah, blah, blah. So she drove me home in the Thunderbird, and we went back to her apartment, near the Hofstra campus.

Veralynn and Peter, who's a *gaboom*—a low-class Guinea—were already there. I saw his car parked in one of the spots. I thought, "Fuck, this cocksucker beat me to the pad." So I gave Linda a kiss goodnight. I wasn't going up there. But then she gave me *that* look. Now I was ready to pop. I said, "Let's go back to the Holiday Inn." And she said yes! So we drove back to the Holiday Inn, which was about ten minutes away from where she lived. Believe me, I wasn't looking to screw her—I mean, I was—but I was going to play her a little. So we went back to the Holiday Inn, and we went back downstairs to the bar with Dom. So I said, "Linda, what do you want to do? I'll get you a room here. You can stay here." I was being a gentleman. I only lived ten minutes from there; I was going to go home anyway. I mean, the first night you meet a girl you usually don't go to bed with her. As far as Karen went, I had it covered—"I was playing cards, shooting crap." I had two kids at the house, so Karen wasn't going out looking for me; she was home with the kids and the maid and shit. And besides, I lived right around the corner from Paulie at the time, so she'd assume I'd be over there.

But Linda made it clear she wanted me to spend the night here with her. I had died and gone to heaven. So I walked to the front desk—we had a guy at the front desk, of course. Soon the hotel owner's came over to me to see what's up and just like that we had our pick of the rooms. I got Linda a nice suite, I walked her upstairs, and she went to the bathroom. She came out. I'll never forget what she was wearing. She was wearing this flower-bikini underwear and a bra. It was beautiful. I took my two-thousand-dollar-suit off, and I couldn't believe what I was looking at. Anyway, she had small tits—maybe a size B—but she was beautiful, drop-dead gorgeous, size 4, pretty, and tan. She was half-Wasp, half-Italian, and a classy, classy girl in her early twenties. And now she didn't want to take off her bra because she had little tits, so I started messing with her bra, this little flower bra. Something like Victoria's Secret would do today. And she was sweet and delicious, with a "10" body. Oh, I fell in love. I hit the fucking lottery.

Now I spent the night with her, and believe me I didn't sleep too much. We weren't doing drugs at the time, so I was drinking a bottle of scotch and we shared a couple of bottles of Dom and made love all night. This broad was one of the best lovers I had had in a long time. Next to my current wife, Kelly, this was my real love. The next morning I took a cab home because I only lived a few minutes from there. I jumped in the cab, and she gave me the address to her house and said, "Call me later."

Of course when I got home I had to deal with Karen, but at this point I didn't care what hell she put me through—it was more than worth it. "Yeah, honey, I was playing cards all night," I told her. For some unknown reason, she bought it. I bullshitted my way through that one.

That morning Paulie weighed in. Now, Paulie lived in Island Park, where there's a little bridge he used to cross to come and get me in the morning. This was Saturday morning. Now Paulie was outside my home honking the horn. I hadn't been home an hour. He was honking his horn, and I said, "Yeah, I'll be out in a minute. I'm coming." He said, "I got to go to Brooklyn." Whatever. I started to tell him, "Me and your son picked up these two chicks last night." Now Paulie was so paranoid. He said, "You sure they weren't Feds?" "Get the fuck out of here," I told him. "I just left the broad at the Holiday Inn. What are you talking about, 'Feds'?" The old prick was nuts. And he screamed, "I got to stop over there. I wanna go meet these girls. They're fucking Feds. I got to see if Pete is still there. Let's go over there. Where are they?" So on the way to Brooklyn we swept by Linda and Veralynn's house.

Now we went there and Paulie saw this big building with a doorman and security and shit. Former New York Senator Alphonse D'Amato owned that building. It was the only high-rise out there—about eighteen stories—and it was an exclusive building. Paulie was just going nuts. Number one, he was jealous. Paulie had a brand new Cadillac with a silver top at this time, but he was jealous. He was mostly jealous of me picking up this young stuff. I saw that right away. I didn't give a rat's ass. "I don't know her. You want to fuck her, you can fuck her," I told him.

I rang the bell and Linda came running down in shorts; she was as bronzed as a shiny penny right out of California. So she came running downstairs and who did she see but Paulie with his shiny suit on. She didn't know what was going on yet, not a clue. She didn't know who I was, who Paul Vario was. She walked down to the car, gave me a big kiss, and said, "Come on up." So we were upstairs and there was no Peter. "Where's my son?" Paulie asked her. "We don't know where your son is," she said. So Linda made coffee, we walked downstairs, and Paulie was paranoid as two fucks. "The Feds!" He ran into the other room where I was making a date for that night. She had *prosciouttas*—Italian ham— and this whole setup, and Paulie was looking for tape recorders and microphones. I was laughing my balls off.

When he came back I wasn't saying too much. He said, "The Feds are setting us up." I said, "Whatever, Paulie. Yeah, yeah." Linda was half-Italian and half-Wasp; these were two college kids. "Okay, Paulie, whatever. Whatever, they're Feds. I won't see them no more." Yeah, right. I went back there the next night. And I went back Saturday night to take her to dinner because I made a dinner date in-between Paulie's paranoid questions.

■ ■ ■

When I met Linda, she was living at this Hofstra house, which is not far from the school where the Jets football team trained. One night, Linda and her girlfriends were making the local bar scene—there's a couple of local bars—and she met Joe Namath because it was spring training and their camp was right down the street. Joe got the hots for Linda's girlfriend, Veralynn, and they got their own thing going. At the time, there was no one hotter, especially in New York, than Namath: "Broadway" Joe Namath. He was the best quarterback in the NFL, loaded, attractive, and single to boot. His club, the Bachelors III, was party central, and guys in my line of work were there every night.

So I came in one night, not knowing about Veralynn and Joe, and pulled into the garage when another car headed for the same spot. Not just another car, the exact same kind of car I was driving: a '59 Riviera, silver with a black top. It was crazy. Then I saw it was Joe Namath behind the wheel. I had the same exact car as Broadway Joe! It was funny. As I was looking over, I was starstruck. Of course he got the spot and I parked outside. I came back in to get the elevator, and who also got on but Joe. We got off the elevator at the same floor. Now I was freaking. When we got to the same apartment, I was ready to lose it. Same car, same floor, same apartment. Finally I got it—he was dating Veralynn, the roommate.

So he and Veralynn went to their room, and we heard them going at it. And Linda was showing me the apartment, so I said, "Let's get out of here." First of all, how could I believe it? This big-nosed, six-foot-six motherfucker was drilling this chick-I-just-met's roommate.

Now we started this affair and I couldn't get this woman out of my mind. I was obsessed. She became twice as obsessed with me. It wasn't long before Linda asked me,

"What do you do for a living?" I told her, "I'm in the union. I'm a union delegate." "Okay." She believed me. She didn't put the Paulie thing together. She didn't get it. So now I began seeing her every night, and Joe's up there every night because he was in camp. One night he said, "Henry, do me a favor. Lend me your car."

"Why?" I asked.

"Well, because you got the same car." See, all the NFL teams had bed checks and curfew. If your car was missing from the lot, they'd come to your room to find you. The Jets' coach Weeb Eubank was a tough-ass coach, and he had his guys on a short leash. So I gave Joe my keys. He planted my car at the camp and put pillows in his bed at night. What did I care? I'd take Veralynn's Thunderbird.

About a month into our relationship, I bought Linda a Triumph, one of those little convertibles, a Kelly-green convertible piece of shit that the chicks loved. And I started paying the rent, of course. Later Paulie's kid Lenny started sleeping with Veralynn. Hey, they were just being normal twenty-one-year-olds. Broadway Joe could care less. He was making it with a hundred broads at the time.

Soon the place is out of control. And Joe is not the only Jet hanging out there—he started bringing his friends up. When Linda found out I was married, she started cheating on me. I think she was screwing their wide receiver. I think she even started up with Namath.

It didn't take Linda long to find out what my racket was. What happened was I started bringing Joe Namath down to Michael's Steakhouse. Now there was Tommy Lucchese, Johnny Dio, Carmine Gribbs, and Tony Salerno, and we were all sitting down and meeting. It didn't take her too long to figure it out. "You motherfuckers are gangsters," she says. And guess what? That even made it better. She was into it.

Namath knew all about me, too, but he was hooked up with this other crew in Manhattan. They were partners in his joint, the Bachelors III. It was the same family, fortunately. He was hooked up at his club with Tommy Teeballs, who was in the Lucchese family, so it was all right. So Joe and I became good friends. We used to party together. But our friendship got me into hot water with the bosses. One day I got the riot act read to me. I can't remember now who called me down to Michael's, but it was either Johnny Dio or Paulie. It might've even been Fat Tony. "Don't bring Joe here no more," they ordered me. See, the wiseguys didn't give a hoot about about Joe Namath; they cared about themselves. I think the Gambinos were partners with him, and the Luccheses didn't want to start anything with them. Eventually Joe had to sell the place because of the wiseguys who were connected with it.

■ ■ ■

When the 1969 Super Bowl was approaching, featuring the Jets and the Baltimore Colts, we all started making plans to go to Florida for the big game. It would be Paulie's son, Lenny, my wife, and Bonesey. The Jets were underdogs, but they were a great team that year, and we thought it was a good excuse for a party and to watch our new pal Joe play. You'd never catch me at Shea Stadium in Queens—too damned cold. I mean, I like Joe, but give me a break. One day Joe said to me, "Henry, bet the ranch." He told me "Bet the fucking ranch, and take the odds." I thought he was nuts—they were seventeen-point underdogs against the powerful Colts.

Now right before the trip, our crew had just made a big score: we wound up with 150 pounds of methamphetamine—pharmaceutical methamphetamine. It came from a warehouse out in Cedarhurst, Inwood. It was the first time

I ever had any business dealings with drugs. We paid $10,000 for it, but it was worth half a million back then. Now I got this barrel for $600 bucks, and I sold it by the pound. The junk was worth $60,000 a pound. I sold it to different wiseguys and stuff. That's when I got my first beef with Sally Fuggo, who's a Bonanno family dude now. I sold his son some pills—like ten pounds.

So I got all this money and I went to bet it on the Super Bowl, taking six-to-one odds. And again Joe told me—he would grab me in the bedroom, in the elevator— "Henry, bet the ranch." Why was he so sure? I don't know. Confidence. His ego. Who knows? I bet about $30,000, taking six-to-one. I spread it around a lot of bookies.

Then on a Friday we got on a plane to go. I had never taken speed in my life, but on that trip I took a teaspoon and stirred it up in orange juice, and we were drinking it on the plane. I didn't sleep for four days. I couldn't talk. My voice was gone. I couldn't get a hard-on either. In Florida we stayed at the Diplomat Hotel, and who was staying there but Vice President Spiro Agnew, so the whole place was crawling with Secret Service. And we were partying our asses off. We got to the Orange Bowl, and we had fifty-yard-line seats that Joe got me. I had hoped to be basking in a luau shirt, unlike the frozen idiots back at Shea. But guess what? It was freezing down there, too, but it didn't matter. We were well-lit and having a ball.

As it happened, the game came down to the wire in the fourth quarter—it didn't help my hoarseness, that's for sure. I couldn't talk, I was so hoarse from screaming and the drugs. But I remember every play of that game. It was a great game, and a great payday for Henry Hill, because the freaking underdog Jets pulled this one out of their asses. I won over a hundred large. And Paulie got shit. In fact, it was Paulie's bookmakers I beat. I took his main guy. They thought it was easy money for me. They were so pissed at me. They didn't believe that the Jets even had a shot. I caught hell for years after it. Fuck 'em. I got the money.

So, the minute after the game, I called New York to one of the bookmakers who owed me about $30,000. I said, "Wire me some money, we're going to the Bahamas." But the bookmaker didn't have the $30,000, so he wired me $20,000. I took all six of us to the Bahamas—me, Karen, Bonesey, and Lenny Vario and their wives. Joe was so busy that I didn't even get to see him after the game. We jumped on a boat and got on one of those cruise ships, and went to Paradise Island.

■ ■ ■

That game wasn't my only big gambling score. I made $420,000 in one year betting college basketball. In 1970, I hooked up Casey Rosado, our president of the Local 57 at the airport. Casey was an unbelievable guy. He was Cuban. Later he was in the indictment with us in Florida. He stood trial in the state trial that we fixed. He died between the state and federal trials; he had a massive heart attack after snorting cocaine one morning. Jimmy and him got real tight. We all got real tight with Casey; me and Casey were partners. Jimmy says, "You and Casey go be partners with this college betting." And that's how we started. I knew nothing about basketball, but we had information. Some of the games were fixed—there was hot information we were getting—but most were just based on brilliant inside stuff we learned about the players.

It all came from Ralph Atlas, who used to move money. He was like a bookmaker's bookmaker. Ralph had these two schoolteachers, Nick "Big Soda" and another guy whose name I forgot—they were called the Soda Twins. Big

Soda and Jimmy were close—Jimmy was like his protector. I heard they wrote books, so I think the Soda Twins are famous now. In the basement of their house out on the Island they had charts of every single school, every single player, their girlfriends' names, what they drank. They were handicap geniuses.

Soda used to call Ralph first thing, because if we got the line early, it meant a point, a point-and-a-half, two points, and that meant the whole game. And he'd move the line. As soon as he got down, the line jumps down sometimes, three or four points. That was the edge. He'd tell us to bet, and he'd give us a number. "Here's Kansas, take Kansas. Don't weigh more than three points." He'd be right eighty-five per-cent of the time. Eighty-five percent! If you get the informa-tion first, you had a huge advantage. We were even betting with bookies all over the world—in London and Monte Carlo. Big Soda helped us bet all over.

It wasn't always a sure thing, though. In 1971, I put $75,000 on a title game between the Kansas City Chiefs and the Miami Dolphins. I was winning all the way up until the end. I made a $75,000 bet; I spread it out with maybe ten bookmakers. And I was winning through most of the game. I remember sitting in my mother-in-law's living room that Sunday and I couldn't believe it—Miami kicked a field goal in the last seconds. It went into double overtime, and Miami won 27–24. It was a potential $150,000 day for me. I'm talk-ing about 1971. Do you know how much money that was?

Some bookies I settled with; some, I didn't. That was one thing great about Paulie. He told his bookies to let me skate on some bets. The first thing I'd ask when I met a bookmak-er was, "Who you with?" In other words, what family are you with? Who was your rabbi? Who was your captain? If he says he wasn't with nobody, then that was like the codeword. See,

I would play the schmucky part, the schmucky Jew. I had it down to a science. As soon as the guy said he was with nobody, I was like, "All right. Gimme a twenty-five-thousand-dollar credit." "Nah, I can't do that." "Okay. Gimme a ten-thousand-dollar credit. We'll start at ten-thousand." And I would win a couple of weeks. We were getting good information. The minute I'd lose to them, I'd lower the boom: "I'm with Paulie Vario, so don't fucking push me on this, understand?" And, boy, they got it right away. Now I could put them off indefinitely. I'd tell them I was out of town. I'd piece them off. I'd send them a little money.

■ ■ ■

It was a neverending well. For a while I would work with the numbers racket. I hated to work that gig, but it was part of the job. It was a two-hour, three-hour job, but my salary there was only like $400 per week. This was chump change compared to my other sources of income. But the numbers were interesting. The gamblers knew they were better off playing the numbers with the gangs than with the state lottery. First, the odds were better. Second, you could charge it. You put a number in for a week or a month, and you didn't have to pay until payday or whenever you told the guy you were gonna pay it. So you had credit. The odds were five-hundred-to-one. The winning number was picked by the last three digits of the total mutual handle at the end of the day. Then you had the single digits—you could bet the single number, the next number that was going to come out. You could do the numbers individually. Guys would hang out in bars and bet them.

And heaven help the juiced guys who didn't pay their vig (gambling debt plus interest). Beat-artists—beatsters, and there were hundreds of them around—we would give those guys an ass-kicking. Same with the shylocking business. You had to crack down on the deadbeats because you didn't want other people taking potshots at you. There were some guys who got away with it, and they'd tell ten other guys, "Hey, I just beat Tommy for five-hundred dollars . . . and I got away with it." That word travels fast in that subculture. That's why they would break legs and whack guys.

A guy wouldn't normally get whacked for numbers, but for bookmaking they would. The numbers were so small; they were nothing. But it was the bookmaking that coughed up some big numbers.

■ ■ ■

Those years were great years. I had three or four other girlfriends on the side. I even had a T-shirt company in my garage, which I used as a legit front for my tax statements— I wasn't going the way of Capone and all the other wiseguy idiots who got nailed for taxes. It also came in handy for laundering any money that needed to be washed. I opened the T-shirt silk-screening thing with my sister-in-law Judy, who was an artist and a schoolteacher and who talked me into it. So myself, Judy, and my mother-in-law all worked there. Three Geminis. We set it up like a corporation. I paid good taxes and all that stuff. I did the T-shirts, hats, and sweatshirts for the Jets, and all their logo shirts. That was a good one. We did probably about fifty percent of their business. It was the stuff that the team would wear. We also had Perrier water and all the nightclubs' logo business. I had salesman going out. That was my job. I was a salesman. I wasn't in a corporation, but I was a salesman. I was successful. I would go make the initial contact with some people. If I had had half a brain, I would have just stayed with this and blown off all the wiseguy idiocy. Like I said, if I had had half a brain.

■ ■ ■

I didn't know that this was insanity, that one day it was all going to end, that I was either going to get whacked or sent to the can, because back in those days, you bought your way out of everything. I just assumed I'd get away with it. We had the power, and we knew it. And we had Paulie, who'd stand up for us knowing we were dead wrong and not give a fuck. And that's the way it was for us, an unending parade of opportunities.

Yeah, right.

CHAPTER SIX

THE FALL

In 1972 it was decided that I was going to become a union delegate—a business agent—for Disney World in Florida. Since I was the only one in the crew who didn't have a felony conviction, I had the best chance of avoiding attention.

This was a big plan to take over Disney World and the food service plan, which was huge. This would've been a major thing for Paulie and the Luccheses. If I'd have gotten the Disney thing I'd have moved down there temporarily, then I would've commuted. I probably would've had to stay down there a couple of days a week. A lot of our guys had houses in Florida, and some moved their families down there.

On Columbus Day weekend I was sent down with my Cuban wiseguy pal Casey Rosado, whose relatives were connected with the Florida mob. So Jimmy, Casey, me, and a guy named Louie Lopez went to Santo Trafficante, the boss of Florida, because Casey was connected with Santo, and Paulie had sent us to Florida for me to get introduced to Santo. We met Santo at the Columbia Restaurant in Tampa, and got the OK there. That night, Casey said, "Let me go see this Tampa bookmaker, John Ciaccio, who owes me $14,000." He wanted to take care of both things on the same trip. At least that was the idea.

Then we went to Ciaccio's joint, kidnapped him, and took him to Busch Gardens. After we beat the shit out of him in the car, he paid us that night. He was partners with a doctor who brought the money the next morning, and we hopped on the plane to go to Miami. We went to the Fountainebleau. I called up Linda, and she flew down there with Jimmy's girlfriend. There was something going on with my kids at home—maybe my daughter's birthday—so I couldn't bring Karen down.

On Tuesday we went back to New York. And then a month later, I was driving down the street—I was living in Long Island at the time—and listening to the local radio station. I listened to 1010 WINS every day. I heard "a big arrest," and then I heard my name. Holy shit! (If only we had cell phones in those days.) I pulled over on the parkway and something made me stop before I got to Robert's Lounge. I looked ahead and saw the cops as they took Jimmy out of Robert's in cuffs. The whole crew was standing outside and they saw my car coming down the street, and they're waving me on, "Go, go, go." I could figure out what was happening—the Feds were making a big arrest. In the headlines I was named, along with Casey, Jimmy, and Louie Lopez—the four of us who went to Florida.

It wasn't long before we got arrested. We managed to beat the Florida indictments. But then forty-six-year-old Casey, the cleanest guy on the witness stand, died of a heart attack, and with him died our chances of beating the federal rap. I was sentenced to ten years for extortion, but my lawyers appealed the conviction for almost two years. The real loss, though, was Disney. Paulie and the Luccheses were never able to get their hooks there, and it was a major defeat that no one has ever noticed. That was when shit started to fall apart. Once the Feds began to unravel the teamsters, there was no way to go back in.

While the lawyers were doing their best to stall my going into the joint, I went back to business as usual. A normal person would have learned his lesson. Not Henry Hill. I was a lunatic criminal in denial like you've never seen. And I wasn't even afraid of prison. That's the last thing that would change a true wiseguy. Prison would only give me more status in the crew. Finally, in 1974, all my appeals were denied, so I had to turn myself in. The night before I turned myself in, I was up all night with Karen. We had a big party at The Suite—a going-away party for yours truly. Then from The Suite we jumped in a couple of limos and moved the party to the Q-Motor-Inn, and then from there to Maxwell Plum's. I was supposed to turn myself in at nine A.M.; by the time I left Maxwell Plum's, it was eleven. The bondsman was going nuts; he was calling Paulie. I was out on a quarter-million-dollar-bail, so he was close to losing the farm. He called my wife and asked, "Where the fuck is he?" What happened was that on my way to West Street, which was where the Manhattan Correctional Center (MCC) was located at the time, I stopped at the Empire State Building, where Linda worked. I went to Linda's office and took her up to the observation deck. And I just told her, "Listen, honey, I got ten years to do, sweetheart. I love you. I'll always love you."

I broke up with Linda at the top of the Empire State Building just before I went to turn myself in, but we stayed great friends from then on.

■ ■ ■

While I was in the joint, Tommy DeSimone began to lose it big-time on the outside. He was always whacko, but he was finally beginning to drag everything else down with him. It was a frightening time.

It all started because of a run-in with Foxy, who was John Gotti's protegé. This guy had like two hundred pairs of shoes and a hundred suits. That's why they nicknamed him "Foxy." He was around the neighborhood a lot, and he and Tommy did a bunch of big mail truck scores and gold scores out of the airport, usually in partnership with Gotti's Gambino crew. They were also partners in the coke and heroin business, until Foxy turned on Tommy. He was furious with Tommy for fucking his sister one night and beating her up another. So Foxy was a Gambino guy, but the lunatic Tommy whacks him anyway.

It went down like this. Foxy put the word out: "I'm looking for this cocksucker. I'm gonna kill him." And I don't even think Foxy was Italian. Tommy found out this guy was looking for him. Tommy said, "Fuck him. I'm going over to his fucking house." This is after Foxy already had warned him. Tommy did it just to rub it in Foxy's face. This is how crazy Tommy was. Foxy went over to where he lived in Howard Beach, in those fancy apartments, opened his apartment door, and saw Tommy. Before you know it, he nailed Tommy with a shot in the mouth. Tommy went down on the ground. This was just what Tommy wanted—he baited him. Now, Tommy carried two pistols. He whipped one out and put it right between Foxy's eyes and let one go. Tommy killed him right in his apartment in Howard Beach, got up, and walked out. Just like that.

That was in 1974—we had just been in the can six months or maybe a year. Tommy was the only one out. Me, Paulie, and Jimmy were in Lewisburg, and Jimmy was in Atlanta. Our whole crew was in the can—except for Tommy. Now Tommy was out on $100,000 bail for some hijacking case, but with all the captains in the federal can, Tommy was scared to death out there on the streets because he had no one to save him. It finally hit him that he couldn't get away with his normal shit with his rabbis in the joint. So Tommy went to Al Newman, who was the head bondsman who used to do all our stuff—all our regular bonds—and said, "Revoke my bail, I gotta go in. Put me in, I'm not gonna make it on the streets."

So Tommy got to Lewisburg, with us. When he showed up in the joint, we said, "What the fuck are you doing here?" He said, "They revoked my bail." It was bullshit. He put himself in. I was living in a room with Paulie and Johnny Dio, and Tommy came walking in the room and told the story of how he killed Foxy. Paulie asked, "Where are all the Lucchese guys?" Now the wink-wink—the next room over from our suite they had another five-man suite, and who was in the next suite but the Gambinos! They had two rooms, we had two rooms, and there were eight rooms on this floor. The Genoveses had another room. The Bonannos had still another room. So we were back and forth, back and forth. Tommy got friendly with Angelo Riggiero, Gotti's right-hand man.

Gotti wasn't there, but his whole crew was.

So Tommy got in bed with these guys in the joint because these guys are coke snorters and Tommy was into a lot of coke at the time. They were a lot crazier—they were kids—so it was a younger, more fun group. And I was stuck with the old cocksuckers, which I didn't mind; I was going to college, literally, while I was there, trying to make the best of a bad thing. So I was going to school and I was minding my own business. They used to laugh at me when I walked down the hall with my books. I could care less—I was getting paid $600 a month from the Veterans Administration. They were laughing at me because they all had a lot of money without having to study. Tommy used to come and mess with us all the time and mess with Paulie. These guys'd be as high as rats on coke. They didn't care that we knew what was happening, and Paulie knew what was happening.

I didn't care if they laughed at me because, believe me, with Paulie and Johnny Dio, it was the best thing I had ever done. Part of me at least thought of going straight. I was the first guy in our gang who ever went into the army. I was the first one who married a Jew. I did everything humanly possible to get away from these people. Anyway, Johnny Dio wanted me to get my two-year degree, which was in hotel and restaurant management, and become an optometrist because he had a connection. They had all the unions, so they were going to put me in the eyeglass business. They had doctors under their thumbs, too. He explained to me that I could make myself a million to two million a year, legitimately, doing this. So he says, "Henry, become an optometrist, the guy that makes the glasses, because you'll get rich."

I was not about to become an optometrist. But Dio was right about getting an education, and I got a two-year degree while I was in the joint. That was the only thing

Johnny Dio ever tried to help me with. He didn't like me because I converted to Judaism when I got married. He used to call me "matzah-crazed." He was a vicious old fuck.

I smoked a little pot in prison, but I didn't do too much coke. I used to get high at night—walk out of the room to go somewhere to toke up. There was this place where we used to get high, Washburn Alley, right behind Reverend Washburn's office. It was a joke.

As far as how the made guys got on with the regular population, there was no tension. They kind of envied us; they were probably jealous of us. They probably ran and ratted us out every chance they got, but so what? We didn't even speak to them—maybe a wave to the white guys. We had the whole damn cellblock. Now the D.C. crew was a big, black crew. Those guys ran that penitentiary. We had the head of the D.C. crew in our corner. This one guy, Wade Brown, and his guys used to do all the killing for us in the joint. They killed nine guys in three months—over nothing, over a freaking sandwich. It was all egos, basically. Tommy killed three or four guys in prison. I was there when he killed a couple of them. They'd find them in the bakery in the huge mixing bowls. The crimes never got investigated. Never. Oh, they got investigated for about five minutes, but there were never any witnesses.

They wanted me to kill a Boston guy, a made guy with the Patriarca family, because he sucker-punched me one day. He owed me some money and he was not about to pay up, so he got me when I wasn't looking. But I was told by Johnny Dio and Paulie, "Fuggetaboutit, we'll deal with it when we get out." And so all I did was just say, "Fuggetaboutit," and we shook hands. Larry Cennino had a sit-down in the joint, and I told him, "It's all forgotten about." But Tommy and this other little guy, Angelo Sepe, went crazy. Tommy was all about revenge and respect anyway. Sepe's uncle was a made guy who was an informant, and he ended up partners with Tommy when they came out. Anyway, this ugly little midget got so mad at me because I didn't want to kill this guy, so he said, "Fuck it. I'll kill him." I said, "No one's killing him." But this little bastard and Tommy were so crazy. I could care less at this point. I said, "I ain't a punk. I was told to leave the guy alone, and you motherfuckers better leave the guy alone." "Yeah, yeah, yeah, yeah—you're still a punk." "Yeah? Well, fuck you." Angelo didn't want me to go with them—when I came out, we used Tommy's midget pal Angelo on the biggest heist ever, the Lufthansa score—and I really didn't have to go. But I wanted to go anyway to make sure these guys didn't louse it up. Jimmy said, "Fuck 'em. You don't have to go. Fuck this little cocksucker." Jimmy was running the show; he, Tommy, and Frenchy were running the crew that was going in. Paulie told me the same thing: "You're gonna get your full end anyway." So I didn't have to go. I said, "I wanna go, Paulie. They're gonna louse it up." "No, they won't," he said. "We got everything down pat." So fine.

■ ■ ■

In prison I met other wiseguys who I worked with later—guys like Robert Venetucci and Bill Arico. Bill was supposed to be a cockroach exterminator for his legit front. But it was his idea of a joke, I suppose, because he was really a human exterminator, doing time for one of his murders. Arico was our money guy; he had the guards, who were on the take big-time, bring him drugs, which he would sell on the inside. The way he did it was to have his wife meet the guards, and she'd pass the drugs to them. Because of his drug sales, Arico always had five, ten-thousand on hand. So he could always front us half-a-G or so to pay off the guards, the prison chaplain, whoever. Then I'd have Karen pay his wife back on the outside. This way we didn't have to exchange too much cash from our wives in the visiting room and shit. The Aricos used to live in a mansion not far from us—this guy was filthy rich.

I got friendly with Venetucci also, and he later got me involved in a huge international scandal, as you'll soon see. His wife used to drive Karen up to prison for visits since we all lived in the Valley Stream area.

Being in the joint with the Gambinos could have been a problem because of the Batts hit, but I wasn't worried about it because the Gambinos came to me in prison when they wanted to whack me over the Manny Gambino clip. They corralled me in a cell. I thought I was dead. I said to the Gambinos, "Hey, listen. I had left early that night. I don't remember . . ." And they spared me. They knew it would've been a big headache if they killed me because of Paulie. So I figured I could skate on the Batts thing. Lucky for me, I was right.

■ ■ ■

In 1976, I was in Lewisburg prison doing my ten-year term when my father got sick with pancreatic cancer. I got a three-day furlough to visit him in the hospital. It was an escorted trip from Lewisburg. The last few days before he died he was down to ninety-five pounds. He was in so much pain I couldn't stand watching it. So I bought him a pint of rye whiskey; I used to drink scotch. There we were, one guy dying and his son practically dead on the inside, drowning our pain with a pint of Chivas and a pint of VO. We sat there for two days and got drunk. I made amends to him when he was in the hospital. I told him I was such an asshole. I realized when I went to prison what a mess I'd left behind. And I also realized, then, what a good man he was. He was an alcoholic, but he was still a good guy. He raised eight kids.

I've got a beautiful picture of him as a fighter. He never missed a day's work. While he was out working hard, I used to steal his pistol to impress my crew. The last job he worked on was the World Trade Center buildings. He was always a foreman or a super. He started Local 3 in New York with Harry Van Osdale.

My father accepted my lifestyle, more or less, and I took care of him financially. I also helped out my kid brother—the crippled one—financially. I put a couple of my other siblings through law school. I'd pay for vacations with my in-laws. I've said before that I would never wind up like my father. But all he ever wanted from me was to graduate high school and to become an electrician. He was a good man. And all he would say was, "Stay the fuck away from those bums. They're going to get you in trouble."

When he died a year later I was then serving out my time at Allenwood, and because I was a practicing Jew, they gave me seven days for shiva. Now here's the punch line: they go to bury him. I see on the mass card that his name is not Hill, it's O'Rourke. His birth name is O'Rourke. He had lived under his stepfather's name. His stepdad's name was Hill, Moe Hill. I have a piece of paper on it. But they had to bury him under the name on his birth certificate, which was O'Rourke. And no one ever knew this. That makes me Henry O'Rourke.

Just before I got out, something happened that I didn't learn about for ten years. See, Tommy was out before me, and for some reason, he got it into his diseased brain that he could have Karen to himself while I was still locked up. I don't know all the details, but Tommy beat the crap out of my wife—tried to rape her right before I got out of the joint. I didn't find this out until ten years ago. All I can say is Tommy is damn lucky I didn't learn about it until years after he was dead.

I got an early parole on July 12, 1978, thanks to my "model" behavior; the fact that I got a degree with the courses I took, and I had a job waiting for me on the outside. Well, the job of course was another union no-show fixed by Paulie through Phil Basile, a disco owner who I had done some torchings for. Nothing at all had changed. Immediately after I got out, Burke introduced me to the world of major drug dealing—pot, coke, heroin, uppers, etc. Of course, this was against Vario's orders, but I didn't care. I was making up for lost time.

CHAPTER SEVEN

THE BIG SCORES

s I recounted the details of my chaotic life for Ed
McDonald in 1980, I wasn't sure he believed everything I was telling him. I know I wouldn't if I were
him. On the other hand, he knew there was a chance I was
the best mob informant he'd ever get, so he wasn't about to
cut me off. And I needed his protection even more than he
needed my information.

I was just a few days into the Program, but I knew that
I had impressed Ed enough that he would become my new

"rabbi"—watching my back and paying my bills—for as long as I kept singing. And at this rate, I could go on like this for years. But as much as he had pushed me about the big scores, the more I diverted him with other gangster stories. I remember the time when I told Ed that I had been in Boston just a couple days after Lufthansa was hit. He asked me why I was there and I told him—to pay the players at Boston College to shave points during the last season. The next thing I knew, Ed was flying out of his chair.

"What the hell are you trying to pull, Henry?"

It turned out that Ed was a BC alumnus who once played on the team, and even went to some of the games we had rigged. He thought one of the other agents put me up to making this up just to get his goat. But he soon realized it was true, and when he caught on, he was just obsessed with it. He'd worried that he couldn't get these guys for Lufthansa, and he wanted Burke badly, so the college fixes could be his ticket because he'd get Burke ten to twenty years for that alone. Besides, BC was his alma mater, so he was really totally obsessed. Of course this would lead to a whole other trial. He tried that case for personal reasons, and that's why he went berserk when I almost sabotaged it, as you'll see.

■ ■ ■

I had baited Ed long enough. Now I felt the time was right to reel him in. So I proceeded to tell him about 1978, the wildest year ever. I had just gotten out of the joint, after having served four years for union extortion, when I started planning to fix basketball games at Boston College. I had heard about the potential in prison from the mastermind, Paul Mazzei from Pittsburgh. He had told me that he and a Pittsburgh bookie named Tony Perla had this kid who played for Boston, Rick Kuhn, who would shave points (miss shots) for a fee. They gave him cocaine and bought him a car and all kinds of shit. He was drugged up, and thought he was half a wiseguy. Perla put this whole thing together; we didn't. I'm sure Kuhn went to Mazzei with the idea. Kuhn was a lot older than the other players. He was originally from Pittsburgh and had gone to high school with Tony Perla's younger brother, Rocco. Mazzei had heard that we had won half a million bucks with the college baskets in one season, and he figured we could win a trainload if we just guaranteed we could beat the spread. See, Mazzei couldn't make as much because he didn't have the bookie network like the Luccheses. We could lay down a lot more bets, so it was a good partnership for everybody. Back then you could only bet a few hundred bucks on a game. Mazzei needed a big outfit to get it moving.

The day I got out of prison on the extortion rap, I went to see Mazzei in Pittsburgh. The main reason for the trip was to pick up some cash he owed me, but it was also to discuss Boston College. My wife picked me up from Lewisburg Federal Prison, drove me to the Philadelphia airport, and I flew on to Pittsburgh. I had to make it fast because I only had twenty-four hours to report to the halfway house. I went to pick up $15,000, and he didn't have it. What he did have were two garages full of pot. So I took two suitcases full of pot home and sold them myself. That's when I got started in the drug business. That's how I bought the house in Rockville Centre, taking the $15,000 I made from the suitcases and putting it down on the house.

Anyway, it was on that Pittsburgh trip that we started talking basketball. Mazzei had already used Rick Kuhn on games, but they didn't have enough juice or people to put it together—that, and he needed more players to play along. But the season was a ways off and I had bigger fish to fry— the biggest fish in the history of American armed robbery.

For the Boston thing, I was mainly responsible for making lots of bets and getting the other players to cooperate. Mazzei knew Kuhn would play along; I brought in more players and set up the bets around New York. One player, Jim Sweeney, claimed later he had nothing to do with it, but I know that he did because I was handing him the money myself. He was always the first one in line with his hand out, waiting to get his. Other players wanted me to bet their money. Ed McDonald believed Sweeney's claim of innocence until just a few years ago. That's why McDonald cut him such a good break later. Ed thought this kid was a victim, and he wasn't.

After the whole thing broke, there was this misconception that we lost money because the players didn't throw all the games we thought they would. Believe me, we made plenty of money. We told Mazzei and the others from Pittsburgh and Boston that we didn't make money, but we were lying. See, they were robbing us blind so it was okay for us to rob them right back. Once, we sent Mazzei to Vegas with a valise full of money, and he told us he didn't get it down on the game in time—and our pick was the winner. Bullshit, he took us on that one. He probably made $100,000 that we never found out about on that bet, but it was whoever could rob whoever first. We didn't give a fuck about those guys. Jimmy wanted to kill them all, and he would have eventually if he hadn't gotten put away himself.

I was also using Mazzei for some small-time gunrunning. I had a shitload of guns in the house from Paul Mazzei. I had six Mac 10s with silencers; one I gave to a major Rockville enforcer named Bill Arico, which I later got back after he got popped. And I had half a trunkload of pistols, about a half a gross. I had supplied all the gear for Lufthansa. Most of it I sold to Jimmy and Paulie; I got the guns dirt-cheap. Somebody from Mazzei's crew drove them in from Pittsburgh. They got them from Smith & Wesson or Colt; I think they had some executive over there who was pilfering that shit. They were brand new, in boxes, and they were beautiful things. At first, I didn't tell Paulie's crew about the machine guns because I was scared to turn them over to the freaking maniacs. I justified it for a little while because I knew how sick those guys were. Eventually, though, I told Jimmy I had a couple machine guns. I didn't tell him how, but it didn't matter.

■ ■ ■

I was becoming McDonald's all-time wet dream of a snitch. With these details, Ed was able to break open the whole Mazzei sports-fixing operation. One of the first things we did was set Mazzei up from McDonald's office. The D.A. in Pittsburgh and the D.A. in New York coordinated it. They were already hot on Mazzei because of the machine guns, which they found out I got from him. They really wanted him, and he flipped eventually. He was an informant years before, and I kind of knew that. They couldn't get him to flip in the beginning, but he wanted to flip anyway. He's hated me ever since for getting him collared. But screw him. He had ripped us off on the Vegas bets.

Now that I was officially in the Program and convinced that Ed would do all he could for me, I decided to give him his second early Christmas present: Lufthansa. There wasn't any way he could get a conviction, since all the witnesses had been rubbed out, but at least he could now understand how it all came about.

Even before the college fixes went down, Burke's crew began planning the biggest score of all, a heist that would make the Air France deal seem like chicken feed. We would be set for life. Yeah, right. Think again, Henry. What happened was that in September 1978, our airport bookie, Marty Krugman, tipped me that one of his most juiced-up bettors, a cargo supervisor named Lou Werner, was about to crack. Werner was a gambling addict who owed us a fortune. But we would look the other way with workers at the airport because they were constantly tipping us to incoming loot. It was a pretty good arrangement that had worked like butter for years.

Anyway, Jimmy Burke paid me fifty large for the tip. The job itself, which went down on December 11, 1978, has been written about before, so I won't repeat all the details except that Burke's crew got five million in cash and another million in jewels that were in transit with Lufthansa Airlines. It was the largest armed robbery in history. The day of the Lufthansa robbery, I went over to my girlfriend Linda's house in Manhattan and stayed there that night. Her mother was there. I had been fighting with Karen again, so where else to go but Linda's? I also made sure I was seen at restaurants and all that sort of stuff.

What Jimmy never knew was that the Feds had been building informants at the airport, many of whom knew that Werner had been planning to hit Lufthansa for months. So they came down on Werner before he knew what hit him. But Lou couldn't rat anybody out because he didn't know how it went down. So he just coughed up his cut, $20,000 that covered his betting losses, and went into the joint. But he got a reduced sentence for his cooperation and eventually went into the Program. And I went back to business as usual—in this case, back to overseeing the collegians up in Bean Town.

■ ■ ■

By the end of 1978 in New York, Jimmy Burke's true colors came out when he had the entire Lufthansa heist crew whacked out of desperation. He knew it was only a matter of time before the Feds flipped one of them. The first two to go were Stacks Edwards (December 18, 1978) and Marty Krugman (January 6, 1979).

Tommy DeSimone was the third one to get whacked, after Stacks and Marty—Tommy's wife Cookie reported him missing in the second week of January 1979. Paulie never liked Tommy. He despised him, but put up with him because Jimmy loved him and he was such a good whacker and such a good earner. So he dealt with him. Paulie would tell me, "Stay away from this motherfucker." There was so much bad blood there. The straw that broke the camel's back was when Tommy tried to rape Karen, which Paulie found out about, and Tommy's killing Foxy.

In my heart I knew Tommy was going to get whacked way before that. I knew Paulie would handle it; that I didn't have to worry about it. So Paulie set him up, but he had to be diplomatic about it. They probably had a big meeting with Paul Castellano, head of the Gambinos. The crews got together on this hit because Tommy was Burke's gut, and Burke was so powerful that he could've been the capo if he was Italian. So Paulie needed an alliance to take out Jimmy's guy.

Paulie and Gotti set Tommy up while I was in Florida to muscle a guy who sold Jimmy some bad coke. Paulie's son, Petey, and this guy, Bruno, two made guys, picked Tommy up that morning. Jimmy actually thought that Tommy was actually getting made. And guess who pulled the trigger on Tommy—none other than John Gotti. Gotti had just gotten made and he knew a good way to move up fast was to take out the guy who clipped Batts and Foxy. Gotti was the skipper of his crew, and they were getting more powerful by the hour because of their drug business and the money laundering. They would have meetings in my joint, The Suite. Gambino

underboss Aniello Dellacroce—"O'Neill" was his nickname—
used to come to my club two or three nights a week in the '70s.
I knew that whole crew—we were good friends.

I first met Gotti when I was fifteen years old. We were
from the same neighborhood. I used to see him all the time;
I knew him and his whole crew. We were three miles away
from each other, but he ran with a different crew. They were
Gambinos, and we were Luccheses. But yet, certain things,
especially a lot of the airport shit, we did with some of their
crew. Crap games and card games were the sort of things we
often did in partnership with the Gambinos. And they
shared with us. It was like General Motors and Ford.

I was told by a former Gambino crew blabbermouth, Sal
Polici, about Gotti being the triggerman in Tommy's hit. Sal
was a good friend of Foxy, the kid who Tommy whacked. He
was the first guy to testify against Gotti in the 1987 trial that
was fixed to acquit Gotti. Polici went into protection, and
then he left. He was a nut, but he still gets checks. "Sally
Umbatz" was his nickname. He got out of the army on a medical leave that said he was crazy. But he wasn't totally crazy.
Obviously he is crazy, half-crazy anyway.

Years later, when I was in California, Sally and I got
hooked up through the U.S. Attorney's office. He was living
in the valley at the time, and I was living in California, in the
ranch on Juniper Hills. I had a house by Magic Mountain.
Right after *GoodFellas* came out, we wrote the treatment for
the movie *Getting Gotti*. We were paid $30,000, and I got
half that. We were supposed to get royalties, but in typical
Hollywood crook style, I have yet to see a dime. Anyway,
that's when Sal told me that Gotti himself had whacked
Tommy. There were no eyewitnesses, so I don't know how
he knew, but Sal was dead certain of it. I even confronted a
couple of agents on it. They may have picked it up on wire-

taps, but they ain't going volunteer anything. Some things they would share with me; some things they wouldn't. But the bottom line is that after I told them what I heard, the agents confirmed what Sal told me. And if I had known what Tommy had done to Karen, I'd have been right there with Gotti unloading on that bastard.

Anyway, who knows where they buried Tommy? Up until 1990, the government still thought Tommy was alive. There were Tommy DeSimone sightings all over the country.

Getting back to 1979, we soon came to realize that the deaths of Marty, Stacks, and Tommy were just the prelude. Jimmy was destroyed over Tommy's murder, but he was too busy killing people himself to go into mourning—he still had more Lufthansa guys on the loose. So in just a few months, Jimmy Burke turned into a Mob serial killer. He next clipped Tommy's girlfriend Teresa Ferrara (February 10), then Tom Monteleone and Louis and Joanna Cafora (March). The Sicilians called this kind of thing "the White Death." The killers took a month off, then got back to work hitting the rest of the heist crew: "Joe Buddha" Manri (May 15), Frenchy McMahon (May 16), Paolo LiCastri (June 13), and Angelo Sepe (July 18). Some bodies, like Tommy's, were never found.

When bodies started showing up after Lufthansa, the whole city knew who the fuck did this robbery. No matter where we went it was, "Hey, Money Bags!" It was no secret, believe me; it was Burke's crew. But they couldn't prove shit. Meanwhile I didn't get any serious money for a few months afterward. But I had what I needed. And if I needed more money I'd go see Jimmy, and he'd put up a sucker's holler. "What are you, shaking me down?" He was getting it from all sides—from the whole crew and everybody who knew him. It's because the whole borough knew he had just made a killing at the airport.

Except for $20,000 from Lou Werner, the Feds would never find the money, and I am always asked if I know what happened to it. I can only tell you what I heard. The money was dispersed to Jimmy and Paulie's families, and they were told to sit on it for a long time. Eventually they laundered it by opening small businesses, especially in Miami. They all had places in Florida, and I heard that's where the money was sent.

■ ■ ■

The investigators could not believe what I was giving them. I had told them where the bodies were buried, and I mean real bodies. And I knew that Jimmy Burke would be digging up those bodies soon. From the beginning, I told the Feds, "Man, you got to go hit the basement of Robert's Lounge, and then underneath the bocce courts. This one's buried there. That one's buried there—guys like Spider and Remo." I even drew them maps. And they looked at me like I was nuts. It took them about three weeks to check it out because they had to convince the U.S. Attorney, who had to convince Washington to give them a search warrant. But they didn't move fast enough. I told them, "He's gonna dig up these bodies." Well sure e-fucking-nough the day they get there Jimmy was in work clothes and the basement of his bar, Robert's Lounge, had been newly cemented—the spots where all the bodies had been. He had dug them all up already. The bozos blew that one.

Back in the neighborhood, both Jimmy and Paulie had figured out what was going down from the get-go. By the time the marshals started showing up at my house, everybody was convinced that I'd flipped. They knew for sure. And I knew they knew. I knew that when Jimmy couldn't reach me he would figure I flipped. I was trying to tell the Feds, "Jimmy knows I flipped by now. He's not going to send nobody near my house, because he doesn't know who's there." Meanwhile, no one's there.

About six weeks into this process they brought me face-to-face with Jimmy, who was back in custody, in the basement of the federal building. With Burke in jail I felt a little safer. The first court appearance was Jimmy's parole violation. On April 13, 1980, life had finally caught up with Jimmy Burke. He was arrested on a parole violation, bailed himself out briefly, but had been rearrested because of my debriefs. They pulled him in on a technicality—consorting with criminals. This was a catch-all phrase that let the Feds keep him incarcerated without an indictment. So they used that to pull him back into custody. Now Jimmy was there and this was my first eyeball-to-eyeball with any of the gang, but I was pissed because I was told I wouldn't have to go eyeball-to-eyeball with anybody. I would never have to go on the stand—McDonald swore to me. Of course I realized, "Hey, there ain't a thing I can do about it." Like I said, I reread and reread and reread that deal I had with the U.S. attorneys in Washington, so I made up in my mind that I was gonna be 101 percent totally honest for the first time in my life, no matter what it took. I'd been living on lies and deceit my entire life.

This was the first time I faced Jimmy. This was not in a courtroom, but it was like a courtroom. They brought Jimmy in, they held him for a few days, and then they had this hearing, but not in an open court. They didn't want to bring me in an open court at this point. I was scared shitless.

So they brought me into this makeshift courtroom of the federal building. I sat there with Ed McDonald and probably six FBI agents, so I didn't feel threatened. Jimmy sat at one table, and I sat at another. He was in prison garb. He didn't look at me once, but I looked at him. I thought, "Well, fuck it. We're both facing a federal judge." Finally Jimmy looked over at me, and he knew. I knew he knew. And we both knew that he was screwed. You could see that look in his eyes: "Cocksucker."

It was pretty simple. Once I sat there, I relaxed, took a few deep breaths, and answered the questions. It was a fifteen-minute thing. In and out. But now they got Burke locked up tight, and I wanted him locked up because I know if he was out there, I was in trouble. He was handcuffed while he was in the joint, to a certain extent. He could always send out messages, mouth-to-mouth, giving commands, because he was good at that. He was good, Jimmy, a brilliant man. He knew every angle, so I'd rather him be in than out.

■ ■ ■

Meanwhile, Karen and the family stayed in the safe house in the Hamptons. Even when I was there, the Feds were constantly debriefing me either in the cottage or while we were walking on the beach. There was an office out in Suffolk County where I would go sometimes, because it was a long-ass haul to the U.S. Attorney's office in Brooklyn.

The whole time Burke's crew was on the move. They figured I'd always be in contact with my girlfriend Linda, and they were right. So the guy who I was partners with at The Suite, Joey Rossano—who today is a wiseguy in Vegas, sent his girlfriend—half-a-wiseguy and real, real close with Kathy Burke to see Linda. They tried to bribe her to give me up. Then they had private investigators checking her phone records. They knew how to find somebody. They had connections in the phone company and credit card companies; they even had cars waiting for me outside the federal building. They had it set up so that it was unbelievable. But the Feds drove me out in a different car every day, with different drivers every day. Tinted windows. Vans. And there was always a car in front and a car in back, so no one could get in between us. But Jimmy's guys had machine guns. I know because I supplied them.

The wiseguys even visited my brother in California, offering him two million dollars. John Savino—a guy whose brother was in the Nassau County jail with me—made the offer. They visited him a couple of times. My brother chased them off: "Get the fuck out of here."

I was worried about everybody. It was a terrible burden. I let the Feds know this was probably going on, so some of them made trips to Jimmy's crew and Paulie's guys. They read them the riot act about any ideas of retribution against me or my family or friends. The Feds went to every one of the wiseguys and told them, "You motherfuckers. You want to play that way? We'll play dirty, too." They'd say, "You stay away from them, because if you think that there was a parade of bodies before, there's gonna be another parade of bodies." The Feds pretty much operate clean, but the FBI used to play hardball—in a heartbeat. There are certain things that those FBI agents won't admit—they can't admit. It was a different organization back then.

The Mob started playing clean when they realized these guys could get tough, too; and I think it actually surprised them. By this time I was drained—emotionally and physically. So when the Feds said it was time to pull up stakes and start the new life, I was more than ready. I couldn't wait to get out of New York.

■ ■ ■

After about a month, we left the Hamptons and were off to Connecticut, where the Program's processing center was, for about a month. After the Witness Protection Program accepts you, they put you up. It's got to be approved by the U.S. Attorney in Washington. It took about three weeks to a month to get our papers. I think they told us to pick a name, and my first choice was Peter Haines. Then the FBI turned us over to the marshal service. That's what happens in Connecticut, around Hartford somewhere. We stayed in motels and hotels until we got our papers. Today, the processing center has its own lodging, so you don't need to stay in hotels anymore. Back then, the Witness Protection Program wasn't as well-known as it is today.

Once we got all our new identifications, we packed to go—somewhere. There was a lot of stuff we didn't take, like all my wife's furs from the airport swag and the jewels from the Lauder deal (not to mention the dope I had hidden in the walls). We didn't know where we were going until we got to the airport. The head marshal, Al McNeil, went with us. One marshal always went with us. So, basically, it was Ed, me, my wife, my two kids, and our pet bird.

CHAPTER EIGHT

BUMBLING

BURGLERS

L ufthansa, gun running, and Boston College. Those were the major deals. But in between, there were dozens of smaller adventures. Our crew soon came to the conclusion that we didn't need to spend six months planning a complicated JFK Airport hit, when all we had to do was snatch-and-grab jobs at the Manhattan apartments of millionaires who were known to horde their private treasures. You could pull them off without having to cut in an army of confederates. It was a piece of cake.

So, despite all that was going down, we found time in 1979 to rob the cosmetics millionairess, Esteé Lauder, at her townhouse off Park Avenue. The Lauder thing came from Bobby Germaine, who was going out with a furrier named Alice. She was Sammy "The Arab" Nalo's girlfriend, too, and hooked up all the scores for Nalo. She was a piece of work. She knew where all the high-class people lived and would go to their homes. After a score we'd cut her in on a piece of the action. Alice was cool. She made my wife this silver fox coat and cap and muff.

For years Sammy Nalo and his crew had been pulling the big one-shot heists in town. That crew was legendary. Nalo had just gotten out of the joint for the Pierre Hotel thing—he and his partner, Bobby Comfort, got almost ten million from that 1972 stickup. They had a great crew, and three of them got away scot-free, with ninety percent of the loot. Although Comfort did time for it, I'm sure that when he got out he put his hands on some of the stash. There was a good book about the heist, *The Man Who Robbed the Pierre*, which I think is being made into a movie. Today there are too many informants to pull off that kind of thing.

Anyway, their basic MO was to stick up fancy New York hotels early in the morning and go through the safe deposit boxes of the bluebloods. They had robbed the Regency in August 1970. In that one, they put the friggin' safe on a dolly and took the whole thing. But they missed Elizabeth Taylor, who was upstairs the whole time with a couple million in diamonds and other gems. Then they broke into Sophia Loren's pad in the Hampshire House and bagged a half-a-mil in jewels—which she had forgotten to insure, by the way.

For the Lauder thing, basically I provided the guns. Bobby Germaine and I were fifty-fifty partners. We brought in Arico and his friend. Nalo had come up with the score, but was with nobody; he didn't have a rabbi—a boss. That's why those guys would come to me; they needed protection from the wiseguys. They didn't come to me because they liked me—they needed me because they knew I could set up the robberies and get the wiseguys their cut.

I navigated the whole deal once we got the logistics figured out. All the parties came to my house. Karen made up one of Arico's crew to look like an Estee Lauder chauffeur. She was an accomplice.

I remember we cased the operation for a couple weeks before going in. We learned Lauder's schedule. She had dinner every Tuesday at Elaine's, a restaurant in New York. We followed her chauffeur with one car in front and one behind. Once we even bumped him, and he got out. It was an accident, but it was no big deal. It was a love tap. He couldn't move. We had him pinned in. Bobby and Bill walked with him. And they told him, "Just stay calm and get back in there," and then the Cadillac moves away. Once we learned that she was picked up by a driver at the same time every Tuesday, we made our final plan. I would not go on the heist, but I was told later how it went down.

Around 5 P.M. on Tuesday, a couple of weeks before Halloween, Arico and Nalo rang the bell to Lauder's apartment. The maid answered, but was really hesitant to open the door. Arico said, "I'm the chauffeur. I'm here to pick up Mrs. Lauder." Then another guy comes to the door and says, "You're not the chauffeur, because *I'm* the chauffeur!" He kind of questioned Arico through the door. But it was too late because the door was ajar and the guys just shoved their way in. After that it was a piece of cake. They tied everybody up. Lauder, her butler, and her people then became cooperative. In her two wall safes she had a huge collection of jewels. She also had pastes—*fugazis*. But she also had a lot of red rubies. Every stone she had was perfect. Nobody got hurt and it didn't take long at all—maybe fifteen minutes. A smash-and-grab job. In three or four hours, they were back with the shit. We split the load in half. Arico got $50,000 from the fences, and me and Bobby sold off the rest, pulling in maybe $100,000 to $200,000.

We missed the tiaras; we missed the big rocks. Lauder had brought them over to her bank that morning and put them in safe deposit boxes. It was a coincidence that she picked that day to move them to the bank. We messed up on that one. But still, we ended up with four or five million. It was really good stuff—gorgeous Harry Winston. The big stones—the three-, four-, or five-karat stones—are easy to fence because you can just take them right out of their settings. But the pieces that are had to get rid of are the small, intricate things.

Bobby Germaine and I took half, and the crew took the other half. Then we brought ours to one guy to fence it. He offered us half a million. We didn't want that: "Fuck you." The newspapers reported that seven million dollars was lifted, but it was like four or five million dollars worth of jewels. So we had to take the stones out of the settings to sell them individually. It so happened that Casey Rosado—the Cuban I got arrested with—had a friend named Pepe who was a jeweler. Casey got Pepe to break them out, and we paid him well. Now Bobby didn't trust anybody because he was half-paranoid. That was Bobby's mentality. So for two days Bobby sat with a .45 on this guy, snorting coke, while he was dismantling all the pieces. Anyway, we put all the stones into one big pile. And every stone was perfect—or so we thought.

So we got all these huge piles of stones, and Bobby said, "Fuck it. We can go to the diamond center, little by little, and get wholesale for them." This was my job, so I took the first batch of these beautiful stones, the highest grade. "Ooh, there's a little chip in it," my diamond fence said. This motherfucker Pepe had chipped ninety-five percent of the stones. He was so freaking nervous because the gun was at his head, being held by a guy who was high as a kite on coke.

Now we had four million dollars worth of stones. They weren't all defective, but about ninety percent of them had problems. We knew we wouldn't be getting top dollar, so we ended up keeping the stones. Since I still had money from Lufthansa, I didn't need the money. That Christmas I had a ton of jewelry made up for people from the stones—stickpins and diamond earrings and bracelets. I gave Paulie a bunch of beautiful pieces I'd had made for Christmas. I don't know if we gave him a cut of the profit; we might have. He didn't care. This was after Lufthansa, so he was happy. But I took care of him. I gave his sons beautifully designed, gorgeous stickpins with diamonds and rubies.

One set of earrings that Lauder had was shaped like a yin-yang symbol. Each earring was an inch and a half across, and it was made with quarter-karat diamonds—worth $35,000, each earring. I didn't even show Karen the earrings. Some shit I kept separate, because if I showed them to Karen she would glom it. So I had two rings made out of them that Christmas. I gave one to Karen and one to Bobby. Everybody was jealous of it, even Paulie.

The week after I gave the ring to her, she had this character, Steve Fish, living with us, who was a gay hairdresser and a fancy Fifth Avenue–type of dude. I was always giving him money because he always owed this one and that one, no matter how much money he made. He used to bring his boyfriends over. We knew his mother. Karen's kid sister, Adrienne, who was wild as a motherfucker back then, first brought him around, and Karen was a typical fag-hag. She loved them. Keep in mind, my house in Long Island was a lunatic asylum by this point. My sister-in-law used to live in the house most of the time, and everybody was on drugs except for the kids, who were at my mother-in-law's most of the time anyway. We used to rollerskate through the living room. I bought about a dozen pair of roller skates, and we used to skate through the damn house. There was a crew of about ten broads—Jewish princesses from the Five Towns—and every one of them couldn't wait to meet me and fuck me. I even had twins. And they all went on to marry well. They didn't have their own money. One married into the Firestones. Another girl I was screwing worked in a bank, and she used to get me the safety deposit boxes.

One day Karen said to me, "Hey, I can't find my ring. Do you know where it is?" I said, "How would I know where it is?" But I started to figure it out because I didn't see Steve around the house. So I said, "That little fucking cocksucker took it." Karen said, "No way. No way. I must've lost it." She was making excuses for him. Now I got crazy because it's worth $35,000 wholesale. But mainly I wanted to prove that he lied to Karen; that was more important than the $35,000. I was pissed off. I figured if he stole it, he's gonna fence it, and I wanted to catch him before he sold it. I went to his mother's house. "He's in Florida with his boyfriend," she said. Now I knew he did it. And Karen was still denying, so I argued with her: "That little cocksucker's got it." So the kid came back a few days later from Florida. I didn't say anything. He came into the house and said, "Oh, what's the matter?" "Steve, sit down," I said. "Steven, did you take the ring?" "Oh, I would never steal from you people." And this went on for a half-hour, because I just kept on interrogating him. So I stood up and I punched him in the head. I hit him so hard I broke my index knuckle. I couldn't close my hand, but I didn't even hurt him. He started confessing to everything. "Where is it? Where is it? I want it back." "Well, I sold it." He told me he got ten-grand for it. Steven said, "I'll pay you back $100 a week." "Take me there," I told him. So we got in the car, and he cried the whole way. "Shut up, I ain't gonna hit you again, you motherfucker. I'll kill you," I said. "You could've asked me for the thing." So I had ten-grand in my pocket, went down to the jewelry store, and bought it back.

The upshot is that Steven is a big-deal hairdresser now. Meanwhile, I still can't close my hand, which is disfigured. To this day I go to a doctor for it. Every time I try to close it, I'm reminded of that cocksucker.

■ ■ ■

When my girlfriend Linda's birthday rolled around, I started to think, "What the hell am I going to bring her for a gift? I'm not going to get her roses." I wasn't even seeing her at the time. By then I had done plenty of other girls, though. I can't believe I lived that way, now that I even think about it. Terrible. But I still cared for Linda, so I went through Karen's stash from Lauder and Karen walked in and asked, "What are you doing?" I said, "I need a piece of jewelry to give to this guy; I owe him a favor." And she went through all this stuff, each one is $10,000, $20,000 a piece, and said, "Here, this choker thing." She never wore it, even though it was 18-karat gold, and with the stones it's probably worth $25,000 today. I grabbed that and I put it in my pocket. I took it to the jewelry store in Rockville Centre and I said, "Give it a quick cleaning." The guy said, "It doesn't need it." I said, "Clean it. Clean it." I went next door, bought a dozen long-stemmed roses, and wrapped this chain around them. I picked up Linda at her place on 84th and York. Beautiful place. Her millionaire boyfriend, Ed Lanso, was there. He was in women's shoes foot fairs—conventions and shows, like fashion shows. "Wait, who's the nice guy?" he asked. Anyway, I hired a limo and took her to the best restaurant in Manhattan; I think it was like $500 for dinner.

Eventually I got some money for my stash. I would get $35,000 for these big, big stones, and I sold a lot of gold. I made maybe a hundred thousand, but I didn't give a shit. I was in the junk business at the time, making $25,000 a week. I didn't need the money. It was just another headache to hide the jewels.

I had about another $50,000 worth of jewels stolen from me by parking attendants. I had just picked it up from the jewelers. We went shopping on Fifth Avenue—to Gucci's—and I bought my wife a whole bunch of stuff and a big pocketbook. I pulled in to park the car in valet at one of the hotels we were going to—the Pierre, or somewhere—and I put all the stuff into the glove compartment. What she couldn't fit in her purse I put into a big Gucci bag. I put it in the trunk; I guess the valets were watching. We went to the hotel lounge because I had a meeting there. She set her pocketbook down on the floor. We sat with whoever I was meeting with. Three hours later, we got up to leave and her pocketbook was gone. I said, "What the fuck? How could you leave the pocketbook on the floor?" My guess is that the valet must've told the busboys.

They never had an Estée Lauder trial—Lauder didn't want to press charges because she didn't want any more publicity. She played it down; she didn't even want the jewelry back. She had so much money and she didn't want to be bothered. She even told the press that only $6,000 in cash was taken, but the cops later admitted to about a million.

But it was a lot more, believe me. I know jewels. Anyway, her insurance company took care of everything. The government still got their share. She never wanted it back—even the stuff I turned in when I got nailed years later. When I got popped years later and went into the Program, I had to turn over as much swag as I had left. That included these packets of Lauder diamonds I had stashed in the house. The Feds knew they were stolen, but they didn't know they were from the Esteé Lauder score.

In a few weeks we figured that Sammy Nalo hadn't cut up the Lauder take right. He had shorted us a couple million; he screwed us. So Bobby said, "We're gonna whack him." So I said, "Fine, let's do it." We set him up to get a call in a phone booth by the University of Natural History café, where he used to hang out. He used that phone booth all the time while one of his guys stood by. We took a different car, with me driving and Billy Arico shooting. We machine-gunned him with one of the guns that Billy and I got from Pittsburgh. But we didn't kill him. He didn't die, that cocksucker. We used the Mac 10, so it's a miracle he pulled through. We had silencers on them and the recoil was terrible, so the bullets sprayed the whole phone booth. He didn't even know it was us who shot him—he didn't see us. This was the second time he had been shot. He was shot up in 1975 for the same stupid reason. I guess he didn't learn his lesson.

■ ■ ■

So Sammy Nalo had recovered from the phone booth shooting, but he still didn't know that we shot him. Now he came to us with another score, and I agreed to unload the take for him. This time he had targeted a Manhattan diamond district jewelry store called Spritzer & Fuhrman. I was like the boss, the kingpin of this score. Bobby Germaine and I supplied everything—guns, suitcases, disguises—plus, I was supposed to move all the stuff; fence it, that is. The deal was for us to get fifty percent of the take.

The stickup went down on Saturday, December 8, 1979. New York City on a Saturday morning is like a ghost town, at least it used to be back then. You could shoot a cannon down the middle of 47th Street and you wouldn't hit anything— the diamond district was run by Jews who observed Sabbath on Saturday. Nalo and his crew went to the store while Germaine and I waited back on the Island. They were supposed to be at my house by ten o'clock. When they didn't get home in a couple hours I knew something was up—no phone call, nothing. Then it was all over the radio, the news flashes. I heard it and I'm thinking, "Uh-oh, something's up." They got caught red-handed and took seventeen hostages to boot. That part was just crazy.

Meanwhile Bobby went over to Nalo's to pick up the jewels, but there was one cop in particular, O'Connor, who was hot to bag Nalo's gang. He knew there was a robbery going down, or he had a good idea there was from an informant. But he didn't know who the mark was. O'Connor was half-broke and was hoping to make a good collar and get promoted. Those were some good cops back in the old days.

So this cop was driving up and down the street, sitting on Nalo's apartment. He didn't know Bobby, but he spotted him at Nalo's place opening his trunk and taking out the suitcases. The cop knew that the suitcases were empty because he saw the way Bobby carried them. It was real good detective work and this guy wasn't even on the job that day; he was just sitting on Nalo because he had a tip. He spotted Bobby and said, "Aha,"—now he was sure. So the cop rushed into the building, but Bobby saw him coming and got out the back door. I skated because I was home.

Nalo got nineteen years in the joint, but he only served about six. I don't know where he is today.

■　■　■

This is when the Feds started showing up at my house with their grisly photos. Apparently somebody saw all these weapons in my house, or knew I had them. Maybe they picked it up from wiretaps. I don't know. The ATF and the Feds—the organized crime Lucchese family Feds—busted my house up as soon as my kids went to school one morning. That was the first time, about two months before I finally got arrested, that the Feds raided my house. They had tried to get me on a lot of different charges prior to guns.

This time about twenty agents showed up. They came to my house about May 10 or 11, 1980. The first time the ATF and FBI wanted to grab the weapons I was getting from Pittsburgh. Believe it or not, at about two in the morning I had moved a couple of Mac 10s with silencers. I didn't even have a buyer in mind. I didn't want the guns. I mean, I wanted them, but I didn't want them. Those things, they could shoot. First of all a Mac 10 with a silencer is only about a foot long. It looks like a little square box until you pull the extension arm out. Then you screw on the silencer, which is about another foot long; you put two of them together. It fires 200 rounds a second, with a silencer. It disintegrates a person in a second; it's scary. This is CIA-type stuff. They don't even use them in combat. They shoot nine-millimeter shells.

Anyway, about two o'clock that morning I said, "I gotta get these guns out." I had seen these cops around and these guns alone could have gotten me a life sentence. The Feds were there all the time, for a couple of months, a little more visible lately and easy to spot. A friend of ours, a friend of Adrienne's boyfriend, had a twenty-four-hour gas station in the next town. I got the guns from the basement, loaded them into the trunk of the car, and drove over to the gas station. I stashed them in an underground gasoline tank vault. They would never think to look there. When the cops showed up at my house I thought to myself, "Wow, you dodged a big one there!" It was all the state agents, Lucchese squad, and ATF.

I had one pistol on me, by the bed, and Karen put that in her panties. That was the only one I was worried about. There was only a little bit of drugs, but they didn't have a warrant so I didn't care. First they said, "It's over. We want to talk to you." They started going through the house. First they put us in a little office room I had in the house, then, after they finished their search, they took us to the dining room. They started laying out the photos of the murder victims from the Lufthansa heist one at a time. With each picture they told Karen, "Your best friend here, your best friend here." They were showing the worst views they had from the crime scenes. These were people I had known since I was sixteen. Those murder scene pictures were horrible. They had me good and mad. "You're next," they said. "This won't go away." So I said, "Just let me call my lawyer. You've got to give me a phone call. I've got to have my lawyer here." I immediately knew it was routine. "What are you calling your lawyer for?" one of them asked. I ignored him and called my lawyer, Richie Oddo, who lived a few miles from me in the next town over, but it was seven o'clock in the morning. He told me, "I can settle this." It turned out that calling him in was a huge mistake.

Meanwhile they had planted the seeds for me to cooperate. They were practically pleading with me, "Please, please." Sweeney and Guevara were the main guys interrogating me. They couldn't arrest me yet, so they were just trying to save our damn lives, basically. They knew we were gonna get killed. They said, "We have information that you're going to be next. We have tape recordings, do you want to hear?" I said, "I don't want to hear shit. I don't believe it." "How the hell can you not believe it?" they asked. "You're the only one, look. You see it in front of you." So this goes on through my lawyer, and it was a whole drama scene. When I realized they found nothing, I figured I had dodged a big one. What were they going to do?

Then my lawyer came racing over to my house while the Feds were showing me and my wife pictures of corpses to scare us. Oddo stopped all that shit and chased them out. But Oddo told Jimmy and Paulie what had happened. After that, every time Jimmy would see me, he'd say, "The Feds were over your house? You been talkin' to them?" What the hell? Where was this guy coming from? He never talked to me that way before. He never spoke to me that way. But he was whacked out. He was taking liquid speed, pharmaceutical stuff his wife was getting from a diet doctor. He was half-insane during this period when everyone was getting whacked. He was also drinking tremendous amounts of booze, because if you take liquid speed you can drink all day and night and think you're sober. So I just saw how crazy he was. In fact, Jimmy at one point made me strip when I went over to pick up a shipment of heroin. Now I don't know if he was checking for a wire or track, because I was losing a lot of weight. And I got real leery then. He told me, "Get off that fucking shit." I didn't listen. I was constantly high and pulling down $20,000 to $30,000 a week. So that's why I didn't give two fucks about the Lufthansa money. I had plenty of money.

A couple of weeks later the Feds visited me again— another visit out of the blue. "We want to talk to you," they said, "Here's some more bodies, man. You are gonna be next. You got to start talking." I told them, "I don't know what you guys're talking about."

So I stonewalled them and said, "Look, do me a favor. I don't want to call my lawyer again, but if you stay here another minute I'm picking up the phone." The Feds left. That time I didn't say shit—I didn't call a lawyer or nothing. I told Karen to keep her mouth shut. When I eventually got pinched, I thought it was the Feds because of all this. But it wasn't. And I knew they were watching me; they were following me all over the place. Usually I'd lose them. I was able to lose them most of the time—if I felt like losing them.

Karen's sisters were real vulnerable—especially Adrienne, of all people. She was around all the time and was friends with my girlfriend, Linda. I tell you, it was a crazy scene. I didn't want Adrienne involved in this although she was involved with a couple of wiseguys, and both of the sisters were doing coke with me. One of Adrienne's wiseguy boyfriends had gotten whacked. I thought he was the one who had first informed on me and could have been connected to this craziness. By now I had finally gotten it into my brain that the other shoe was going to drop soon, and the fewer the victims the better.

All along I thought it was the Feds who were watching me for Lufthansa, so I was stunned when Nassau County narcs collared me. I was told the informant was a guy from Gotti's crew, but I had no doubt who had fingered me. If it wasn't for my constant home improvements, I might not have gotten caught, at least not then. You see, wherever I spent money, I knew the people I was paying and I paid cash. That goes for the contractors I had at my new house—I knew them. I had just bought a fixer-upper, which it really wasn't—it was a solid, good house. I bought it from an old Italian contractor, and even got the mortgage through a friend of ours who had a bank. Karen had a blank check to decorate and buy clothes. Unbelievable. The guy who used to decorate all the nightclubs for our crew was an architect, and he pitched in his two-cents' worth. This one bedroom that I built—"The Moon Room," I used to call it—looked like a discotheque. It had solid push-open doors with no knobs on them.

I put it in my sister-in-law's name, and transferred funds to her account. She's still got the house and now she's the principal of a nearby school. But believe me, I rebuilt it from the roof to the lawns. And it was the lawn work that was my undoing. That's how we got popped.

At the time, Bobby Germaine's son, Bobby, Jr., did all my lawn and garden work. He and another kid were working for me, but basically they just dug everything up. Bobby, Jr., had gotten popped six months before and was cooperating with the DEA, unbeknownst to yours truly. So he gave me up. He didn't know I was partners with his father, or maybe he did and didn't care. When they came to get me they thought it was just cocaine, because Bobby had seen five kilos of cocaine. I think I actually used him to transport some coke to Pittsburgh or to Cleveland—I had another connection for heroin in Cleveland. I used Billy Arico as a courier also. Thanks to Bobby, Jr., the Feds were tapping into my phone calls to Paul Mazzei's dog-grooming place in Pittsburgh. Paul had a friend who owned a golf shop, and we decided to use golf terms and pet jargon as code words for drug deals. So I'd be talking on my tapped phone, jawing with Paul about golf balls and dog collars instead of kilos and ounces—like we were fooling the Feds. And, unbeknownst to me, they were listening to all of this talk on wiretaps.

Danny Mann was the head of the Nassau County narcotics squad, and he popped me. He took me to his office that night after he popped me and said, "Man, you're the fucking best." He's a nice guy. We became friends. He's retired somewhere in North Carolina. I ended up spending about a month in the joint, first at the Manhattan Correctional Center, then the Nassau County jail. I didn't tell them I was on drugs. In other words, I had to quit cold turkey. It was pretty tough because I had been using heroin for seven or eight months—just snorting a lot of it, because Italians have a thing about injecting drugs; a lot of guys don't want to do that.

I was facing twenty-eight-to-life for Lufthansa, but I didn't think they could get a conviction, even though half of Queens knew who did the Lufthansa job. But at the same time, Ed McDonald and I both knew I was next on Burke's (or Vario's) hit parade, because he couldn't take the chance of me ratting him out. That first weekend in custody, I thought I was gonna get whacked in the joint. Knowing my number was up, I had them put me into protective custody. I was well aware that Jimmy could have me killed in Fort Knox if he wanted. I called my parole officer after about a week in jail and told him I got arrested. They had a special squad of parole officers that just took care of the wiseguys. They're really cool dudes, and they're no longer parole officers—I think they're attorneys now. They had this special three-guy team, and all the wiseguys had one or the other.

Then it was in all the papers, and after a few days in the joint I started thinking, "Why ain't Paulie bailing me out? What's going on here?" And my bail wasn't that high. I think it was $50,000 or $100,000. I was out on a quarter-million-dollar bail or $350,000 bail before, and they had taken care of that. Since I was already freaking because of going cold turkey, I was paranoid as anything. I was even more certain they had decided I had flipped, even though I hadn't. I knew I was gonna die, and all because of this heroin business. I was only in that business for about a year, but it was a huge mistake from every standpoint.

Soon they picked up Jimmy for the Lufthansa robbery, but they couldn't hold him. So he skipped out of jail and, with no witnesses, figured he'd got that beaten. He had killed everybody now except me, so he didn't have to worry. But he had to worry about all the other crimes I could connect him to. I'm totally sure he was worried about it.

I wasn't worried about Paulie, Lenny, and the rest of the Luccheses. They knew me all my life, and they knew that I would put a gun in my mouth and pull the trigger before I'd ever rat on them. But Jimmy would've chopped my wife and kids up and fed them to me. That's the way Jimmy Burke was; he'd lock them in refrigerators until they suffocated. Jimmy used to say to his captives: "You have four minutes to live, whattaya wanna do? You don't do what you're supposed to do, I'm gonna lock your kid in a fucking refrigerator." That's how vicious this man was. I knew what he was capable of, so I was more worried about Burke than Vario. Absolutely. Vario knew I wouldn't hurt him too much, and I didn't. I could've got Paulie for murders and shit, but I loved Paulie. It wasn't only Vario that I would protect as long as possible. I skipped over a lot of people because I knew they weren't bad people. I might give up killers like Burke, but that's it. And when I finally ratted, I went for their jugulars because even a guy like me had some kind of twisted moral code. Burke, I knew he was a sick mother. I had seen nine or ten months of his violence. I was so pissed off at him for killing Marty, because he promised me he wasn't going to kill him. The other guys

I didn't care about. I guess he had to kill Marty. I can see it now—but he swore to me he wouldn't.

When they didn't bail me out, I knew. They were pennywise and powerful. They didn't want a trail leading to them. They hadn't seen the information from the district attorney's wiretaps yet, so they had no idea. But once they saw them, forget about it; it was a death warrant. And Bobby's son had a death warrant, too. Because on these tape recordings they put the informant's name and number, so and so and so and so, residing at the same address as Bobby Germaine. They don't black that out. How dumb was that? It was idiotic. That's how dumb cops are sometimes. It was insanity for me at this point. If narcs hadn't caught up with me, I would definitely have self-destructed within months. Even without the Feds' visits, Jimmy was so paranoid I'm sure he would have whacked me before the year was out. I guess I should thank Bobby Germaine, Jr., for setting me up. I know now that it saved my life.

Finally, I bailed myself out, using Karen's parents' house as collateral, and the DEA turned over two months of wiretap transcripts to my attorney. I read through them in horror, because they had us cold. And Jimmy was all over them. I was talking to him like I had a radio license. The drug dealing was all there. I knew once I got this material from the Nassau County District Attorney's office, Jimmy would get the same material. And both of us were all over those tapes. Paulie's son was all over those tapes. Everybody was all over those tapes. All of these guys were goners. The only way they wouldn't get indicted is if there were no trial, and for that to happen I had to be dead. It's not rocket science. But I didn't say shit to anybody. I didn't say shit to Jimmy, but I refused to go and hide. I just kept quiet all around to see if this cat had one more life. The trouble was that Jimmy's attorney also had the transcripts, so Jimmy was frantic that I was going to flip to save my ass. He asked me to meet him at the Sherwood Diner on Rockaway Boulevard. We kept it casual, but I was certain that I was not going to walk out alive. I knew it. Jimmy proposed that I go to Florida to whack the informant, Bobby Germaine, Jr., but I smelled a setup. The guys he wanted me to travel with were the very guys who were heard in the wiretaps telling Jimmy *I* needed to be clipped.

But almost immediately the Feds rearrested me on material witness charge for Lufthansa. Their guys were furious at me. "How could you meet with Burke? You're gonna get whacked." I knew I was gonna get whacked. When I met Jimmy at the diner, I knew for sure, no ifs, ands, or buts about it, that I was gonna end up eating lime dust in a shallow grave. But I didn't care. I lived my life. I lived those last years of my life knowing I could go any time. I knew it wouldn't come because of my actions. I thought I was intelligent enough not to get involved in a lot of the mistakes that a lot of those guys who got whacked got involved in. I was afraid of getting whacked, but at the same time I was ready for it. I wasn't afraid of dying, but I sure didn't want to give them an excuse to do it. I'd seen so much death to that point in my life I didn't want to die, but who does? The tough part was that I loved my children and my wife. I loved them as a unit, although I wasn't in love with my wife anymore. I was most worried that I didn't know what would ever happen to them if I got clipped.

Soon they rearrested Burke, who by now knew he should've killed me that Sunday in the diner. He knew it was over. They also pulled in Vario, and a month later, Lou Werner was found guilty for his role in Lufthansa. But before he was to be sentenced to a twenty-five-year term, he started cooperating. He then became the first of our guys to go into the Witness Protection Program. I wasn't far behind him, and I knew a whole hell of a lot more about Jimmy and Paulie's operations than Lou.

That's my dad, a hardworking Irishman (note the bandages on his right hand), with my kid brother Joey on the left and yours truly on the right. A rare photo of me while I'm still an innocent.

Visitors' Weekend in the Federal Pen. Karen, standing behind me, came out with a couple of pals from Rockville.

Would you believe Wimbledon? OK, it's actually me and the legendary Johnny Dio (kneeling) in prison.

Rabbi Mark and I kicking back at a hotel near the Federal Pen.

A "class photo" from Wiseguy College, otherwise known as prison.

Karen, Greg, and Gina visit me at Lewisburg.

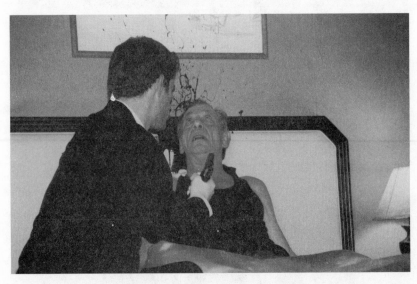

Here I am acting out a scene for film students at a local college. This picture brings back a lot of bad memories. I am still amazed that this never really happened to me in real life.

With Robin Quivers and Howard Stern. It was Howard's admiration for
GoodFellas that convinced me to get out in the open—for better or worse.

Brilliant actor Ray Liotta captured me on film better than I
ever thought possible. And he's a great guy to boot.

My first day at Fort Dix, a feeble attempt to break away from the life.

In this surveillance photo, Paulie leads the way through a chop shop with Frank "The Wop" Manzo on the right, and a Pizza Connection guy on the left.

More surveillance in Brooklyn.

By the '90s I began to lose my girlish figure. Standing next to me is my hero, Rabbi Mark, along with other pals from Beit T'Shuvah.

A Wiseguy Christmas in the early seventies. That's Karen with me on the left, and Greg and Gina in front.

CHAPTER NINE

BIG SKY COUNTRY

After a long day of recounting the details of my life of crime for Ed and his boys, I would lay awake at night while the events of the last couple years played out in my brain over and over again. I found myself hoping that I could create a life in Witness Protection that would cut me off entirely from my past life. Wrong again, Henry.

The Feds' job was to find a town in America that was safe from the wiseguys who wanted to kill me, a place where they didn't have spies who could track us. But it also needed to be near a major airport, because I had to roundtrip it to New York a lot to give testimony.

It took them a number of weeks to get all the paperwork done to relocate us. In the meantime, they had to keep moving us around. Every couple of days, we'd be in a new place, so we wouldn't even bother to unpack. It was Bonnie-and-Clyde time. We couldn't go anywhere, couldn't make a phone call. And we were scared to death, since we were still on the East Coast—much too close to Paulie and Jimmy for me. They had never hesitated to whack somebody who crossed them, and I wasn't just going to cross them, I was going to put them away for the rest of their lives, if I lived to testify.

After I was accepted into the Witness Protection Program, the first place they relocated us to was Omaha, Nebraska. It was a pretty safe bet there weren't a lot of wiseguys in Omaha, but there were a lot of cows—feeding pen after feeding pen after feeding pen. They raise them in Omaha and send them up to Chicago to get whacked. Oh, and there was something else—corn; cornfield after cornfield after cornfield to feed all those cows. I thought I'd landed at the end of the world. It was like a foreign country where they happened to speak English.

Except for a brief hop to Vegas, I hadn't spent any time west of the Mississippi, just up and down the East Coast, always for some scheme; running cigarettes from North Carolina, down to Miami on business for Paulie. But I was never in those places long—I'd do my job and leave. This was completely different. The first thing I noticed was the sky. It was huge. It took up more than half of what you saw any time you looked around; it never seemed to end, except that the place was so flat that the land never seemed to end, either. There was nothing to cut off the flat land but the sky, and there was nothing to cut off the sky but the flat land. No tall buildings, clubs, subways, or street signs—no noise even to break up the monotony. Just a bunch of cows.

■ ■ ■

The first few nights we stayed in a hotel that was right opposite a racetrack named Aksarben, which was Nebraska spelled backward. It would turn out that every place they sent me had a racetrack across the street. They put us in the Embassy Suites, and we looked for a house and found a nice, generic-looking new house in a generic subdivision. It was about ten miles outside of Nebraska in a nice, up-and-coming community. The Feds had stashed us in this tract house in the middle of a lot of other tract houses. The houses were so alike that I had to count from the beginning of the block so I'd to go to the right one. My whole family was miserable. We were completely separated from everything we'd known all our lives. Karen was miserable without Fortunoff's, and the kids definitely had no interest in the 4-H Club. Actually, I had it easier because I would be in New York being debriefed most of the time. But I had a lot to learn. I didn't even know how to write a check or read the phone book. Stand on line at the grocery store? Me?

I fit in like an Eskimo in Miami. It looked like it was going to be horrible. But, in fact, the action wasn't all that bad, and I could understand the people. To my surprise, it went pretty well, all in all, and no one knew we were there. I didn't tell a soul.

■ ■ ■

In Nebraska I wasn't really there for the family. Before my bag was unpacked they had me back in New York for more debriefing. Even when I wasn't in New York, I was constantly on the phone with the Feds and the attorneys. So I was still in constant action, but a different type of action. And when I wasn't doing that, I was drinking a quart of Stolie's a day because I couldn't live with myself when I thought of the situation we were in. I went through a God-awful process.

I also spent a lot of time at the local bar and met a couple of guys and played tennis with them. I made friends pretty quickly, since I'm a pretty talkative guy. I hadn't changed all that much—still hyper. I always hit the ground running. What else was I gonna do? Sit home and look at my wife and kids? I needed an outlet, too. So that made it even rougher on Karen and the kids. It created so much stress in the family for the first few months.

Meanwhile the marshals told me to "invent some type of cover," whatever that meant. They told me I needed a fake career to tell my new friends. So I told my neighbors and the people I met right away that I was an insurance investigator, to explain why I was out of town probably three weeks out of the month. I figured it was the home of the insurance people—Mutual of Omaha—so I said I was an arson investigator. I knew a little bit about it since I torched probably about a half-dozen places in my time. It was one of my areas of expertise. Philly Basile, for instance, owned a big nightclub out in Oceanside, Long Island, and he had leased the place out; it took off like you wouldn't believe. So then he wanted the place back, and the only way he could do that was if the tenants broke the lease—which they weren't about to do. So Philly asked me to torch the joint—either for the insurance, or at least to chase out the current tenants. So I did it. When this shit came out later on, I guess through the "3500" material (U.S. Code 3500 refers to discovery evidence that must be given to defendants) that the Feds turned over to their attorneys, the tenants tried to sue me or my book and movie money. I think I gave an affidavit, then Philly died, and it kind of went away.

So this was my cover, and I made friends with local insurance guys: "Hi, I'm Peter Haines, insurance investigator." It was nuts. At first my insurance pals would tease me about cooking. These were the kinds of guys who only went into the kitchen to get a beer or a dish of ice cream. But they loved my food and I could see them trying to figure it out— "a macho-type guy who can cook?" It made me laugh. Just because I had gone from my boss Paulie's great table at Rao's to the end of the line at Burger King (God help me) didn't mean I was completely uncivilized. The Feds had let me keep my pots and pans and one gallon of imported olive oil. They took everything else I owned except my appetite and love of good food and cooking; I was ecstatic to share it with my less-fortunate new insurance pals. It ain't just about the food. With Italians it's also about the experience of group eating, and the bigger the group, the better.

Going back and forth and being debriefed became major insanity for me. I flew out on a Monday morning and came home Thursday night or Friday. I sat in the U.S. Attorney's office in New York every day. Every other week the U.S. attorneys would take me somewhere beautiful to debrief me: we went fishing in places like Colorado or Wyoming—states I had barely heard of back in Queens. Sometimes we'd meet in Kansas or Houston. I was seeing parts of the country I'd never seen. It was terrific. Now I, Peter Haines, was on a run. I was constantly moving while Karen and the kids were stuck in a white-bread time warp.

Although most things in my life had changed, some things remained the same. I was still a substance abuser, a problem I will have to fight for the rest of my life. In Nebraska I quickly located an unlikely source to feed my habit. I lived right near an Air Force base, and I was walking down the road one day and found a couple of joints that one of these Air Force guys had thrown out his car window. On another walk I learned that marijuana, or hemp, grows wild in Nebraska—at least it did in those days. It grew on the medians of the parkway, and I would go and pick it. But it was like ragweed. You had to smoke an entire cigar to get a little buzz. After I found those Air Force doobies and hemp patches, I started walking that highway every day. My neighbors and insurance buddies thought I was on a fitness walk. Yeah, right.

When I would go to New York I'd take along a sandwich bag full of marijuana and hide it in the ceiling of the "hotel room" in the conference building where I stayed. But they started messing with me and changing my room around. They had like a dozen rooms and I'd tell them, "I want this room. I like that one. I'm comfortable. It has nice pictures on the wall." The walls were like murals, and each one was a different scene. One was a snow scene; another was a seaside thing. But I could care less—I just wanted to be in the room where I hidden my stash.

■ ■ ■

Meanwhile the kids enrolled in school; we bought a car. This marshal in Nebraska is a sweetheart-of-a-guy. He had a female partner. The marshals had connections in all these towns with everything. One marshal took us to a car lot where they had a connection, so they cleared my credit immediately. I had no credit history at all under my new name—I didn't have bad credit, I didn't have good credit. The marshals took the kids into school and told the teachers, "We can't tell you anything—this is government business. These kids just came from a location that we can't disclose." They never told people that we were in the Witness Protection Program, so the principal of the school—or whoever they spoke to—didn't know if I was a

CIA agent or what. I couldn't participate in their school-
ing, though, so Karen did all that stuff. I tried to give
them everything, and yet it was nothing. We were a loving
family, but I felt like a piece of shit.

■ ■ ■

At home, Karen had bought so much furniture that she had
to have garage sales. The marshals looked out for her also
and made sure we lived somewhere that had a strong Jewish
community. In Omaha there was a Jewish beach club. It was
a beach club, but there was no beach—just a pool and a
health club. Karen kind of got into that with the kids, and
my son got into tennis big-time and even came in second in
the Nebraska Open. So it wasn't too bad. It was like the only
Jewish community that we were ever involved with.
Apparently they took that into consideration when they
moved us there.

Omaha turned out to be pretty decent, once we all
assimilated after a few months. I was cooking more and
more and Karen and the kids were inviting new friends over
for some dinners, so it really wasn't that bad. We were there
less than a year when the tornado reared its ugly head and
none of us were ready for it. How could we be? We lived out
on Long Island for decades. There was the occasional hurricane every couple of years, but a hurricane was child's
play in comparison to what we saw outside the kitchen window. In New York, hurricanes made their presence known
and merely knocked over some few-hundred-year-old trees
and some phone wires. But tornadoes were crafty; they
were the snakes of the weather. The houses across the street
were still under construction—it was completely barren for
as far as I could see. It was so still outside, which is what
made it uncomfortable. I looked up and saw this massive
grayish-black funnel trotting across the earth. I thought I

was going to die right then and there. I'd been scared by the wiseguys, but this twister was more ruthless than anybody ever sent to kill me. It was like a big, spinning wrecking ball sent by God himself.

We got lucky and the twister touched down a few miles away, and we went on like nothing had happened. We were a little shaken up, but life went on.

CHAPTER TEN

BLUEGRASS AND BEDLAM

Not too long after the 1981 tornado, Witness Protection called and told us to pack our bags and get ready to move. The head marshal said, "We'll be there in half an hour. Pack enough for three or four days. We'll explain later." We had no choice. They had hinted that something like this might happen and we'd have to be ready to drop everything and leave. Now they were actually ordering us to do it. I hung up the phone, and they were already outside. They never took any chances. Part of the reason that they were so worried was not because of my well-being, but because we had been working so hard preparing for the upcoming trials. They knew if I got whacked, then all that hard work would've gone up in smoke.

We ran around like scared rabbits getting together whatever we could carry. By the end of the day we were packed into the marshals' cars and speeding off into the unknown. We got out of Omaha in the blink of an eye. What the hell was going on?

The Feds transported us to a "safe house," which is really just another word for a place where they can watch over us for a short time. There wasn't a whole lot safe about it. The safe house was a lodge like a Regency Suite, miles away from Omaha. It wasn't much, but it had a small kitchen. That was the only thing worth mentioning about that place; we'd been at so many of them before and after that. We were all really high-strung, anxious about Jimmy, and more importantly, where we would be shipped off to. The tension was killing us because we were pretty vulnerable. Anyone could have spotted us, so we had to stay inside. Safe house, my ass.

Our first stop on our way to the airport was the marshal's headquarters. That's where we got the bad news; Jimmy Burke, possibly the most cold-blooded of all my former gangster colleagues, was overheard saying while being transported to a court or prison, "We know that rat bastard Hill's somewhere in the Midwest" (you don't have to use your imagination much to assume he was a little more explicit than calling me a "rat bastard"). But I knew Jimmy and that he'd stop at nothing to have me—and maybe even my family—in an unmarked grave. It was a chance that neither the Feds nor I were willing to take. Jimmy's reach was virtually limitless, and who knows what would have happened had we stayed there another night.

The weird thing about moving was that we were really beginning to call Omaha home. A lot of the things we had sent for from our old place in New York, like furniture, had just arrived. We left everything, including the cars—the only things we took with us were two dogs we had rescued and, as always, the pet bird. Everything else, if we were fortunate enough, would meet up with us when we got to wherever the hell it was we were going now. But I had to hand it to them, Karen and the kids were champs. They put on their best faces and packed what they could.

Once again, I had to tip my hat to the marshals. Their timing was impeccable—like clockwork. In Witness Protection they were almost unrealistically fast. Who knows how close Burke was to finding us? They kept in mind that Jimmy had snitches everywhere, and I wouldn't put it past him to have a guy on the inside of the Program. There was even a rumor that someone in jail heard Jimmy say, "The fucker's in Nebraska." So I naturally worried that one of the Feds was on the take. That was one of Jimmy's specialties. Looking back now, I don't believe he could've ever infiltrated those guys, but back then I would've believed anything about Jimmy Burke. But the Feds were quite sure that he knew where I was, and he had good P.I.s and good this and good that.

■ ■ ■

Once we were flying out of Nebraska, the marshals let us in on the secret and told us we would start a new life in Lexington, Kentucky. In the back of my mind, I knew something wasn't kosher about that location. I went down the list of reasons of what could be wrong with Lexington. It wasn't because of the racetracks—it was something else. I was recycling all the crap from my brain on that plane and I almost dropped dead when I realized what the problem was: there was a huge federal penitentiary in Lexington! I must've known almost two-dozen goodfellas in that joint, and their families visited them frequently. In fact, some families and girlfriends of wiseguys moved to Lexington just to be close. I knew that if we were spotted by any of those visiting family members near the area—at the track, a bar, or in a McDonald's (like I'd eat that shit)—we'd be signing our own death warrant. Word would spread like wildfire, and that would be it for us.

Paranoia hit me like a bucket of water when I realized the horrible possibilities. When we landed I must've looked like I had seen a ghost. Our location was so bad that I was sure there was someone in the airport ready to whack me at the baggage claim. So now I had to meet my new babysitter from the local marshal's office, and he read me the riot act. Each region had different marshals. I always traveled with at least three armed marshals. The nicest, most decent guy I met was in Nebraska. The rest of them were bastards. And I didn't make their life too easy. But this new guy would be my nemesis.

The Kentucky head marshal was a guy named Al, who was like the stereotypical fat sheriff in old westerns. This guy was six-foot-four, red hair, 240 pounds, and looked like he played tackle for the Wildcats. This surly, red-faced, tobacco-spitting Southerner and his crew were going to be watching out for us. "This is your new home," he said. "The Bluegrass State." I didn't have time for formalities and bullshit like that. "Get us outta here now," I said. "It's too damn dangerous." How the Feds missed this one was beyond me, and this fat prick looked at me like I was out of my mind, like I was some tough guy barking orders because of some macho thing. So I informed him about the penitentiary and its inmates and all the bad things that could happen. Instead of actually listening to me, the schmo was sizing me up. He didn't want to be embarrassed by a guy like me in front of his team, so we just stood there, staring each other down. It was ridiculous!

"Well, I got news for you, guys," I said. "There's a federal prison eight blocks from here. And I know about a dozen guys doing time there. There ain't no fucking way on this earth that I am staying in this town."

"What're you talking about? They're in prison," Marshal Al said. "They're locked up." He didn't instill a lot of confidence in me with this comment.

"What about their families?" I asked. "I know every one of their families. I know every single person and their families." Back then, in the federal prison system, you could get a visit seven days a week. So these guys did their time in the visiting room. And in those days, you could do anything you wanted in the visiting room, including smoking or getting laid, drunk, or stoned. It was like an airport waiting room with a bar area, because every woman who walked in there had pint flasks or drugs or food. They wore these special coats with pockets on the inside. It was a joke and nothing like prison today.

There were definitely guys from New York doing time in Lexington. I knew them from West Street or from different prisons. They moved them from Lewisburg directly to Lexington. It was a hospital, also, so if you were sick you went to the federal medical facility in Lexington, and I knew ten guys who were doing time there. The biggest mobsters in the country, the ones who were elderly, were there. And some of them moved their families to the outskirts of the nearby town because they were ill. So Big Al and I really got into it. It went something like this:

Me: "I'm not staying here a fucking day!"

Al: "What are you talking about?"
Me: "What are you, crazy? I might bump into somebody."
Al: "Well, the chances are a million-to-one."
Me: "Yeah, right."
Al: "Well, you're staying here."
Me: "Yeah? Nah. This isn't happening. You guys are crazy."
Al: "Yeah, well, we're crazy; well, you're drunk."
Me: "Yeah, right. I'm drunk. But that's beside the point. You guys are nuts."

So I walked over to the telephone and I got Ed McDonald on the line. By that time Ed and I were pretty friendly and functioning on the same level, especially since he knew I was more valuable to Witness Protection alive than the alternative. Ed said, "But what are they, crazy?" He got it right away. I told him about the families that I knew there, and he said, "Just hang loose, call me back in a half-hour." He called Washington while I told Marshal Al, "I ain't leaving this fucking airport. I ain't going in the street. You're crazy." I got my wife and kids to go sit by themselves, and I had all these animals and shit also, like a circus, or a zoo.

We awaited the verdict from Ed, with Big Al glaring over at me the whole time. I was almost expecting to hear the theme from *The Good, the Bad and the Ugly*. To all this drama and nervousness, add the fact that we stuck out like sore thumbs in the Lexington airport. The Jews from Long Island and their pet menagerie were supposed to be traveling incognito. Yeah, right.

Soon Al got a message on his beeper from the top FBI marshal in D.C., whom McDonald had called on my behalf. So after about two hours Al was ordered to send for two more cars. There were three or four marshals in the airport, and it was total chaos. Finally a van and a few cars pulled up. Another marshal said, "Alright, we're gonna take you closer to between Cincinnati and Lexington." I said, "We'll see how it looks over there." So we wound up in a town called Independence, about twenty-two miles from Cincinnati, and also ten miles from Covington, which is the hub of organized crime in the south. I said, "These assholes are looking to really get me killed." And, of course, it was right across from a racetrack. I was within walking distance to the racetrack near my house in Kentucky. "Perfect," I thought. "I'll get whacked while I'm juiced up to the local bookies." By then I believed it was somebody's idea of a joke, so I started thinking, "Okay, I'll play along." But honestly, I had given up on these federals. I was tired of arguing with idiots, and the whole family was just anxious to get into our new digs.

■ ■ ■

So they took us to an Embassy Suites Hotel, and I didn't waste any time. This hotel had a big nightclub in it, and on the second or third night we were there, while Karen and the kids were in the room, I went down to check it out. I started talking to this guy at the bar, and we picked up on these three broads who worked for General Motors. This one that I was with, Rose, was young—twenty-five or twenty-six—with a statuesque figure; a beautiful blonde. I couldn't believe it. I made love to her the first night I met her, and she was just terrific. Her girlfriend was a local politician's secretary. This just fascinated me—women who made these kinds of salaries working beautiful jobs, driving brand new cars, owning homes, but still blue-collar. We made a date for the next day to go to a GM picnic. We went to this picnic, and I was like a fish out of water again.

We continued to go out for a few weeks, and she was wild. Karen actually caught me with this broad, but we had kind of an open marriage anyway; Karen always knew about Linda in New York. Anyway, Rose had this beautiful house with big old round turrets. The minute I used to walk in the door she was on her knees, if you get my drift. We used to go out to the American Legion, or the Eagles Club. It was twelve dollars for the night, and I was buying drinks for everybody. But she wanted me to stay there with her. Later on, I kind of told her who I was, but she didn't take it seriously. So I stayed a couple of nights a week, but it was just too miserable because when I got home I'd have hell to pay with Karen.

I later found out that guy that I was with when I was picking up these broads wound up going out with the councilman's secretary and marrying her. And there was another guy who we met, I forget his name, who became my pot connection. The councilman's girl was my Quaalude and coke connection. It was so funny.

■ ■ ■

We couldn't find a decent house in Kentucky initially, so we found a condo. Finding it was horrible, but it was nice and new, about 1,600 square feet. In Omaha, we had a 2,300-square-foot house. Here we had a little yard, while in Omaha, we had a huge backyard where we'd have barbecues. There were no Jews in Kentucky, and Karen had no friends. Omaha was starting to seem like heaven.

In Kentucky, this new marshal was already pissed at me because I showed him up at the airport. But he got salt rubbed in his wounds because he lived in Louisville, and he was my driver whenever I had to go anywhere. And I was going back to New York every week at that point, so this guy had to drive 120 to 130 miles from Louisville each time to bring me money or deliver mail. Not a word was said during the many rides to the airports. I'd take a joint of marijuana and light it up. We'd get to the airport and sometimes have to wait around three hours for a flight. So I'd hit the bar. This drove the Feds crazy because they weren't allowed to drink: "Hey, you can't go to a bar." "Fuck you," I'd say. "What are you gonna do, handcuff me? I ain't in custody." I used to terrorize these local marshals. I never got on or off a plane sober once.

I had to deal with this guy for the rest of our stay in Kentucky. Every time this idiot saw me, his face turned red, especially when he had to bring me large sums of money that I got later from the book deal. When he had to count out $20,000 and $10,000, I'd make him count it three times just to bug him. And he was such a moron. He had an IQ of 64. These marshals were like defective FBI agents.

He also had to check all the other mail that came in. My family could write to me in care of a certain post office box in Connecticut, and then they would have to send it to another place where it would be X-rayed and searched. That was how Karen communicated with her family. They were really careful.

■ ■ ■

When we left Nebraska we had to change our names again because the marshals were more paranoid than I was. I could never get them to spill how much more they knew about what Burke knew. We had to wait for a new name change, so for a month we used a generic name. But after about a month, I became Martin Todd Lewis. We were the Lewis family. For the next ten years almost everyone called me Marty Lewis, so much so that I actually got used to it pretty fast. Over the years we used two or three other names briefly, but the two main names were Haines and Lewis. I said, "Screw this. I ain't changing my name anymore. It's crazy."

Kentucky was like a foreign country. They'd speak in that real Appalachian, Southern accent. *No capiche.* I was like Joe Pesci in *My Cousin Vinny.* So we tried to fit in as much as possible. I didn't start going to a Goodwill store yet. I would go to the local K-Mart and buy a carload of goofy clothes like they wore down there—mostly polyester. It was like a costume I had to wear. I even bought freaking cowboy boots! The red alligators and green lizard loafers didn't go over too well here in Grand Ol' Opry land.

I also quickly realized that everybody owned horses in Kentucky. People in Kentucky are *crazy* about horses. And I mean crazy. If you're not a farmer, the only other thing to do in Kentucky is to have horses, or be in a business that has to do with horses. I guess it's the Kentucky Derby fever. It was just as weird as Omaha was with the cows. I started thinking that, except in Brooklyn, all over America animals were more important than people. So I start planning to buy the kids horses to keep them amused. When I went into the Program I had maybe a hundred-thousand saved, so I bought them horses. I bought this big, beautiful Palomino we called Banana Split, for my daughter. And then I bought a horse named Flash for my son. We paid $200 a month for the boarding, and they had a big corral and a lot of riding places. The kids really enjoyed it.

I got lucky with those kids. I could see right away that my son and my daughter were anti-drugs and crime. They were what the wiseguys called "goody-goodies." I didn't have to worry about a thing with them at all. My wife and in-laws did such a wonderful job raising those children, so that wasn't even a question with me. I knew that they would never follow in my path, which was a relief, because the kids of the other wiseguys all aspired to be like their fathers. It was like any other normal kid, who just wants to be just like his father— no matter what his father does, whether a cop or a gangster.

And they knew what I did for a living. They knew when everybody started dying and getting whacked, like

Marty Krugman and Stacks—these were family friends. They were like uncles to them. Almost all the adults the kids knew got whacked at one point, and that was a heartbreaker for them. They'd seen it all, but they didn't talk about it. I couldn't imagine how bad it was for the kids, but they were incredibly understanding.

I'd take my son to play miniature golf and a lot of tennis. I wasn't getting along with Karen and was sure she hated me. Actually, she really loved and hated me at the same time. I was always on the go, and she was just stuck there. When I was home, I was not the easiest person to live with. If I wasn't in New York I'd be on the phone with New York prosecutors all day, who would call from secure phones. I was constantly on the phone with one of them, or with the NYPD or with different branches or different organizations—everybody in the world, actually. And I was constantly on the make. It was a hard habit to break. In no time at all I had two girlfriends, so I hated myself even more. Karen knew all about them. Hell, I'd invite them to come home at night. She would bark at me and I would just drink a bottle of Stolie's at night at home, feeling sorry for myself. I was becoming just like my father. If I could get my hands on drugs I took them. It was a horrible life, so thank God we took the children because otherwise Karen would have lost it.

I used to cook and try to make things as civil as possible. That's when I really got into cooking because it was the one contribution I could make to the home life. Lugging my favorite pots and pans from one airport to another was proving to be just as important as I thought it would be. My attempts at domesticity had an important side benefit—my and my family's health. Just looking around at the kind of people in our neighborhood, I began to think that my life expectancy would have been longer if I had taken my chances with Jimmy's crew back in Queens: the food in Kentucky was fried death on wheels. I was chowing down so much Southern food that pretty soon I had to loosen my belt a couple of notches. I was on my way to looking like Paulie.

■ ■ ■

I found out about the racetrack the first night we were in Independence. In those days I'd learn about a town by heading straight to a local bar, having a few drinks, and talking to people. It turned out the racetrack was a stone's throw from our house. I couldn't believe it—I guess the Feds weren't thinking clearly when they put us there. This was the drill: take a guy out of a life where he's been hooked up with numbers rackets, don't let him do anything like have a job because people might recognize him—basically try to bore him to death—then drop him next to a racetrack, tell him to behave, and see what happens. Puh-leese! I was hooked up with the racing crowd in a flash.

The track was my kind of place, and I was there every day. I bought a bunch of cowboy boots and dungarees, trying to fit in. Now I was not only an Italian Jew, but an Italian-Jew cowboy. Right away I met a girl there who had a job at the track— she was what's called a "hot walker," meaning she'd walk horses around when they finished their workouts or a race to cool them down (if you put the horses in the stall right after they run, if they're still hot they get sick). And I discovered she was a hot walker in more ways than one. This hot walker was a fox, and only about twenty-one, and I of course was a whoremaster. In the backstretch they got these little rooms, where the people who work there live. They're like little motel rooms, but we used them like a whorehouse. Right away she introduced me to the backstretch at the track—which was where the real horse people hung out—not the owners, but the trainers, water boys, vets, people who lived and breathed horses from dawn to midnight. But most important, it was the "world of the little people"—the jockeys. They were the kings of the backstretch, and everybody bowed to them. They got whatever they wanted—girls, drugs, hard-to-get tickets, clothes, you name it.

Despite their royal treatment, most of the jockeys didn't seem happy. They were bastards to anyone beneath them. They were under constant pressure to perform—one bad race, and a string of good ones were forgotten. They also had to stay rail-thin, and if they gained even a quarter of an ounce, they'd be on drugs to get it off, or they'd do the throwing up thing. You'll never catch me wasting good food like that! But I learned a lot being around them, including respect for what they did. Think about it—you have a tiny guy who weighs eighty-five pounds, but he can control a half-ton animal. That was worth something in my book. Thanks to the backstretch, my betting average got pretty good. After I hit a $6,000 trifecta one day, the track officials barred me from the premises. They were convinced there was a fix. I was eventually allowed back on the grounds, only to be barred again. I was still a problem guy.

But the bottom line was that Kentucky was hell. My family couldn't even understand what the locals were saying. These people chewed tobacco and spit. A Jewish family in Independence, Kentucky, was like being a Martian on earth. We were the only Jews within a thousand miles. I think the closest Jews were in Cincinnati. Karen went into a complete state of shock, and the kids weren't happy either. Instead of getting better, it got worse; I caught the wrath of hell from my family. Consequently my personal life started to really deteriorate. I began looking for every excuse to stay out of the house.

The sadness at home, coupled with my hyperactivity, made it impossible for me to sit at home at night like a normal person. Even though I had been off hard drugs for a few months now, I was still pretty much of a frantic person. I guess I always will be. So I opened up a business in Cincinnati. I didn't go through too much money in Omaha, and then I earned some, so I opened this business in Cincinnati with Jack Vance, a guy I met on the backstretch who had a pool for rehabilitating horses. He was quite a character, like most people on the backstretch. Anyway, he talked me into opening this horse-drawn carriage business around downtown Cincinnati.

At one point I had gotten temporarily barred off the track for getting drunk with the hot walker who Vance had set me up with. That's how Jack Vance got me. He fixed me up with her because she worked for him. And that's how he kind of sucked me into going partners with him and fronting him money. Don't get me wrong, it wasn't all Vance's fault. It was the typical Henry Hill screw-up of letting the little head do the thinking for the big head.

I ended up buying my kids' horses from Vance and then I almost bought his ranch. I gave him a bunch of money down, but it became a fiasco. Jack was supposed to pay the original owner another $700, but he never did, so this guy demanded a check from me. I gave him the check and Jack swore he would make good on it, but he never did. Jack Vance became a real asshole about it and we got into a screaming match. Next thing I knew, Flash disappeared. There were a lot of horse rustlers down there—redneck bastard animals who would take horses to the auctions where there were "killer" buyers, meaning they'd buy for slaughter horses. I went to every auction looking for my son's horse. I was crazed because my son was really upset. I later learned that it was Vance who had the horse taken away.

So I continued to finish this trolley business by myself.

And I went about it all wrong, fixing all the parts instead of starting with the chassis and building it up from the ground. Someone told me that Governor Brown had a dozen restaurant-trolleys in Louisville that could be made into tour trolleys if I just gutted 'em out. So I bought one of them from him and had it shipped to the Cincinnati train station. I took the restaurant apart and made a trolley out of it. I mean, this is how insane I was. I didn't know what the hell I was doing. I invested about $75,000—serious money.

It took me six months to finally get this forty-seat contraption built. Then I had to deal with the city council for zoning variances because after it was built it was six inches too wide to be on the streets. Then I had to fight City Hall to allow me to let this horse-drawn trolley go from the train station downtown, around the fountain, and to all the historical sites. Luckily my little sweetie girlfriend Rose, who I was still going out with, worked it all out with her girlfriend, the one who worked for the councilman. So I got a permit. We hired a teamster and a couple of Clydesdales and christened it the Queen City Trolley. We dressed my son up like a conductor and we'd just ride along, or I'd hang out at the bar at the terminal with Rose. It was a nice tour. We took the whole scenic route, picking up tourists at the train station and taking them to all the store areas in town. We'd go by WKRP in Cincinnati, which was a big TV show at the time. But what we didn't realize was we had to go through the black section of town to get to downtown. And every time we'd ride through there they'd attack us like cowboys and Indians.

The business wasn't bad; we paid our bills and made our salaries. But the truth was I didn't care, because it kept me out of trouble. It was funny; we had newspaper articles about it and everything. The newspaper photographers came out one day and they took a picture of me, and I ran so he wouldn't catch my face. It was ironic: I needed publicity for the business to succeed, but I couldn't really have any because I was supposed to be in hiding. I don't know what I was thinking when I got into this.

It was now the fall of 1981, and although much had changed, some things never would. For instance, I still had this uncanny ability to attract interesting people, like I did with Namath in New York. One day I was just having a couple of drinks at Roosevelt Raceway in Cincinnati, when who do I see but Pete Rose. I knew everybody at the backstretch and in the clubhouse, so he'd seen me around. He didn't know who I was, of course. Eventually his gorgeous girlfriend, who managed the Cincinnati train station, introduced us. So he would be there every day in his white Rolls double-parked outside the track, and we'd hang out and bullshit. Anyway, after I met Pete I'd give him horses that had a better shot than the nags he would bet. He didn't know me that well, but I sort of felt sorry for him. He was a degenerate gambler, betting with two hands at the track. It was sad. And no, he never told me to bet on his baseball team.

■ ■ ■

While this was all happening I had a problem in Nassau County. When the prosecutors realized that I didn't know beans about Governor Carey, they indicted my wife because she used to take messages and give me messages on the phone. McDonald had always told me, "Don't worry about Nassau County. They can't do anything." But I got nervous anyway. I called my attorney, Bob Simels, and told him, "Bob, I don't care how much the government pays you. I want you to drop all your other cases and work on this hearing." Simels was also hard at work trying to find me more sources of income. First he put a *Sports Illustrated* deal together for me to talk about the Boston College fixes. He snuck the *SI* writer into the U.S. Attorney's office so we could meet. We talked only for a few minutes and then we just talked on the phone. Simels was also talking to Simon & Schuster about a book deal. I wound up giving him thirty percent of the rights to my story in exchange for his services. At that point I wanted guarantees. I believed in paying attorneys. He's still taking $20,000 a year from me—like he needs it.

Since we didn't have a book deal yet, I was happy when I signed the *Sports Illustrated* deal. I think that was my first big payday after going into the Program—ten large. I said, "This is too easy." They had all the basic information; I just added a few things to fill in the holes. It came out February 16, 1981. We were just hoping the notoriety would attract a book deal. Bob was pretty smart when it came to that. The magazine contract was a secret from the marshals. No one knew about it. When McDonald found out he went crazy, and so did the U.S. Attorney in Washington. I made a big mistake in keeping the *SI* thing from the Feds. McDonald didn't even know about the *Sports Illustrated* article until the day it came out. The worst part of the whole thing was how it would play out in court later that year.

CHAPTER ELEVEN

NICK
& NORA

hile I was in Kentucky from 1980 to 1981, I met up with Nick Pileggi, a talented writer who would change my life in a huge way. My attorney had been pushing me to hook up with a writer and get my Mob story down on paper. Michael Korda from Simon & Schuster got Nick and I together. Korda sent me a packet of five different writers and their styles. I met with three of them, and it was no contest—Nick was the guy for me, a top-notch writer and editor for *New York Magazine* who completely understood the world I had just left.

I had known Nick's writing because of his magazine work, and especially because he used to write about us guys all the time—he and Breslin. Breslin wasn't one of the writers in the packet, though. So I met two of the writers at different places, but after I was with Nick for five minutes I knew he was the guy. If I had a couple of conversations, I could just tell if somebody had it. We just hit it off and got a deal very fast. I don't even think we had to write a proposal— that's how hot Michael Korda was in the business.

For our first meeting, we were flown, very indirectly (Nick from New York, me from Lexington), to the Cleveland airport. From that point on, we spoke about five times a week by phone. I'd call him collect at his office at *New York Magazine* or at home and rack up thousands of dollars worth of calls, which we never had to pay. The magazine covered it: we had no expenses. We'd go for a couple of hours a day. Nick and I would work early in the morning, then I'd be gone. At first there was only a one-hour time difference, and I'd start work about 7 A.M. Later, after I moved out west, I'd be talking with Nick at 5 A.M. I always said that I was on East Coast time; I could not shake the gene that controls this internal clock. There are a lot of people out at five o'clock in the morning, jogging and stuff. I was sort of like that, only I'd be up early to hijack a truck at JFK. I never got more than six or seven hours of sleep per night in my life. I probably get more sleep these days than I did then.

Every few months Nick and I would meet, against orders, often in Vancouver. As a result we became good friends, and he became like part of our family. Years later, when one of our mares foaled a colt, we named it Nicky P. We had a pass on our deadline because of my being constantly pulled away to help the Feds in New York, or anywhere else, for that matter.

If they wanted me in Arizona to stop the Columbo family's liquor companies from moving in there, I'd go and tell them who the players were. If they applied for a liquor license in Arizona I had to go, but I got paid extra for that.

There was a funny sideline to my work with Nick. At night, I'd get half-gassed and call Nick in New York just to bullshit. It was like therapy for me. Sometimes Nick's wife, Nora, would answer the phone and tell me, "Hey, Nick is sleeping. What's the matter, Henry? This is Aunt Nora." Meanwhile, she was picking my brain for a script she was writing. I had no idea. She was on the other end taking notes. She was a piece of work. She is best known by the name Nora Ephron and used to be married to the Watergate news guy, Carl Bernstein. She later had a lot of her scripts produced and they were big hits: *When Harry Met Sally*, *Silkwood*, *Sleepless in Seattle*, and *Michael*, to name just a few. In 1990, the same year my movie *GoodFellas* came out, she had a little movie released called *My Blue Heaven*, starring Steve Martin, about a New Yorker in Witness Protection out west—just like I had been in Omaha. When I saw it I flipped because she used some of the stuff I had told her on the phone for her movie scenes. She took a combination of me and Michael Franceze, another rat she had read about in the papers. I never got a penny for it, but Nick had been so generous with me that I just let it slide. Had it been anyone else's wife. . . .

There would be no pictures in *Wiseguy*. We were going to have twelve pages of pictures, but in the end Nick said it would cheapen the book. He began working the book with everybody in the literary field for good press. It was a great book. But until about a year or six months before we finished, Nick didn't even have a title for the book. Nora came up with the title about three months before it came out. She said, "They're a bunch of wiseguys. Call it *Wiseguy.*" And I never knew who came up with the movie title *GoodFellas.* We couldn't use the same title because there already was a movie called *Wiseguys* with Danny Devito.

Our partnership was a risky business—for both of us. There was always the chance the wiseguys would try to use Nick to find me, or that he'd become a target himself. The government was afraid they'd kidnap him and force him to reveal my whereabouts. So they tried like hell to keep our contact to a minimum. But we were still constantly on the phone.

Meanwhile, the whole Kentucky thing was coming apart. I kind of helped the process because I wanted to get out of there, and I was also tired of doing business in Cincinnati and living in Kentucky. Neither was the kind of place where I wanted to spend the rest of my life. And my family was so miserable in Independence. Also, I was worried about the New York crews getting wise to my location. I went over to Covington a couple of times with Jack Vance, and when he started introducing me I knew that I was in trouble; Covington is the hub of organized crime in that region. But there was more. By this time I realized that the horse-drawn trolley business wasn't going to make the kind of money I thought it was going to make.

The problem that really got things rolling for us to leave was the hot walker I was seeing started telling everybody at the track, "Ooh. This *Sports Illustrated* article's gonna come out." So I had people approaching me, having figured out I was Henry Hill. I remember when that *Sports Illustrated* article came out (February 16, 1981), I bought every last one. There was this one little store that carried it, and I bought every one off the shelf because my picture wasn't in there, but my name was, and these Kentuckians had known who I was at the time. My feeble attempt at damage control would become apparent when I went back to New York for the first big trial. That was the Boston College basketball fix trial in late October 1981, and I would soon find out how stupid I was to have spoken to *Sports Illustrated* without telling Ed McDonald.

The funny thing was, at the time I didn't know who their other witnesses were. They didn't share that with me—the U.S. Attorney's office, or the FBI. So it was me against the world. At the murder trial with Burke, which came later, I was the only witness. I didn't know that would be the deal. They didn't tell me that the whole case was riding on my testimony. They said, "Go there. Just do your best. Don't lie."

One of the big problems I had on the witness stand for the college fix was that the dates I gave under oath and those in the *SI* article were inconsistent, but not intentionally. The trouble came about because I spent very little time with the writer. That's why I screwed it up so bad—I wasn't even concentrating. Sweeney had circled a bunch of stuff on the Boston College schedule card and I had given it over to Ed McDonald, so I had to go by memory, and I didn't remember it right. I knew it was a shitload of games, but at that point there was so much other garbage going on in my head that I couldn't remember what dates I had told the *SI* writer. It was my own fault, and they almost threw that article at me. But I went toe-to-toe with Jimmy Burke's defense lawyer, Mike Corio, which was ironic because he represented me in Florida on that kidnapping. I knew Mike—an ex-cop piece of shit, that guy. We did things together; we hung out. And he's throwing facts at me that he knows because he was on the fringe himself. I said, "Hey, Mike, if you know that, then you were there with me. Why don't you fucking spill?"

Anyway, Jimmy's lawyers jumped on the inconsistencies. Then they had a torture-Henry party for the next ten or twelve days—every day. It's funny; the lead attorney, Mike Corio, went on to become John Gotti's first attorney, and he wound up in prison himself. And then it came out that I made ten grand. The U.S. Attorney's office wanted to pull the plug on me for that, and Ed McDonald had to go to Washington and beg for me. I was scared as shit. And I didn't know, until McDonald told me recently, how close I came to having that deal pulled on me. If I'd have gotten kicked out of the Program, they would have charged me with accomplice to murder in a heartbeat. I was present for a half-dozen hits—and I'm talking pre-Lufthansa.

Of course Burke's crew now knew I was in town, thanks to all the news coverage. But the security was the best. I took the judge's elevator from the courthouse. I didn't feel threatened at all, at least not physically. It was more like a psychological thing. Everybody and their wives were sitting there in the visitors' section. The courtrooms were jammed. The left side was packed with FBI agents and marshals and off-duty cops—everybody and anybody. On the right side were the wiseguys and their families, trying to stare me down. It was like a wedding—one side was the groom's, the other the bride's. It wasn't pretty. I'm sure they didn't have assigned seats, but it was close. There wasn't a vacant seat in the whole federal courtroom.

When I was on the stand I saw all these goons there, anybody they could muster up, who were just aching to blow my brains out. Anybody that knew anything about me, or the skeletons in my closet, was in that courtroom. They'd intimidate me with their eyes, so I was taking Valium to calm down. That was when one of the FBI agents threatened me, telling me, "Stop taking." He went through my pockets and took my Valium tabs away. He said, "Your memory is critical to this case. Don't screw it up." They wouldn't let me drink, except two beers at night. I couldn't even unwind before the next morning. I was also talking to Nick about the book before being driven off to the courthouse. It was insanity.

It was so hectic I didn't even get to see my family while I was in New York. I wouldn't allow my family to come to the trial. Before the trial, my little brother came to see me a couple of times. But I wouldn't allow my mother or my sisters to take the chance. Linda came to see me a few times.

■ ■ ■

My testimony against Rick Kuhn got him ten years in the joint for the college fixes, and Tony and Rocco Perla got sent up, as did Mob-fixer Rich Perry. This was one of the few crimes I committed that I had genuine remorse over years later. A lot of the stuff we did was rob from people or companies that were insured, and since the insurance companies were basically thieves, we figured, "What the fuck?" It was a stupid way to think, but that was honestly where our heads were all those years. But with this thing I was most upset about how it ruined the kids' lives, because when the jury came back, Kuhn got ten years. Last I heard, Rick Kuhn was living in the woods in Pennsylvania with no running water. I think Sweeney became a missionary.

When I finished with that trial, I went back to the U.S. Attorney's office; I'd have to sit in front of another U.S. attorney and get ready for a different trial. And in the beginning I didn't realize what was going on with these trials and the debriefings until I'd read about the indictments in the paper. They wouldn't even tell me. I had opened a can of worms. Then they had all these agents asking me, "How's the best way to do this? We got to put a wiretap. Where should we put the wiretap?"

And then all these other agencies come in and wanted to solve all these murders and robberies.

Well, I skated on the *Sports Illustrated* thing, but not for long; my days in the Program were numbered. I had gotten a DUI in Kentucky and been arrested for passing bad checks. I could've made them good, but I figured this was another nail in the coffin to get me the hell out of there. The check I bounced was to Jack Vance, the guy who stole my son's horse. That's the reason I gave him a bad check. He said, "I'll take you to court." I said, "Fuck it, take me to court." So he had me arrested. I couldn't believe it. When I got arrested I'd never use the name Henry Hill at all. I was booked as Marty Lewis.

I started using heavy drugs again, especially cocaine. Ed, the marshals, and Nick Pileggi—they all looked the other way as far as the drugs went. Nowadays, they call them "enablers." But they knew I was hurting. I was so depressed that the drugs actually saved my life. I would have blown my brains out without them.

I broke other Program rules as well. One of the rules was no contact with the family you left behind—your siblings, cousins, aunts, and uncles. Phones are way too easy to tap, and phone records were a snap. Paulie always had AT&T employees on the payroll. In the Mob, we could get anybody's phone record. At first I was good about not calling anyone. But, little by little, I started making calls back to New York. The few times I did, I'd use a pay phone. It took rolls of quarters to call Queens. But as time went on I called more and more, and I got sloppy about it. Besides that, the quarters were a pain in the neck, and after I got the DUI I really didn't care. I started calling them from home—a big no-no. I was calling my sisters a lot—"scoccing" them, we called it (pronounced "scotching"). *Scocciare* is Italian for annoy, or nudge. To me, scocciare basically means, "You're bugging the hell out of me." And boy, was I bugging them! I'd interrupt them at dinner and want to have a nice long chat. I'd get drunk and call at two in the morning. There weren't a lot of answering machines in 1981, so if the phone rang, your choice was pick it up or let it ring, both of which were lousy choices when someone else is sleeping. Brother Henry was becoming a pain in the tush. I started calling almost every day, using any excuse I could think of to be on the horn to Stella, Marie, Lucille. The truth was, I missed them. When I first got into the Program a year-and-a-half earlier, I had taken the rules very seriously and knew I had to follow them to survive. But it was getting old. I couldn't imagine being cut off from my family for the rest of my life. It broke my heart to think of it.

Even though they were annoyed I was calling so much, we had some great late night conversations (or at least I thought so). We'd reminisce about Brooklyn in the old days, our Mom, catch up on family news. Or we'd talk food. Food talk made me feel right at home. We'd been cooking all our lives, but our recipes weren't written down. We learned from my mom the way most Italian families do—we cooked with her. Lucille and I would talk about stuffed veal like we were standing at a stove together. Or Marie would tell me about the great recipes my niece Bonnie came up with. But subconsciously, I was just trying to get kicked out of Hicksville. I wanted out of Kentucky bad. I kept pushing for it. So what happened was that in 1982 they kicked me out of Witness Protection—but not really.

The marshals approached me, made me sign a new agreement, and then told me I was out of the official Program. But I really wasn't. They still had to take care of me. They still had to transport me. So I went off their payroll and went on the FBI's payroll. But the paperwork still came through the marshals. The fact was that since so many of the Feds' upcoming trials depended on me, they still protected me and took care of my security. They couldn't afford to lose me. When I first got out of the Program, I had to get permission to appear in the media. In the late '80s, I wore a beard on shows like *Geraldo*. And even back then I had to get permission. I was out of the Witness Protection Program, but I *wasn't* out of the Witness Protection Program. The marshals went away, but the FBI still needed my cooperation. So they still protected me, and they kept the money flowing. I was in "Henry's special protection program." I was protected and paid, so nothing really had changed.

Anyway, when we got the word to move, thank God, we packed our things without hesitating. Again we didn't know where we were going until we got to the airport. By this time the Hill family menagerie included horses, dogs, cats, a cockatiel, and my son's new ferret. It was a mess—like something out of the Arabian Nights, with caravans and animal cages. We had two dogs, three cats, and two birds. Al McNeil came to Kentucky and moved us—including the animals. They shipped the furniture after boxing it themselves. But McNeil told us, "You can't take the horse." The only horse left was my daughter's, but I made arrangements because I knew how to transport horses. There was no way my daughter was leaving without Banana Split. I told her, "Don't worry about it, we're not taking the horse now, but I'll get it sent out soon." So later, when we reached our new destination, I made arrangements to get my daughter's horse sent to us. We stabled her with a horse-owner friend of Karen's near our next home.

I got half-drunk on the plane with Al McNeil. He wasn't drinking, but I kept sneaking back to the bar—you know how they put the bars in the back after you take off and they serve one round of drinks—and I kept getting a couple of shots of doubles. I found out that even leaving a place you didn't like brought out mixed emotions. I did make some friends there that I would never see again, and I left the business that I had worked so hard to start. So I was kind of sad I was leaving. Anyway, a big part of me was glad to get out of there; so was the family. The Jew in Kentucky now felt like Moses in Egypt, and this was my Exodus.

So this entire circus (minus the horse) flew from the Cincinnati-Kentucky airport to St. Louis on our way to God-knows-where. The animals were shipped through cargo and all that stuff. On the layover in St. Louis, as we were taking them out for walks, my son's cockatiel got loose in the airport terminal and terrorized the other travelers. McNeil was pulling his hair out.

And Marshal Al—I was ecstatic to be leaving him behind.

CHAPTER TWELVE

THE GREAT NORTHWEST

Seattle. That's what it said at the boarding gate. I knew as much about Seattle as I did about the theory of relativity, which is to say zilch. All I knew was that it was a cross-country trip from New York and it was known for lots of rain and aerospace companies. I didn't care about that part, really; I just wanted it to be better than chaw-chewin' Kentucky, where Karen had only made one real friend in the year we had been there and the kids had felt alienated. With this move, it truly felt like another chance to begin again. It was December 1982.

Washington State would be another first for this wiseguy—I had never been to the west coast, so I once again had no idea what we were in for. Physically we were as far away from our old lives in New York as possible. It seemed like there were traces of us across the country. The plane arrived in Seattle and we did the usual "two-marshal plan," which meant a duo of Ohio marshals were on the flight with us. When everyone else was off the plane, including the pilots and stewardesses, they brought us to our new Seattle marshals and the newest place we'd call home. The new local marshal, Bob, looked like Tommy Lee Jones in *Men in Black*. I was half tuned-up when I got off the plane with McNeil and he handed Bob the baton. Bob knew that I had screwed up in Kentucky and this was my third move. He wasn't what I would call a nice guy, but he wasn't bad. Still, there was no love lost between me and Marshal Bob. It was his job to "watch over me," and it pissed him off to no end.

As far as Bob could tell, I was living the life of Riley on the government's dime, and he couldn't do anything about it. I could see the smoke coming out from under his collar whenever he had to deal with me. I tormented this guy, I really did, because I knew what an uptight, straitlaced dope he was. I didn't even have to do much. The slightest thing would bug him. I'd just lift my pinky and then sit back and watch him steam. For instance, it was his job to transport me to and from the airport for the New York trips, so when he showed up to get me, I'd make him wait outside in the car. Even if I was ready, I would make him wait until we barely had time to make the flight. It drove him nuts. But he was bearable, and compared to Marshal Al in Kentucky, he was a darling.

I saw a rainbow as soon as we got off the plane. So I had a feeling it was an omen of good things to come for us. My kids were kissing the freaking ground. We all did. A couple of days later, as we were riding on a ferry over one of the little islands, there was another rainbow. It was a moment. And I thought, "Everything is going to be fine." I said, "This is home." It just felt better. Walking around in the terminal, we saw what looked like one thousand lumberjacks catching planes: everyone dressed like Paul Bunyan, in plaid flannel shirts, jeans, down vests, and hiking boots. We thought we were going to a real city-type of city, so we had our sport coats and heels. Instead, we hit a half-city and stuck out again. So much for blending in. But at least Seattle was a city where people spoke normally and didn't have chewing tobacco dripping down their chins.

We all got on a ferry and checked into a hotel. They put us up in a nice hotel downtown that allowed dogs and cats— I don't think we told them about the cockatiel and ferret. We had a suite, with a room for the kids and one for the animals. We were so cooped up before that we dropped our things at the hotel and made the Feds take us to a mall. Our first stop was a waste of time. We went to Pendleton's and outfitted ourselves with Timberland hiking boots and jeans. But it was all new and stiff. Everybody else's clothes were worn in, and we were like the undercover cops in Brooklyn, who you'd spot a mile away just by their clothes. So we went to Goodwill and traded all our new stuff for used.

■ ■ ■

A week later, we found a little ranch for rent in Redmond, which we rented before moving to a big ranch later on. Within a week I met a couple of townspeople. One night I went into town to a Mexican restaurant, and I met Len Frail and Sherry Anders. I said, "Len, listen, I just moved here," and then I told him who I was. I don't know why, but sometimes I just know when I can trust someone. If the marshals knew I told my real name, they would've moved me again. But I had to talk to somebody and get it out. It wasn't the first time I'd let on who I was. I'd get drunk and tell a woman. Len was astonished because he'd heard my name. I said, "Listen, you've got to be my eyes and ears around here." Even though they knew my real name, everyone there called me Marty, Marty Lewis. I was Lewis ninety percent of the time. My family, even Karen, used to call me Marty. My new girlfriends all called me Marty. But, little by little, I was starting to let some people know who I was.

■ ■ ■

Len's friend, Sherry, became my girlfriend immediately. Len also introduced me to a lawyer friend of his, Jim Slagel. Together, they were into real estate developing. Jim was a real cool guy who loved to drink. They introduced me to other locals. There were three brothers I met: Jim, Bob, and Rich. Bob was a dentist. Rich was a carpenter—a dropout psychiatrist, actually a pothead, but the nicest guy in the world. Jim was a nuclear engineer, but I wasn't too friendly with him. But the three brothers, and Len and myself, would start drinking at nine o'clock in the morning—we were all alcoholics. They didn't serve hard liquor there, so we just drank beer and wine. Then we'd go fishing, and in the afternoon meet at a bar called the Workshop Tavern in Redmond, which had a pool table and served great burgers. All the computer geniuses hung out at the Workshop, so we'd harass the tech guys from Microsoft.

We had a ball. Those guys taught me a whole lot of stuff—how to live life, how to slow down. Those guys, for some reason, had a lot of compassion for me. They indoctrinated me and took me to used clothing stores to buy normal clothes.

They were great guys, and I'd never met guys like them in my life. I used to amuse them, too. We've kept in touch every once in a while. They've all gone through divorces.

Of course my past was still very much a part of my present, especially since I was still working with Nick on the book. He came up to Seattle a couple of times, and we'd drive up to Vancouver and work for two or three days. All the while the trials were going on as well as the travel for the debriefs. I told my buddies the truth about where I was going. They knew. I told them all.

Although most of the trips were an enjoyable escape from suburban boredom, the returns to New York were a royal pain since I could never fly direct. I'd fly to St. Louis or Dallas first, and I would always be the last one off the plane. That was the deal: I had to be the last one off the plane. And there'd be two armed marshals at all times, but you wouldn't know they were armed. Sometimes they'd switch me twice, and each leg had a different name. I'd fly to Virginia to St. Louis to Seattle. They were pretty good about that.

We were always worried about Paulie or Jimmy's crew waiting for me at Kennedy Airport, so I never flew into Kennedy. After many diversion connections, we'd eventually land in Newark, or sometimes Philadelphia, or D.C., or Boston. Then we'd drive to the city. I had to hand it to them—the marshals did a superb job. In New York they catered to me and treated me with kid gloves. When they realized how valuable a witness I was, I got carte blanche and took advantage of them. But it was always a relief to hang with the New York guys, as opposed to most of the ones I was assigned to out in the sticks.

If I had to stay over the weekend, they'd fly me anywhere I wanted to go and I'd meet up with girlfriends. It was pretty sick. Linda used to visit me and bring basket lunches, because they used to lock me in the conference room or the library and I needed some company. After the first time, they'd let me have a couple of beers with dinner. McDonald had these miniature liquor bottles—they used to call them "airport bottles," the little two-ounce ones—and he'd always toss me one.

■ ■ ■

Back in Seattle, I started to go crazy again. This time I took out my lunacy on my marriage. I started dating Len's friend, Sherry, a makeup artist. She was only nine years younger than me, but about thirty years younger in experience. Actually, I had been flirting with her since day one, but now I started to get serious with her. She used to go to Carson City about every other weekend and work, and she'd "fuck-nap" me on the way. But she seemed so young that it was just insanity on my part. After a couple of months, I went off with Sherry to Virginia City, Nevada, on a major bender, and decided in a drunken haze to tie the knot. I just ignored the fact that I already had a wife and family. Part of me never thought I could get a marriage license, and another part did-n't care. So I couldn't believe it when they handed it to me. I got married under the name Martin Lewis, and Sherry's eight-year-old son gave away the bride. It was insane, alcoholic, irresponsible behavior on my part. I called Nick and Ed McDonald, and they thought I was crazy or kidding.

Now, Nick knew Karen. He knew her well. He knew I'd been married to her for seventeen years, and still was. At which point I explained to him it wasn't bigamy—I married my new wife using my Witness Protection Program name. Nobody said I couldn't, did they? I remember the conversation went something like this:

Me: "Hey, Nick. Congratulate me. I just got married."
Nick: "What?"

Me: "I just married my girlfriend, Sherry."

Nick: "Henry, you lunatic, you're already married to Karen. It's bigamy. But considering you've committed almost every other major crime, I guess you decided that you might as well add bigamy to the list."

Me: "No, that's Henry Hill who's married. I'm Marty Lewis, and this is my first wife. So it's cool."

CLICK!

Oh, was I in trouble when we got back. Sherry lived a mile-and-a-half from me, and I went straight to her house. We both knew the marriage wasn't valid when we sobered up. But I moved in with her for a short period of time; it didn't last long because I kept going home to Karen and the kids. My attempt at bigamy was a complete failure. I don't think it lasted more than a month, and it brought about an ugly breakup. Sherry threw all my clothes out of her second-story bedroom window right into a pile of snow. And it very seldom snows in Washington, but it did that night. It was a nice neighborhood—upper-middle class—so this really made a scene. Then she called me up at Karen's and screamed, "Don't you ever fucking come back here!" But of course I did—I had to get my clothes, which were full of dirt snow and mud. All my Brioni suits from New York were ruined. Amazingly, Karen took me right back—she thought I was crazy. And she was probably right.

■ ■ ■

SHERRY'S VERSION: I was thirty-one then, but still going on twenty-one, if you know what I mean. I was raised in a very strong Mormon family—there was no smoking or drinking in our household. The city where we lived is still unincorporated. I was very protected, and my mother took in foster kids and raised thirteen children.

I knew Henry as Martin Lewis. It was hard for me to get used to calling him Henry. We met because I had a horse issue. I'd always had horses, and my horse hurt herself. I had to give her injections every day, and I was afraid of needles. So I had gone to a Mexican restaurant called El Toreador's in Redmond. I knew the family that owned the place. I was sitting there having dinner in the lounge. I asked Wayne, the owner and bartender there, if he knew anybody that knew how to give shots to horses. And Marty popped up and said, "Yeah, I do." And he said he used to have racehorses. And so we started talking and talking and talking, and we were together about every day after that until he went to New York and had to testify.

It was probably love at first sight. We just hit it off because he was funny and he was smart. His attraction for women is that he's smart, worldly, and he talks a great game. I didn't realize until I went to the John Gotti trial years later (strictly out of curiosity—it had nothing to do with Henry) that he had the same smile that Marty/Henry does. They have that charming, innocent, little-boyishness about them. And there's that charisma. It's a con-man charm, is what it is. I presume after seeing *GoodFellas* that he's had that charm since he was about nine years old.

He told me he was a writer for Simon & Schuster. After we met, we were inseparable. He moved right into my place. We were together every minute unless I was working. He was working on his book, talking into a tape recorder and sending those little tapes to Nicholas Pileggi. Nicholas came and stayed at our house. We all went to Canada together. Marty kept claiming that he was a writer and that he had a thirty-thousand-dollar-advance, a forty-thousand-dollar-advance. When Nick showed me his business card that said *New York Magazine*, it seemed like Marty was validated. They were drinking bottles of Dom Perignon, but I didn't drink so I just dumped mine into the plants at the restaurant and probably killed them.

Seven weeks after we met, we decided to get married. He had woken up one morning and said, "Let's go get married today." And I said, "What? What do you mean? I have appointments." And he said, "Well, cancel them. Let's go get married right now. Come on, get dressed. Get packed." So he drove while I did my makeup and hair in the car. We put his clothes and my son in the back seat, and away we went. I married him on November 21, 1981, in Virginia City, Nevada.

When I met Marty he drove a little green car, but he usually drove my new 1981 Honda Prelude to drop me off at work and pick me up. Well, one night I was coming through Redmond and I passed that green car and thought, "Oh, that looks like him." I pulled alongside at a stoplight and a gal rolls down the window and she said she's married to Martin Lewis. "Wait a minute," I said. "I just married him. We gotta talk." He was at my house. I followed her over to her house, which happened to be just a couple of miles from my house, and talked to her until six o'clock in the morning, until their kids got up to go to school. That was when I also found out he was Henry Hill, a mobster. I thought I married a writer, and then he turned out to be a mobster.

I found out later that the Feds were always parked outside our house, keeping tabs on him the whole time.

So I went home and got him. I grabbed him and his clothes and his pots and pans and his favorite pillow, packed him up, and took him over to her house. I told her, "No deposit, no return."

A couple weeks later, I came home from work one night and my girlfriend had brought him back to my house. She had run into him at El Toreador's. He talked her into taking him to my house. When I got home he was smashed and in my bed. I said, "Get up and get out of here. I don't want anything to do with you." And he wouldn't leave; he was too smashed to drive. So I said, "Okay, shut up and roll over and go to sleep then. We'll talk tomorrow."

Karen came over the next morning while I was in the shower. She broke in the door and came in and grabbed him out of bed by his you-know-what. She started beating him with this old antique phone—a real heavy, solid-metal type of deal. And then she came into the shower and attacked me while Marty was in the other room getting his clothes on. Now she was a very big Jewish girl, and she had a mouth on her—oh, my gosh. I was never afraid of Marty. He was like a teddy bear. But Karen . . . There I was, naked in the shower, and she whipped open the shower curtain like in *Psycho* and started beating me with the phone and calling me every name in the book. God, she was worse than a truck driver. It was unbelievable.

I traded him in for a dog, a little Maltese. Oddly enough, some woman had lost him in a divorce.

Karen dragged Marty home. Right after that, they moved again and I couldn't find him for the divorce. I paid attorneys' fees for years, but I still couldn't track him down. It took me almost ten years to find him. I finally got him through a private detective. But the detective reported his bigamy to the authorities right away, and I think that had a role in getting him booted from the Witness Protection Program.

■ ■ ■

So I was back with Karen—and a dozen other girlfriends I had at the time. I tried to be a good boy for a couple of months and thought the second marriage went away— never getting an annulment or nothing. Four or five years later, Sherry sued—for child support, and this and that. I thought she was a nut job and had gotten rid of her. In 2002, when I returned to Seattle, I did make amends with Sherry. I hadn't spoken to her in years. She had done a bunch of TV shows and was trying to write a book and a movie. I had lunch with her and apologized. It was something I felt I had to do. Now she's a big, successful real estate agent with her own mortgage company.

During this time I was in pretty good shape, financially. In Witness Protection, we were only sent a monthly allowance of around $1,500 a month, and a normal guy couldn't live on that, even in 1982. But a family certainly couldn't live on that, especially in a new place. Plus, I could blow that much dough faster than Marlon Brando can inhale a meatball hero. But, luckily, I was working with Pileggi at the time and we got about $175,000 as an advance, which I received in increments of $30,000. We split the advance fifty-fifty. So I had a little cushion, with about $20,000 or $30,000 in the bank.

I was also getting money at the time from my brother Joe and Donald Brown. These guys were smugglers. Don Brown was one of my oldest friends, who I grew up with. He would smuggle hash and weed. I put them together, so Donald always took care of me. A couple of books were written about him. He was a character. When I hooked up Joe and Don Brown before I went into the Program, they were in California, importing hash. They were big-time, doing five to ten million dollars at a time. I was a silent partner, not really doing anything more than giving them credibility with other drug buyers and wiseguys. I saved Donald's life a couple of times when he crossed some connected guys. So out of respect they always cut me in for some profits. Every four or five months I was getting a nice package from my brother in California, and I had a lot more money due me when my brother got pinched. Funny thing, my brother Joe never got nailed for smuggling, but they got him for state tax evasion. That was the only thing they could get him on. So I was getting money from those guys, the Feds, and the publisher. Plus, I was getting money from the state. I was shaking everybody down so I could get a ranch.

Even Karen was contributing to the nest egg for the first time, instead of depleting it on shopping sprees. She had been training and studying for her cosmetology license, and aspired to open a beauty parlor and bring in some income. She was starting a legitimate business and was a talented woman; by then she had worked in dentistry, dog grooming, and had training as a nurse. We figured that while the money was there, we should look around for a real home and get situated. I talked to a friend of mine who was in real estate, and he helped us pick out a ranch. Right after settling on it, I bought four more horses, thinking they would be something we could all do together as a family.

Our ranch was on a beautiful piece of land, loaded with pear trees, in Redmond, the "bicycle capital of the world"—like I'd ever ride a bicycle. There was a barn for our horses. The house was gorgeous and spacious, with at least five bedrooms. The ranch looked out over a polo field, and beyond that there were acres of fields cut in half by a river. Next to that was a company I'd never heard of called Microsoft. *Marone*, if I had known then what I know now! And not just about the stock, but if we still had that ranch today we'd be sitting on a goldmine. I'm sure that ranch is worth a fortune.

I was still a little antsy about not working, but being a house-husband wasn't too bad. Transforming the ranch into a home was my mission; of course, I was the cook. A new semi-permanent houseguest was making things interesting, too. This came about because, while Karen was making eighty-five-year-old ladies look ten years younger, she had landed a nursing position that was our cash cow. Karen and her gay nurse friend, Bill, started taking care of a loaded old man named C. P. Middleton. Karen and Bill were caring for the guy around the clock, and she was bringing in $2,000 a week—which, in 1982, was pretty damn good.

Middleton was a trip, that guy. He was nearing one hundred years old, and nothing got past him. He claimed to have been "in textiles," and he was the oldest living Harvard alum, but that didn't stop him from going back to march in Harvard's annual alumni parade. He was a little flimsy, but the guy was ninety-five, for crying out loud. I hope I live to see ninety-five, let alone be in that kind of shape. C. P. didn't need Karen and Bill looking after him all the time, but he could afford it. In a way, he sort of paid for company more than anything else.

At first, C. P. was living in a really extravagant nursing home. But he didn't like it because he was scared he was going to die of boredom there. Karen brought him over to the ranch one day to give him a change of scenery, and he was like a kid in a candy store. He wanted to stick around. It caught me a little off guard, but I didn't care. We were used to having strangers in our houses. So we made up one of the bedrooms, and he lived with us for a few days at a time. Since he was at the house, it meant he'd pay Karen for the full twenty-four hours. No one objected to C. P. staying as long as he wanted.

C. P. was so old, but he wasn't a cranky old fart. I actually really liked him, but it was as if he was from a parallel universe. He was a classy, classy guy. It was obvious that he'd come from money just from the way he talked and acted. Even his table manners were refined. The way I figured it, he spent $20,000 a month cheating death. But the amazing thing was that his well hadn't dried up. All the money I had from gambling, dealing, and busting heads were gone. Those stacks of hundreds I once had may as well have been whisked away with the tornado in Omaha. I really admired the way C. P. looked after his finances.

The irony of taking care of C. P. was that he reminded me so much of the people I used to rob back in the old days with Arico. C. P. would've fit in real well with the Upper-East-Siders we'd steal from, like Estee Lauder. We'd bound and gagged them and stolen their jewelry; had we known better, we would've noticed the Picassos on the wall and taken those, too. That I was sitting with a guy with the profile of Hymen Roth from *The Godfather II* was a hoot.

Since Karen was taking care of C. P. all the time and he was basically a stool in my house, I became his cook by default. I didn't mind. He never shouted orders or anything like that. He was more like an extra mouth to feed. But he didn't even eat at the table, claiming that he didn't want to disrupt our family time. We were no Rockerfellers, but our table manners couldn't have been that bad. It would have been a little more fun to cook for him had he been able to eat all the good stuff—but because of his age, he needed bland food. So I'd make him tortellini with just a touch of sauce, or a chicken without spices or garlic. Karen had a table set up near the window, and he'd have a grand view of the polo field. From where we were sitting, it was like something out of a Hemingway piece—the clichéd old man eating all alone—but he seemed content. C. P. had the best of both worlds during meals; company and privacy. In time, he had to be hospitalized, and we heard he eventually died. He was a great guy, and it was a pleasure having him share our home.

■ ■ ■

I loved it in Seattle. Everything was great, except I still had no job. I wanted one badly, not because I'm a goal-oriented person or anything like that; it's just that I feel useless if I'm not busy or on the move. If it's a fault, then blame it on my upbringing. I worked at Tuddy Vario's cabstand when I was just a little kid and hadn't really taken a day off since then. I guess I'm just one of those people who likes to be busy. Tons of guys would've given an eye to be doing what I was doing— nothing. Early retirement? To me, it's a death sentence. I want to be doing deals when I drop. Being out of the official Program freed me of the restrictions, but I still received protection and the FBI picked up my monthly payments. So I was free to look for things to do, but practically speaking, it was impossible since I was flying out every week, and often with little notice. Full floor. Pedal to the metal.

With so much going on with the ranch and my work with Nick and the Feds, I was starting to get stretched a little thin, so I tried to hire people, especially to help with the horses we had bought for the kids. One example was a girl named Gloria who my wife had become friends with. She was a divorced horse trainer who came from a good family. She was on the lam with her son, also using a different name. She wasn't in the Program, but she was hiding from her ex-husband, who was a stockbroker in Manhattan. The Feds were also looking for her for stock fraud. I gave Karen some money, and I went into partnership with her and a couple of horse breeders. I was mainly doing it just to keep occupied. That was like Karen's escape—she wanted to get seriously into the horse business, and they became good friends.

But almost everybody else I hired screwed me, just like Jack Vance. Everybody. And it was kind of insane.

■ ■ ■

Back in New York, we started the next major trial, which was for the phony job scam indictments against Paulie and Jimmy. These took place in February 1984. They were going after Paulie and Jimmy simultaneously, so it was difficult for me. I felt absolutely horrible, but these guys were going to have me whacked, I had no doubt about it.

I knew the whole Paulie thing was affecting me badly because I started to get back into cocaine in Seattle. I'm sure it had something to do with being anxious about the trial. I started getting into drugs with my Seattle friend, Rich, who was a pothead, a dropout psychiatrist, and a pool bum— Rich could play pool. He was big, tall, thin, and lanky, and owned a big home where he lived by himself after his wife left him. We did a little drugs on the weekend—if we were going fishing, we'd take a gram or two of coke, and I abused all that garbage.

I didn't bring the coke with me to the trials, but I always showed up at the airport high and toting a carry-on with at least a quart of Stolie's and a baggie of pot. I did this on every trip I made to New York. When I got to the Witness Protection hotel, I'd hide the pot and booze in the ceiling— they had these drop ceilings—because they'd come in there and go through my bags. I swear, eventually there were fifty empty whiskey or vodka bottles in the ceiling and a few ounces of marijuana. I'm sure that they had the fingerprints, so they knew the stuff was mine. But at that point I knew that I could play them good. I had seen what they were doing with me (lying to me that I wouldn't have to testify), so I could care less.

Paulie was pretty subdued, never once trying to stare me down or anything. His family eyed me to death. In court, we just looked at each other like, "Hey, this is what it is." We knew what the consequences were. It wasn't like in the military, where you know off the bat that you're offering your life. In my case, as far as Paulie and Jimmy were concerned, it was the old karma routine.

Paulie's son, Paulie, Jr., never even showed up for one day

of the trial. It was very weird because I was so close with two of the Vario kids. Right before he died, Lenny rode with me to North Carolina so he could be my best man at my marriage to Karen. And I was his best man; I was all the nephews' best man. I still have all those pictures. Lenny died when I was in prison, getting burnt to death—they were torching a union job. After Lenny died, Paulie, Jr., who I was partners with as kids, became real close with me. He even married a Jewish girl like me. The last time I saw him, this kid and I were real good friends. But he's vanished. Petey was the asshole-wiseguy and he was like a punk, but Paulie, Jr., was the brains.

The trial lasted a couple of weeks. The highlight of it was when Senator Alphonse D'Amato walked in, kissed Johnny Dio and hugged Paulie—in the federal courtroom, in front of the jury. You know what that does to a jury? D'Amato was so dirty. To my horror, I was the strongest evidence against Paulie. But they never told me that. I thought they had other evidence wiretaps and so on. The government played me like a violin. If I had known, I probably would've been more scared than I already was.

Paulie got four years for the job fix, and later he'd get six more for the Kennedy Airport rackets. He was done. After the trial, I never saw Paulie again. First of all, I wouldn't call him—I couldn't even if I wanted to because he didn't have a phone in his house. Just like the movie showed, he'd go to the phone booth, or he'd go downstairs to the bar, around corner—like the Feds didn't have those phones tapped. But that was the mentality of those guys. And then they would talk in Italian, like the Feds couldn't understand. That's the way those idiots would think. By "those idiots" I certainly include Henry Hill. We were all in gangster denial. These days, it's the same thing.

Not long after that trial I went back to testify against

Jimmy Burke for the murder of coke dealer Richie Eaton. That was the big one, because Jimmy had only gotten ten years on the job trial. On the Eaton thing he got life, and I was glad he got it. The bastard had done some horrible things to people—and I stood right there and watched a lot of it. Helping put a big fish like Jimmy away made me feel empowered.

■ ■ ■

Back home, things looked pretty good, on the surface anyway. I had a beautiful family, a gorgeous ranch, and five horses. But my marriage to Karen was hanging by the slimmest thread. I really loved her (and still do), but in too many ways we weren't a good match. Hell, I'm probably not a good match for anybody. But Karen lived in a completely different world from me. Unlike me, she worked at being a parent, and when she wasn't doing that, it was all about shopping. B-O-O-RING. I needed a continuous fix of action, and not the kind that involves a Labor Day sale at Bloomies. But we held it together, mostly for the kids' sake. Then I met Kelly Norblatt on St. Patrick's Day, 1985.

I had like five girlfriends at that time. I knew Kelly's ex-husband, and he had tried to keep her away from me. She had two little girls, Rochelle and Shannon, but was separated from her husband; they were going through a divorce at the time. Even though he was her ex, he was still very protective and knew I'd be attracted to her. Kelly's ex was a carpenter, and he was a half-assed dope dealer. He'd deal a little bit here and there. He first started working on my house. Every time I looked around he was there, and if I was drunk I said, "Hey, drive me." So he'd drive me. But he didn't know what would happen between Kelly and I. And neither did we.

I had first heard about Kelly through Penny, a local store owner whose home was right over the hill from mine. For months Penny had been telling me how beautiful Kelly was, so by this time I was prepared for an anticlimax. I used to go over Penny's and we'd play Yahtzee all night long and joke around and play silly games and just kid around and laugh and get high with her husband. One night Kelly stopped by, and I was floored. I had heard about her for six months, but this was the first time I'd ever seen her.

We locked eyes and felt it in an instant, but it was a year before we had anything to do with each other. That was really not typical for me, taking time moving in on a chick, but something told me this was different and I had to go about everything just right. Since it was a small circle of friends in Redmond, our paths would soon cross again, so I just bided my time. Somehow she wound up over at my house—I think her ex introduced her to Karen. At the time, our kids weren't taking care of the horses properly, so she started coming around the house all the time. She would go out to the barn and muck the stalls and exercise the horses for us. She became like a fixture. We had a big house with a finished downstairs that we didn't use, so she'd come over and stay a couple of days with the kids.

For a while, Kelly was just a friend who would drive me around when I was drunk or high. She drove me to different girlfriends. It was crazy. We became good friends, but the sexual tension must have been apparent to everyone within miles. Karen said she was "weaving the web."

Kelly was impressionable. She was different from all the bimbos I had known in New York and all the girls I was screwing in Washington. She was a little ace, she really was, and a good mother. Kelly's ex-husband used to constantly accuse her of cheating, which she wasn't. He also accused me, six months into me knowing her, of sleeping with her. I would laugh at him and say, "Are you crazy?" I got so taken with her and her situation that I plunked down some serious cash to buy two horses, Paulie and Penny, for her daughters. (Before you get the wrong idea, the horses were already named. The Paulie thing was just a coincidence.)

So Kelly was living at my house at the time. And it was tough. Plus I had a bunch of other distractions. I thought I was hip, slick, and cool in those days. Unbeknownst to me, I was an asshole. I reflect back on it now, and if anybody had ever done to my sister or aunt or cousin what I did to Karen, I might kill him. There were a lot of women in my life, but I tell you, I didn't bullshit them—I didn't bullshit those broads. They used to come after me. What the hell, I'm human. Four, five times a day with a different woman—from one to the other—without Viagra. I've slowed down a little since then.

As far as intimacy with Kelly went, it was a long time coming, but there was so much flirting going on that it became excruciating. I'll tell you how crazy it used to be. We used to go places—me, Kelly, and her ex driving. I'd sit in the back or she'd sit in the back. I'd stick my hand against the door in the backseat. She'd grab it and hold it and squeeze it. And I'd be sitting there getting a monstrous hard-on. This stuff went on for months. We were playing a game, like kids. I tried to kiss her once, I guess about six months into knowing her, and she wouldn't let me. I said, "Fuck it." Now it was my turn to play hard to get.

But it was there. I was in love. I was hooked before I was sleeping with her. Finally, after months of this hard-to-get bullshit, we gave in. It eventually came about when I went over to her ex's to pay him back $600 for some cocaine. Everybody was giving me credit if I didn't have money, because I was good for it, with book royalties due and everything. By then, the book was out and climbing up the

bestseller lists, so they all knew I was in line for a big pay-
out. I got some money and I paid him back. He said, "I owe
this guy for some pot over in Renton." So we drove over
there—me, him, and Kelly's friend, Jane. Jane and I stayed
in the car while he rang the guy's doorbell to pay him. The
guy opened the door and punched him in the jaw, sending
him down with his face smashed in. Now we didn't know if
his jaw was broken, and I jumped out of the car—I think I
had a gun in the car, too, at the time; a shotgun or a pistol—
wanting to shoot this guy. My old instincts were never far
below the surface. Part of me was itching to get back in the
game. But they said, "No. No. Let's get the fuck out of here."
He paid the guy, I think.

Kelly's ex was driving, and he started to faint on us.
"Pull over," I screamed. He didn't realize his jaw was broken. I knew it because in my former line of work I had
seen more broken jaws than you can count. And I knew
that guys with broken jaws usually go into shock or pass
out. So I got behind the wheel and he starts passing out in
the car. I said, "Oh shit." So we ran him to the hospital in
Bellevue, Washington, which wasn't far away. I had called
Kelly and she came to the hospital, also. They checked him
and the doctor told us, "Yeah, his jaw is busted." No shit,
Sherlock.

It got to be late in the afternoon, around six or seven
o'clock. I was hanging around in the emergency room, and
I knew how long this would take. I could have cleaned out a
loaded, hijacked eighteen-wheeler in the time it would've
taken to get him treated. I said to Kelly, "Fuck this. I'm going
to go home and take a shower. I'll come back and get you
later if you want." She didn't want to leave. As big a prick as
he was to her, she still felt sorry for him. So I left. I returned
about midnight after he came out of surgery. Kelly was in

the waiting room in intensive care, sitting there, dozing off. I guess she was waiting for me or just lost at that moment.

I came walking in, all refreshed and all coked up, and saw her sitting there glowing. I reached my hand out to her, she reached her hand out to me, and I grabbed it. We just walked out of the hospital together. I got in the parking lot and hugged and kissed her. That was it. I knew, as soon as I was kissing her in the parking lot. It was hot. About a mile away there was this place called Tub's, private, real high-class hot tubs, and you would rent beautiful rooms there by the hour. It was, like, a three-hour minimum for, like, twenty-dollars an hour. First we had a couple of drinks at the piano bar upstairs, but I just couldn't wait to hit those hot tubs with Kelly. That was the first night we made love, and I was hooked. That was a red-letter day for me.

That was it. After I started with Kelly, I was finished with Karen and all my other girlfriends. There was no turning back. It was very simple—we fell in love. Falling in love with Kelly changed my life. We tried to hide it, but we couldn't. She was at my house all the time. It was unbelievable. She'd saddle up the horses and we'd go for rides, and we'd have our spots. I was in a bubble. Right from the get-go, my relationship with Kelly was so beautiful to me that nothing else mattered. I met Kelly, and all the bullshit stopped.

And then it got so obvious. It was the only time Karen started to rebel against us. She didn't mind me making it with two or three different broads, but she saw that I was in love. This was 1985, and the book was out. I had got $20,000 in the bank. When the book was delivered, I got a check for $33,000. I signed it and made Kelly go to the bank and deposit it. Karen had opened up a beauty salon at the time. Karen knew it was over.

One day, Karen and my daughter Gina went to my niece's wedding. My son Greg was in Washington University. While they were away, I moved Kelly in. She was already spending occasional nights there, but now she would just stay. I called Karen and told her, "Don't come home." Karen said, "You know what? You and Kelly can live in Greg's room, but me and Gina are coming home." So it was just Gina and Karen, Kelly and me. We lived together. It was crazy. Karen only agreed to it because she thought Kelly was just another meaningless fling. Her attitude changed when she realized we were serious.

CHAPTER THIRTEEN

THE VATICAN CONNECTION

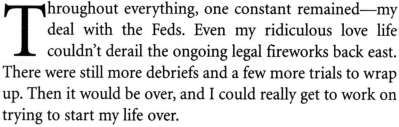

Throughout everything, one constant remained—my deal with the Feds. Even my ridiculous love life couldn't derail the ongoing legal fireworks back east. There were still more debriefs and a few more trials to wrap up. Then it would be over, and I could really get to work on trying to start my life over.

Luckily for me, my next courtroom appearance would take me out of the country for the first time in my life, and to the country of my heritage to boot. I had always heard how beautiful Italy was; when I laid eyes on Milan, the reality actually exceeded the hype. What happened was that the whole Vatican Bank scandal was blowing up. And guess who was right smack in the middle of it?

It all had to do with an Italian investigation into the way the Mafia had been using the Vatican Bank to launder drug profits. My connection to the whole shebang came from the fact that Jimmy had decided to put me in the drug business, believe it or not, right while all the Lufthansa craziness was going on. He told me to go partners with Bobby Germaine. Bobby had been in the joint with Jimmy and was part of the Purple Gang from Harlem. It was Bobby's connection, the "Pizza Connection" as it later became known, that had the dope, and we had a big network that could push it.

Jimmy called me down one day, in the middle of the robbery and all the Lufthansa crew getting whacked—all this insanity. I was looking to stay away from everybody, but Jimmy got me involved with this dealing, throwing down an ounce of pure heroin on the table; he knew I was dealing coke, pot, and Quaaludes by the thousands. So he threw me this ounce of pure heroin, knowing that I could move it fast. But I looked at him like, "What the fuck?" I never expected that. Petey and Frenchy were at that meeting, too, and Jimmy said, "Frenchy's your partner. I want you to use some of your connections to move some of this stuff. It's pure heroin." And he explained the whole process to me, which I didn't know nothing about. I'd never seen pure heroin.

The heroin was coming in from Italy. Basically the Bonannos, Gambinos, and other families had this deal with the Mafia in Sicily to import pure heroin. It went on that way for decades. A lot of the dealers on this end owned pizza parlors as legit fronts. That's where the name the Pizza

Connection came from. The details of the operation that later came out in court said that they had brought in almost two-billion worth of heroin. That was one of the trials that Donnie Brasco testified in. But, let me tell you, even though they ended up sending over twenty hoods to the joint, other guys, like the Gambinos, just took up the slack. It was a joke.

So I took this one ounce and shot up the whole load. I got these guys in Harlem—this one black guy, who I knew from the joint and sold some coke to now and then, and a couple of guys from the Purple Gang, and this other guy from Harlem who I knew was a smack dealer. And these guys saw this shit was pure. Now they weren't used to pure shit. They did the math: for each pure ounce you can make twenty-five street ounces out of it. So if they were paying $6,000 an ounce, multiply that by twenty-five. They were getting it in by the hundred kilos. And it would dry up—the whole city would dry up. Not often, but it happened maybe once or twice, and I knew it was coming. Bobby or whoever was supplying would tell us, "Hey, the suppliers are running low and we're expecting the shipment but. . . . " I prepared them both times. I stocked up.

I would meet Jimmy and Bobby and this one guy used to deliver it to us. He didn't even hand it to us, and we didn't exchange money face-to-face. I was getting it up front in the beginning. I'd leave the money in the trunk of my car, in a parking garage at a shopping center. I'd leave a bag of $60,000, and there'd be a quarter-pound of heroin.

At least I had enough sense to keep my ass out on Long Island. Everybody was watching Queens. And I was dealing drugs out of my house. I was selling China White. I was brilliant. But I was also doing a ton of drugs, and dealing with Paul Mazzei up in Pittsburgh. I was making pretty good money even before the heroin, but just with the cocaine and bullshit, or some bales of grass. But I had a whole slew of crazies hanging out at my house. I was eating ten, fifteen Quaaludes a day and maybe snorting a couple of grams of coke a day. But I was anesthetizing myself, to be perfectly honest—I figured if I'm gonna get killed for Lufthansa, I didn't want to feel it. I think that was a big part of my drug-taking.

I was supplying dope to Paul Mazzei in Pittsburgh, who was giving it to all his crew. I already had a whole network of cocaine to deal with, but it's a whole different ballgame with heroin. The money, though, was about twenty times more. You don't have to screw around with kilos; you can sell it by the ounce. The money is addicting. Anybody who ever got into the heroin business could never get out of it. The only way to get out of it was to go to prison because the money was too easy—there was so much, it was mind-boggling. I had safety deposit boxes in other peoples' names, like my wife, and my sister-in-law.

I was strung out big-time from snorting heroin and cocaine at the same time. I actually got hooked on heroin by accident. What happened was that I was cutting so much of it to sell that there was no way I could avoid inhaling it. The stuff is light and floats right up into your nostrils. I overdosed a couple of times. And I would just get up and put some more in the spoon because I was so high. I went to the hospital a couple of times with seizures. Drugs would take me to a place where it was like watching a movie. I didn't have the patience to watch a movie, and the only time I've ever read was in prison. So the drugs took me to that place normal people get to when they read.

Paulie's son, Peter, was a partner, too, in the heroin business. And Paulie knew it. It was, "Don't sell drugs—wink wink." It was the same thing all over: "Don't get caught." The wiseguys were in the drug business when heroin was invented, but they would never own it. Johnny Dio's brother, Tommy, went away in the '50s for drug-dealing. This guy was like an underboss of the family. Crack came in much later, so we used to freebase back in the day.

At one point, Paulie's brother Lenny began shaking me down for a piece of my drug money. I would give Lenny five thousand every couple of weeks. I'd walk into Robert's Lounge, three, four months after the robbery, on a Saturday night with my wife, and they'd say, "Hey, here comes the big heroin dealer!" They'd bust my balls.

I couldn't believe Jimmy and Paulie put me in the heroin business in 1978. It was against my better judgment. Honest-to-God. I had never done heroin. I wasn't a heroin addict. I knew heroin addicts were considered rats. If you were a heroin addict, you were a potential rat. You *would* rat. Period. And I knew everybody in the heroin business who got popped got whacked. So I said to myself, "Man, if they pop me, I ain't taking this beef. This is insane." I had been in the Lufthansa robbery and had seen maybe fifty large from that. I was supposed to get Marty Krugman's end after they whacked Marty. So I'm still looking for my half-million.

■ ■ ■

I was dealing with all this when Bill Arico called me for a favor. By the summer of 1979, Bill Arico and I were practically neighbors. At one point he told me to get him a stash of untraceable guns, which I did: an M-11 submachine gun and a half-dozen .38 handguns. Later that summer I was at his house, and he pulled out news clippings from Italian papers and showed them to me. He was bragging. "Henry, check this out. This is the guy I hit with the guns you got me."

The "guy" was an Italian bank liquidator named Giorgio

Ambrosoli, who was brought in to clean up the Vatican Bank mess made by Venetucci's pal Michele Sindona. Within two weeks after Ambrosoli was hit, two prosecutors and a judge in the case got whacked. Six months earlier an Italian judge involved in the case had been killed. I wouldn't be surprised if Arico pulled those, too, but I don't know for sure. I knew about Venetucci and Sindona being connected because Venetucci told me about it in Lewisburg. It was Venetucci who hired Arico for Sindona.

A lot of other details I only learned years later. As I pieced it all together, it became clear how important my little transaction with Arico was to the whole case. It's a complicated story, but I think I finally came to understand the main parts of it. Michele Sindona was a financial consultant hired by the Vatican Bank in the late 1960s to oversee its foreign investments. Now the Vatican Bank had been corrupt since Jump Street. Even before the bank was formed after World War II, the Vatican had made deals with that fascist bastard Mussolini that gave them a half-billion dollars and a tax exemption on their investments in exchange for letting Mussolini run the country. Then, after the war, the Vatican started up this bank to take advantage of the tax exemption. The first thing it did was launder $500 million looted from Yugoslavia. When the tax deal was finally repealed in the late 1960s, they had to bring in Sindona to prop up their cash flow.

So Sindona started laundering Gambino, Lucchese, and Bonanno drug money through the bank, but he was also a partner in the drug smuggling himself—that's the big cover up. I'd heard about the Sindona thing in the '70s from Venetucci in prison. They were smuggling this stuff in the frames of paintings. Venetucci brought the paintings to my house. Sindona was involved in the heroin trafficking through his olive oil business, which was a cover. It was easy to ship over the frames with his regular containers. Sindona somehow had diplomatic immunity, so he could bring over anything he wanted with no customs check. The Pizza Connection was a multi-billion-dollar heroin-importing scheme, but the Feds never hooked Sindona's name to it. They only thought he was getting a kickback on the money he laundered, not that he was actually involved in the smuggling. Anyway, I think that's half the reason why I didn't get whacked in prison for the Billy Batts murder. The Gambinos had no way of knowing who else I'd told and they couldn't take the chance on this whole thing coming apart, which of course it would.

So next, Sindona bought the Franklin National Bank in New York and started defrauding investors to the tune of hundreds of millions. While all this is going on, a new Pope comes in, John Paul I, in 1974, saying he is going to investigate the Vatican Bank shit. He lasts a month, and some people think he was whacked by Sindona's pals. I don't know one way or the other.

Anyway, when the Franklin Bank started to fail in America, Sindona tried to muscle the most powerful Italian banker, Enrico Cuccia, into bailing him out with a loan. Sindona told him if he turned him down he'd get the Sicilian Mafia to rub him out. But that Cuccia had iron balls, baby. He said, "Fuck you," to Sindona, and even got away with it.

So Franklin failed—my own mother-in-law lost a ton on that con—and the next thing that happened was Sindona had the Bonannos put out a contract on Cuccia and the U.S. prosecutor in the case, John Kenney. A hitter named Luigi Ronsisvalle, who had been in the joint with us, said they offered him a hundred large for the hits, but he didn't go through with them because Sindona refused to give him thirty Gs up front. At the same time, the Italian courts tried Sindona in absentia for bank fraud and convicted him, and they were just starting to unload on him. They were just beginning to investigate his Mob connections, and they appointed Ambrosoli to clean up the bank. With so much heat coming down, Sindona had the Bonannos stage a fake kidnapping on him. That didn't last long and he handed himself over the U.S. prosecutors, but he was really worried about what might happen in Italy with the murder charges.

That's when Arico used my guns to hit Ambrosoli. When he came to me for the guns, he told me they were going to be used to get rid of these judges and prosecutors. I later read that one of the prosecutors who was whacked, Boris Giuliano, had just delivered evidence to Ambrosoli that proved Sindona's connection to the heroin network. So they both had to go. But that was just the beginning of the whole Sindona mess and my involvement in it.

By the time I was in the Program, Michele Sindona had already been sentenced to twenty-five years in the U.S. for the Franklin Bank scam, the largest bank collapse in U.S. history, and the Italians hadn't even gotten in their two cents' worth yet. They had indicted him for the smuggling deal with the Gambinos ($600 million a year), and defrauding the Vatican Bank, but they wanted him for the Ambrosoli hit, too. This was the Pope's money he was messing with. He cheated the Pope out of about a half-billion dollars, so the Italians wanted their hands on him bad.

So they had to make a special treaty to send me over there, knowing that I had already told the U.S. prosecutors that I knew Sindona hired Arico for the killing. It was called the Treaty for Mutual Assistance on Criminal Matters. Now ever since, the U.S. and Italy have been exchanging witnesses in organized crime investigations, mostly drug smuggling. The

Italian prosecutors came to America three or four times and made this special treaty with the American authorities for me to go to Italy. It was the first treaty ever like that. The Feds told me I wasn't obligated to go to Italy and testify, but my mother-in-law had lost about $100,000 in the Franklin National Bank scandal so I had a hard-on for Sindona anyway.

One of the big controversies in all this has been whether or not Sindona hired Arico for the hit. I know that when Arico was in prison, he told interviewers that he killed the guy in Italy, but he said it wasn't Sindona who hired him. Guess what? It was Sindona. I don't care what Arico claimed. By the time of the trial, Sindona was just looking to save his kid and some other guy. He had so much friggin' information, they weren't looking to give him a pass or nothing, but he was just looking to protect his son, his daughter, and this other bookmaker. The p2, which was a secret group of Italian moneymen, were deathly afraid of Sindona because he would open up a whole other can of worms.

The Treasury Department was looking for the $400 million from the Franklin National Bank and thought that the Italians might locate some of it in their investigation. So the U.S. agents started telling the Italians that I knew Sindona was behind the Ambrosoli whacking. That's when they offered me a percentage of any monies recovered (I never saw any of it). I also got this document from the Treasury that says I'd never have to pay another penny in taxes. That was the deal they gave me. The Treasury Department gave me a pass, a document that said I don't have to pay taxes. But stupid me, I lost it. It was written on a yellow piece of paper—handwritten, on a legal pad. So I don't know how official it was. It might have been just a con to get me over there.

It took about a year of negotiating, but eventually I made the big trip. Interpol flew over with me after the FBI picked me up in Seattle. I flew from Seattle to New York with the FBI, and Al McNeil took me to customs, where I got a passport in fifteen minutes. On the plane, two Interpol agents took me over, and I flew over with them. We flew Air Italia, and the pilots came out and upgraded us to first class. We landed in Italy, in the middle of the runway, and four cars escorted me from the airport to the hotel. One of the Interpol guys spoke English, the other guy didn't. They turned me over to two different squads—Italy's version of the Feds, and the locals.

I was put up in The Congress, the best hotel in Milan, where all the local congressmen stayed. My babysitters had a room on the side of me, and I couldn't go anywhere without these Interpol guys and a four-car caravan. As I said, it was scary in Milan because Sindona was going to start cooperating, so the security was intense. We would go into a restaurant and they would clear out the restaurant, for us so we could eat in total security. Everywhere we went, these guys showed their AK-47s and Uzis. To me, it was a circus. I mean, everybody around me carried machine guns.

Everywhere you go in Italy, you drink. In the morning you start off with the espresso and Sambucca. And I was already lit because I had brought an ounce of pot with me. What'd I care? Drinking that coffee and the Sambucca gave me a speed trip, so I was a nervous wreck. I was lighting joints to calm down, and the Interpols were telling me, "Put the *spinache* away." To top it off, I was wearing a red shirt and a white suit with red boots—red lizard cowboy boots. Hell, I was living on a ranch, and we did not have a lot of nice-looking clothes. Compared to those guys in Redmond, they were really conservative shoes. Forget it, I was acting like a nut. I was looking as wacky as I could.

Every night, my babysitters took me out to eat and

drink. "Where do you want to eat tonight?" they'd ask. "I want to eat seafood." We'd go to the best restaurants. Anywhere I wanted to go, they closed restaurants, and they'd send six guys in to cordon off a whole section. Three guys would be outside with these Uzis, and they loved it. Meanwhile, those wacky sirens wailed everywhere we went. Christ, if JFK got half this protection, he'd still be alive and chasing broads today. And every restaurant I went in, the owners would give me sausages and big pork salamis. We used to go from the court to the restaurants. And wine? Forget about it. Wine up the wazoo. Those guys drink over there. Then if I wanted to go shopping, they'd close down Gucci so I could shop. Every day it was, "What do you want to do?" "I want to go sightseeing." So we'd go into these museums where the Last Supper painting and other things were located, and they'd close the museums down so I could go in and check them out. Meanwhile outside, the tourists were screaming at me. Hey, it wasn't my fault.

■ ■ ■

There was a whole bunch of other guys on trial, too. In court, they had cages up against the wall. I'd never seen a courtroom like they had in Italy. It's like a circus. It's set up like a forum where you have one main judge who sits in the center, a semi-circle of judges, and attorneys who sit in the audience. All the prisoners are in these cages along the wall. This was a huge case in Italy, and it was in the headlines every day.

They wanted my testimony to go after Sindona and two other guys, including Sindona's son, at this point. They gave me an interpreter who was an opera singer—literally, an opera singer. They have a big opera house there and I guess the singers moonlight as translators for the Italian Feds. But the problem for me was that I didn't understand shit that was going on, so I was scared to death.

Billy Arico, Ambrosoli's killer, was dead at this point. That's a weird story, too. He had been arrested just before me in 1979 for bail-jumping and sticking up a jewelry store. But, can you believe it, Arico escaped from prison—he swam from Riker's Island to Manhattan. That's the kind of shape this guy was in. When I knew him in New York he used to run five miles every morning. He looked like an accountant, but he was ripped. Initially, the Feds thought he was dead. By 1982, I was in the Witness Protection Program when a guy from the fugitive squad of the marshal service came to me and said, "How can we nail this guy Arico?" He was good, this guy. I said, "I'll tell you how to nail him—all you gotta do is just sit on his wife, because he visits her every weekend and on the holidays. Follow her, and she'll take you right to him. It's that simple." I told the Feds exactly how to pinch him. And it just so happened that some holiday was coming up and they got him—just like that. And when they nailed him, they nailed him with his stepdaughter. He was screwing his stepdaughter. Sick. They never gave me credit for that arrest.

In 1984, the Italians were set to bring Arico to Italy to stand trail for the Italian killings. But I felt bad about ratting him, so I decided to help him escape. I got a jeweler's saw to his wife. Two days before he was to go to Italy, he broke out of MCC with a fat drug dealer. When they were caught on the roof, Billy jumped first—something like forty feet—and then the fat guy jumped and fell on Billy, crushing him to death.

So Billy's son was on trial for helping him with the Italian murders. I had said that I thought I recognized his son's voice on a tape recording. A couple of years later, I had to recant that—it turned out it wasn't his son; it was another guy, some bookmaker. I did that here in the States and I said, "Well, it did sound like the kid." But anyway, I got the kid off the hook. Now Sindona was another matter. I gave them enough to hang him.

■ ■ ■

In the Milan courtroom, all the prosecutors kept screaming, "You should be on trial, too, for murder." I don't understand Italian—except for the curse words, so I was only getting bits and pieces. And they're screaming and yelling and throwing shit and . . . it's a circus, those Italian courts. There's no order. "Murderer!" they're screaming at me. It was insane. And then the other defendants' attorneys started jumping up, screaming in Italian that I should be prosecuted because I supplied the weapons used to kill one judge and two prosecutors. Now I'm getting scared half to death; on top of it all, I was half in the bag from partying with my Uzi-toting babysitters. When I was back at the hotel I called Ed McDonald and my lawyers in New York. "Just relax," they kept saying. Yeah, easy for you.

They let me stay for the whole trial. All in all, I was in Milan about four days, but my testimony was considered crucial. Before I left, I wanted to go shopping. I had about $5,000 in my pocket when I went over there, and I knew I wasn't going through customs. We never went through customs; we went right through to the runway. Anyway, I wanted to go to Gucci's and Farucci's—there are a lot of beautiful stores there and the prices are a third of what they are in America. So they closed down the high-roller stores like if Madonna was going shopping. Honest to God, a whole street was roped off so I could get some goods to smuggle home. Amazing. I ended up going home with suitcases full of gifts—shoes, sweaters, salamis. I couldn't take food or wine out of Italy, so I had the Interpol boys carry it for me. Screw customs. And the whole time I stayed high on the pot or the coffee.

Before we left, I told them I had never seen the mountains, so they took me sightseeing to Switzerland—right across the border. It was fun. I made a party out of it.

After I came back, Sindona was found guilty and sentenced to life, but his son walked, which was what he was most concerned about. Sindona was sent off to the Vaghera Super Prison, and wouldn't you know it, two days later he turned up dead—poisoned. There aren't a lot of people who think it was suicide. He knew way too much to live—about the Gambino drug deals, about the Vatican Bank corruption, and about this right-wing p2 group that was running Italy behind the scenes with the Mafia.

Even with all this bad publicity, the Vatican didn't clean up its act, from what I've read recently. In 1982, the Vatican paid out $250 million to investors for its part in another bank collapse. A year later, a Venezuelan lawyer named Alberto Berti said he laundered hundreds of millions through the Vatican Bank for businessmen in Caracas and Poland. In 2000, twenty-one Sicilian Mafiosi were arrested for hacking into corporate accounts, stealing $100 million, and then laundering it—guess where—in the Vatican Bank. And last year the bank was charged with helping an American financier named Max Frankel launder $150 billion. I assume they're still at it. I guess they don't have a RICO law in Italy.

CHAPTER FOURTEEN

FROM KAREN
TO KELLY

Then it was back to Redmond, Washington. I brought back stuff for Karen, Kelly, and every other broad I knew. All that good shit. But practically before my bags were unpacked, I had to go back to New York for the Philly Basile trial for getting me the no-show union job that got me out of Lewisburg on early release. He got five years probation and a fine of $250 large. There was one more big trial, in 1987: the Kennedy Airport Racketeering trial—KENRAC. That was a big, big trial. We got the president of the union in that one. Paulie and many others just gave up and pled guilty to extorting Kennedy Airport.

By this point I had worn that marshal out. I would only go off occasionally with them to meet prosecutors, and then it was to the point where we would usually meet at neutral sites. We'd meet in Denver or Wyoming—wherever they felt like going trout fishing. But, for the most part, my work with them was really slowing down. There were no more east coast or international travels.

■ ■ ■

Finally, after what seemed like a thousand courtrooms and a million conferences with prosecutors and marshals, Kelly and I were finally going to get some time to start planning the rest of our lives together. We had one immediate problem—there was no money left from *Wiseguy*. I was still getting $1,500 a month from the Feds, which the marshal delivered. Now, the book with Nick had been out, but the royalties were being withheld because of the Son of Sam law. One Monday morning I walked into the library, opened the *New York Times*, and the book was number one. "Wow."

So with that little bit coming in, Kelly and I drove to this little town called Monte Rio. It was supposed to be a little getaway. What we thought would last a weekend became a week, and then two weeks, then three, and so on. We were going there to get clean. The marriage was over, and I was going to try my best to start a new life. In Monte Rio, these two gay psychiatrists from San Francisco had this motel and recovery center right on the river. Those two guys are whacked out—high—right out of the birdcage. Two doctors, and they'd fight like husband and wife. They'd come up on the weekend. We were staying there and Nick was picking up the tab most of the time for me. Nick was sending me $500 every couple of weeks.

For a period, I didn't tell Karen where I was going. She had a business at the time in Redmond, a hairstyle place. So she was doing her own thing. I figured that the only way I was going to break away from her was to have absolutely no contact with her. I got in the car, filled up the backseat with clothes, went to the bank, and took out three-quarters of the money. I didn't call for one month. She would call Bob Simels, who was like my manager at the time, and Ed McDonald, and this one and that one. Nick was the only one who actually knew exactly where I was. Karen later told me she thought I was dead. She figured her worst fears had come true; that Jimmy or someone had found me and the Feds were clueless as to where I was. In reality, Kelly and I were just like two teenagers going against the wishes of the unhappy parents.

When we hit Monte Rio it was spring and it felt like we were having our own rebirth after a long winter. Monte Rio was a small town with a lot of dropouts. It's where the Bohemians meet every summer. It was maybe ten miles from the coast but it's right on the Russian River—this little, one-horse town on the river. They let all of these artists and Vietnam vets live there ten months out of the year, and they grow their little pot patches—everyone had a patch up in the mountains from which they earned their thirty to forty grand a year. And they wouldn't bother them—they'd just let them live. Ninety percent of them were on military disability and social security.

They had a resort there where all the Trilateral Commission people—the Kissinger crowd—go and party and run around the woods naked. It's a huge resort, and they go on retreat once a year during the summer. The Secret Service would come in about two or three weeks before they arrived. They'd make themselves present. Everyone knew to hit the beach or go find a place to stay for six or eight weeks. And the town would be squeaky clean. You'd see the limos pulling up with their bimbos. This went on every year. It still goes on, I'm sure.

Kelly and I moved out of the motel because we couldn't afford it any longer and got a little dilapidated shack on the Russian River. Every thirty or fifty years these houses get washed out. So we rented one of these little places, a little one-bedroom with half a wall gone. The owners let us stay there while they repaired the place—real nice people. We just hung out, going down to the beach in a little town called Duncan Mills every day. We'd sunbathe and just be hippies. This was around the time I started to work on the screenplay of *GoodFellas*, so I was talking to Nick and director Marty Scorsese on a daily basis.

We weren't doing much coke, although there was plenty of marijuana and alcohol around. At least I wasn't doing the massive amounts of cocaine I was doing in Seattle, which was a pleasant change for me. I had gotten all that shit out of my system. But if you wanted a little bit on the weekends, you could always get a gram or something. The problem for us would always be that we were both addictive people, and there's nothing worse than two addicts living together because you just keep feeding off each other and enabling your bad habits. If one of us was clean, we would be tempted back in by the one who was still using. We would have to deal with this off and on for the rest of our lives. I have to admit, Kelly has been much more successful at it than me.

So we stayed there, and we kind of cleaned up. We had a little kitchenette in this nice place. I finally got in touch with Karen about five weeks after I moved away. It was a couple of weeks before Easter when I started communicating with her; I had started feeling guilty. So I said to Kelly,

"Let me go back and settle up with her. I have to figure out what she's going to do with the house because we got the ranch up there, and I got a business up there." I told Kelly I'd be back in a week or so. It wasn't easy or pretty. You don't leave your wife and kids after twenty years, and, boom, start a new life. But Karen finally understood that she finally had to let me go.

I went through what everybody else with kids goes through in a breakup. I felt selfish choosing between my kids and my own happiness. On the other hand, if I didn't leave, Karen and I would have eventually been throwing steak knives at each other, and no kid should see that. I knew I would miss them a lot, but I promised myself I would see them constantly and do everything I could to contribute to making their lives better than mine

While I was back in Washington dealing with Karen, some things happened that caused my new fairy-tale life to go into a tailspin. The deal was so bad that pretty soon I was facing the prospect of going back into the federal joint, where a pack of Gambinos and Luccheses would be waiting for me with their razors and switchblades.

Kelly remembers how it got started:

KELLY: Henry had gotten that guilty feeling and left me high and dry in California with no money, no house, no nothing. He had to go home and take care of his wife, but what he didn't realize was he was going home to one great big set-up, at least in my eyes. When he got there, Karen had gotten herself into a mess with certain people staying in the house. I think Henry's son Greg was gone already, and his daughter Gina was in high school. There were people in the home who shouldn't have been there, and so he was crazy over that.

Henry got involved in what was going on in the house—a big drug scene. Karen had some drug dealers there from Peru, and they were doing deals out of their house. One of the guys involved was a Texan who Henry was suspicious of the moment he laid eyes on him. I know Karen has been presented as an innocent bystander, but I used to sell drugs to Karen, so I know better. She didn't do a lot, but she did use, I think to watch her weight. She was a very large woman, so I used to secretly give her speed. She was no saint—I mean they were doing *big* deals out of that house. At one point the Peruvians were stuck with fifty kilos in the house.

When I finally got a phone call from Henry, I said, "What am I going to do here? I'm stuck here. What do I do?" Then he had a brilliant idea. One of the Peruvians, Juan, had a cousin, Walter Alor, who was not legal in the states—he was a missionary in the Mormon Church and a real good guy—not into the drugs or anything like that. So Henry said, "Kelly, Juan, the dope dealer, has a cousin who needs to get married in order to stay here. Would you come up and do it?" Juan was Juan Tirso Hernandez-Leon. And, of course, I would get an ounce of coke and all that stuff. Cars. I don't know what would've been the case if that wasn't offered. I'd probably still be stuck in Monte Rio, California. So of course I said, "Sure."

Henry had gotten me a ticket to come back. We left our Volkswagen there and then I flew in. I was staying in a hotel at first, then I moved in with my sister. I was also pregnant, and Karen and Henry persuaded me into not having it. But that was devastating for me. The whole time was just total insanity. Just drugs and bad behavior. All that.

I had a bout with breast cancer just before I met Henry, and now I was invited to live with Karen and Henry while I underwent treatment. Karen used to come and get me from treatment and bring me to her house. One day she came over to my sister's and picked me up and said, "Get your stuff, you might as well just stay at our house. This is where he's going to be anyway."

Soon Karen realized that I wasn't just another girl in Henry's life. That's when Karen started getting scared, because she knew Henry had feelings for me. When Karen thought it was just an affair, it didn't bother her. But once she knew the feelings were there, she became real hostile, actually. I got bashed in the head with frozen peas once. Another time she knocked me out in my house when she snuck up behind me and hit me with a metal beer stein. I was out cold for a few minutes.

She had a room made up for me, and Henry slept in there with me. It was really weird. There was one time we were supposed to pick her up at the airport and we forgot and she came home and we were in her room, asleep. She came in and said, "Hey guys, it's time to wake up. Could you move to the other room?"

No surprise—Henry got into trouble with all this drug-dealing going on right under his nose. He said he was trapped because he was in debt to these people. He got in debt to them at least partially because of Karen—they were doing it out of their house.

It all started because I got $9,000 into debt to Peruvian dealer friends of Karen's. They had been supplying me coke, and I had run up my marker. To work it off I agreed to help them move some stuff. I didn't want to be involved with it, but I had to. I knew from five minutes after I met one member of the conspiracy from Texas that he was a rat, an informant. He'd come to buy two kilos of cocaine from me, and he had no money. He had a couple of hundreds in his pocket. He said, "Well, my partner's down the road, sitting in a car. He's got the money in the trunk." And it was only fifty to sixty grand, but I knew this guy was full of shit. I told the Peruvians, "Don't bring this guy to me again. I'm out of it." But it was too late because the Feds were tapping our phone calls.

KELLY: What happened was that on May 1, two weeks after my divorce became final, I actually married Walter, and by the same judge who presided over my first marriage. The judge was Judge Love—believe it or not. And he was looking at me like I was nuts. Henry was my best man and my witness. So after we got married we went over to the El Toreador restaurant in Redmond, and my new husband's looking at me like, "Wow. You're a tramp." And I explained to him that he didn't marry your typical, average American girl. "So you better hold on."

It wasn't but two seconds later that the cops came in and scooped up Henry for this conspiracy thing with the Peruvians. It turned out that Fernando Sergio-Borgo, not his cousin Juan, had set Henry up. Fernando was the one who was staying in the house. It turned out that he was cooperating with a cop who brought the deal about from Peru. And Henry knew all along it was a set-up, so he didn't go through with it and he was waving at the cops; he's driving off like, "Ha-Ha. I didn't do it."

I was not the original target. Fernando was the target. Fernando and this other kid, Casey, another big dealer, were the main guys. They were the targets. Then when the Feds found out who I was they switched it. They changed the whole plan because they knew that those guys would turn on me to cut a deal, and they figured they were going to get headlines with me. Once again, my name and reputation were big liabilities. And since I was out of the Program, I wouldn't be protected from this bust. I was as scared as I had ever been because I was looking at forty years in the joint (they were going to try me on two counts) and a two million dollar fine. I tried to post the Peruvians' bail by putting my ranch up as collateral. And it was that damn second phone call about the bail when I put my ranch up. I was the only one who had any money. The other guys were petty dealers, moving a couple of kilos here, a couple of kilos there, every week. But my friend, Fernando's cousin, was hooked into one of those big families down there in South America. So now, because I'm communicating with them by phone, and it's tapped, I was raised to the status of drug kingpin. The cops set up an entrapment on that second call. That was my defense, and it was the truth.

KELLY: They had a tape recording of Juan okaying the bail, I guess. Then they scooped Henry up and told me not to go anywhere. Legally they could pick me up for the same thing, but they weren't going to.

Karen didn't get arrested. Karen never got nothing. They targeted Henry because of who Henry is. They wanted a big collar, so midway through the investigation they made him the target instead of the main guy. There was a snitch for the cops, a D.A. informant from Texas. He was big, heavyset, with a pock-marked face . . . yuck. He wasn't one of the Peruvians. He was the one who was setting up the deal, buying two kilos. Henry had told them, "Don't sell it to him because he's with the cops." But nobody listened and they went behind his back and they did it. Sometime during this point, a friend of mine gave me a little pistol because I was so afraid of this ugly Texan. He came looking for Henry once, and when he couldn't find him he came into my room. He stole my marriage papers and all that kind of stuff. Then he started talking to me about what a lovely woman Karen was and what a bitch I was to be doing this to her. He proceeded to attempt to rape me. I reached in to grab my gun, and he grabbed it. For the first time in my life I was that scared—I would've shot somebody. And then he held me down and put a cigarette out on my neck.

Henry was locked up so he never could have tracked this guy down. In fact, when it went up to go to court, we were not allowed to be within so many feet of each other. I didn't have to go into the courtroom if he was in the courtroom. They imported this guy from Texas. It came out in court what this guy did to me—I had pictures from the doctor and all that kind of stuff.

So I moved in with this guy who had a room for rent, while my "husband" Walter was financing me. This was in Redmond, just above Karen. I couldn't go anywhere because I had to be there for court. I devoted myself to sobriety for a very long time. I went to a treatment center and then I went to this sober-living house, and then I went to an out-patient program, all geared toward being able to be with Henry because it had gotten to the point where I wasn't allowed to be with him. But I would visit him. I went to treatment in Everett where he was being held and got into a sober-living house that was just two blocks away. I could look out and see his window. I would spend my days out in the parking lot, waving at him, showing him a little leg. And on the weekends I would get a hotel room right there and me and my kids would sit in the window and wave to him. On his birthday we'd go into the parking lot with a banner and a cake and sing "Happy Birthday!"

I went to visit him, but it was behind glass. When he was in Federal prison, we used to barbecue and all kinds of stuff, but not in county jail. I went in there one time with just a little teddy on under a big coat and told him to sit down and whipped off my coat. He was getting frustrated. And he got so mad that he made me go home. Eventually, a judge denied me access to California altogether.

I moved into this sober-living place for about four months. And then I moved into this mansion—you just had to be a sober person to live in it, and I got a job, and that's when I started . . . what happened from there was I devoted my time to getting legal papers from counselors and things like that stating that I was sober and clean and that they and I felt I would be a good influence on Henry.

I was still married to Walter for a few years, but I worked it out with him. He was a great guy. He was literally a missionary in the Mormon Church. He gave me credit cards, cars—two or three cars—he always gave me money. He would come and visit me. We've sort of lost touch. I think he threw in the towel because he was having problems with his kids getting their residency. This man worked hard, starting out as a janitor, then he owned his own company. My name was on it—it was because of my name that he got a lot of it. He opened a detail paint shop, played in a band. He did really, really well. I stayed married to him for an extra year-and-a-half to help get his kids permission to stay. But it wasn't working and it was just too difficult, so he was already thinking of going back. The last time I was in Washington I tried to locate him, but I couldn't.

So I went down to the jail and it was obvious that Henry had not been being honest to Karen or to the Program about me. When I went down there, we legally got to see each other, and once, when he was out with his Program group, we saw each other without permission and they found out about it. I had happened to go to the same meeting. It was a set-up, because they knew Henry and I wanted to see each other. And that's when the treatment center had him taken back to Terminal Island. Karen was called down, and I was asked to leave California. At Terminal Island, Henry had to say, "Oh, I'm so sorry, Karen." I mean, it was always, "I'm so sorry, Karen."

Henry shouldn't have been in prison in the first place. I don't think he should've been. I mean if Henry should've been, I should've been, and Karen should've been. We both knew just as much as he did. The Peruvians got deported and Fernando got time. Henry ran into him at Terminal Island. [Fernando] made some kind of deal. They all made deals, I think. And it's amazing—the amount of coke that was seized and what was actually presented in the courtroom. Amazing. I couldn't believe it. There was, like, two kilos at the house, and when it got to the courtroom there was, like, six ounces. We were talking the real stuff. We were talking the stuff that people would die with if they did it. I went overboard a few times.

I wasn't the target until about midway through the investigation, when they found out who the hell I was. This kind of bust got the DEA headlines. I could not believe what they did to me. After all the cooperation I had given the Feds for the last eight years, I was stunned that they would target me like this—even if the DEA wasn't technically linked to the FBI. They wouldn't give me bail, so I did a year in confinement until the trial came up.

Then the Feds did the craziest thing—they had me sent to Terminal Island to do my time. As for me, I was focused on the word "terminal," since this place was like a death sentence for me because of the Gambinos there. They ran Terminal Island. They were not only associates of Paulie's, but they were still pissed at me for the Billy Batts thing. I had no idea how many of them were now doing time because of my KENRAC testimony. While I was imprisoned in Terminal Island, there were two attempts by associates of Paulie's to whack me. But while I was there, I ran into Michael Franceze, the sports-fixer for the Columbos, and he called Ed McDonald and told him, "Get this guy out of the population, or they're gonna whack him." So they had a tip, thanks to Michael. Ed went berserk, and they moved me out of the cellblock right away. I was able to escape getting locked down in the cellblock, but they locked me down in the prison hospital for a couple of days.

So, thanks to Michael and Ed, they got me out of that death sentence. And then the Bureau of Prisons would not accept me. When I went back to court, the Bureau of Prisons said, "We cannot handle it." They decided it would be easier for everyone if they just got me into a drug program while I waited for the trial.

When it came to trial, I got a severance because I didn't want to be in the same room with that snitch—he had too many ties. I got one of the best drug lawyers, Richard Sherman, to present my case, and he did a great job. Nick Pileggi, Ed McDonald, and other Feds wrote letters on my behalf. The judge, Judge Francis Whalen, was a ballsy, eighty-two-year-old guy, and he saw what was going on. He saw that it was a setup. He gave me a suspended ten-year sentence and one year in a federal "impact house" to clean up. I also was put on a five-year "special parole," meaning I had to submit to drug testing every goddamned week. But I wasn't about to complain. It was better than forty years in the Big House trying to avoid the Luccheses and Gambinos twenty-four hours a day.

So around the spring of 1988, I got sent to a halfway house in Pasadena. It was an impact house which the Feds have a deal with. While I was drying out for the umpteenth time, I heard that they found Paulie dead on the floor of his jail cell in Fort Worth. It was May 6, 1988. He was seventy-three years old. When I heard the news I was sad about it, but I was also relieved—one of the main guys who would have wanted to whack me was gone forever. It was a big weight off of me. Now I had to wait out Jimmy Burke.

KELLY: So I went back up to Washington and moved in with my sister—I got smart. It was just a matter of waiting for Henry to get permission for me to come down. This was before *GoodFellas*. What happened was I had a really good job. I was even offered shares of Microsoft, which I kick myself in the butt for not taking. But I took a leave of absence to come down and help Henry, and then I just stayed.

When Marty was released in 1988, he finally left Karen, and we lived in his brother Joe's big house in Woodland Hills. Joe's wife was getting ready to lose it because they were about to lose the house after Joe got busted for tax evasion. So we were caretaking the house. And then, I became pregnant. And then we moved to Valencia. We still drank, occasionally. I didn't use and didn't drink while I was pregnant. And this is all when all the movie stuff was going on. Our son Justin was born in 1989. I was still calling Henry "Marty" at this time. I called Henry "Marty," up until three years ago. I did that because I always believed that I didn't know Henry Hill and I wasn't going to judge him like that. I knew Martin Todd Lewis. Whenever I'd see Henry start to surface, I would tell him to go back. I'd say, "Henry, get back in there."

I knew who he was all along because my then-husband would tell me about his background. I knew it before I met him. I used to drive him around to all those different girls—twosomes, threesomes, this and that. I used to tell him how disgusting he was. "Ew, you're just disgusting. How do you do that?" And I yelled at him because he was cheating on his wife. But I didn't let it influence me. I just chose to hang in there—it was a denial thing. I didn't care, because Henry was different with me than he was with anybody else. I knew the real, the soft, the gentle, the kind, very romantic, very giving, Marty Lewis. He swept me off my feet. But the way he would look at me, I knew. We were really, really, really good friends. He would try to make a play, but I'd be like, "I don't think so." He had a way with women, a ladies' man.

Henry wasn't divorced, so we couldn't get married. That's when Henry's quickie-wife Sherry Anders popped up all of a sudden. This was the first time it was laid on me that he had another wife. She probably heard he had a book and film deal, so she popped up for a piece of the money. He got out of prison, and she showed up and sued him.

SHERRY: When I finally realized Marty would never show up, I went to court without him to get the divorce in 1989. Of course, bigamy was a felony, but because he was protected, he only got his wrist slapped. I had wanted to get some money, too. Marty had gone through all of my savings. He went through thousands. The gal from the bank said she had never seen anyone go through the cash machine as much as he did. So I just wanted to be reimbursed for what he had taken from my checking account. When he left, my son and I had to move in with my mom and dad. I was so sure that I was going to be reimbursed because we had the proof of the bigamy right there on paper. But I had no idea how well-protected he was.

In February 2003, he called me to have lunch with him—I thought he was dead. I thought maybe Paulie got out of jail and whacked him. I said, "Hey, you owe me some attorney fees." Needless to say, I never got the money back.

Sherry claimed that she didn't know I was married, when, in fact, she used to come to my house and cut my hair. She would come to my house in a full-on mink coat, naked underneath. Anyway, we had a big court case. I had some money from *Wiseguy*, and I was in pretty good shape at the time. Sherry tried to tell this judge that she didn't know I was married and this other lunacy. I never even went to court. Karen went and testified on my behalf. As far as me spending Sherry's money goes, what happened was Sherry wanted to build a house on property she had in Fall City. She had illusions of grandeur. I spent over $27,000 getting the property cleared and having a foundation put in over a three-month period. At the trial, all Sherry's friends testified and said that I hired everybody and paid them for their work. The judge was so pissed off at Sherry that he threw her out of the courtroom and made her pay for my attorney. He knew what it was. I had a pretty good attorney, so the bill came to about $20,000. But it didn't cost me anything; she wound up paying for my attorney. Karen said that this broad was full of shit. She knew I was married, and it was a set-up. It was so bizarre: I leave my wife, marry somebody else, and then my real wife is my defense witness. But, you see, Sherry would've taken some of Karen's money, too. And it didn't take her ten years to find me; it took her ten years to find a lawyer who would do it. Everybody knew where I was from 1987 on.

■ ■ ■

By 1989, we were practically adrift, moving around southern California. Kelly had left her family in Washington—her daughters stayed with her ex—and I'd left Karen, the kids, and my Seattle pals. All we had was each other, and we'd just learned that a new little one was growing inside Kelly. We were more isolated than we'd ever been. Of course I looked to food to make us feel at home. And I soon discovered one of the best things about southern California: the sun! Almost any day of the year you can get a tan! It's like a joke to have a weatherman in southern California—every day, it's the same thing; beautiful weather, no clouds in the sky—perfect! You get so you love it when it rains just for the change. But all that sun also means that things are growing all the time—you can get fresh fruits and vegetables year-round. Peaches, apples, tomatoes, basil: there's so much of it, and it's incredibly cheap. There are still growing seasons—even though you can get them almost any time of year, things like artichokes and strawberries are fresher and cheaper during certain months.

We lived in tons of places in southern California. Being near a big city meant there was a better chance of someone spotting me, so the Feds were a lot more cautious and would relocate us at the drop of a hat. We'd lived in Pasadena, Woodland Hills, Alta Dena, Palmdale, Venice, Santa Monica, Valencia—all over the place. We never knew from month to month where we'd be.

CHAPTER FIFTEEN

UNCLE SAM AND THE SON OF SAM

After I was released from the Pasadena halfway house in 1989, Kelly came down to join me and we were broke again, taking turns living with various sponsors from all the treatment programs we had been in. In any event, I was more determined than ever to straighten out my life, if only for my unborn baby's sake.

But as I said, I had no money coming in, except for the occasional handout from Nick or the Feds, who still sent me a check if I helped them on a case. The Feds were paying me because I cooperated on the Sindona investigation, but it wasn't a lot of money. At first they tried to bring me into that case for free; they tried to tie it to my original deal. Those guys were getting paid $80,000 a year, those prosecutors and investigators. "So why the fuck would I hand them the case on a silver platter for free?" That's the way I looked at it. Business was business. Once again, Ed McDonald stood up for me. McDonald knew the lifestyle I led, and he knew that it was hard for me. But most important, he didn't want me to backslide and commit any crimes. McDonald said, "Hey, the guy needs a little help. See what your office can do." When they hesitated he told them, "Listen, if you want this guy not to hold back, then pay him." And they helped. They gave me $5,000. As I said, they promised me I would get a percentage of any money they recovered from the $300 million embezzled from the Franklin National Bank. But it never happened.

To make ends meet, I started chipping away at all the CDs I saved for taxes. I almost got on a plane to see Simels one day because he wouldn't cash a CD in for me. Some of this can be blamed on the fact that my advance for the book was long gone, and my royalties were being held in escrow by New York State because of the Son of Sam law. Back in 1977, this asshole David Berkowitz had clipped six innocent people because he said his dog Sam had told him to. Then, after his conviction, he wanted to get a book deal, and that was like rubbing salt in the wound. So New York passed a law saying that he or any criminal, *whether he was convicted or not*, couldn't make a cent from talking about his crimes—the money had to go to the victims. So my cut was held back since the book came out in 1985. Nick, God bless him, sent me some of his cut whenever I asked.

But I was tired of getting handouts. I had always earned my money since I worked at Paulie's cabstand, so I had a certain amount of pride. As the wiseguys would say, I was "an earner." Now it was four years since the book's release and I know the book had made a ton of money, so I wanted my cut so I could buy some land for Kelly and myself and our about-to-be-born baby.

Then lightning struck again. Nick called to say we'd gotten a green light for the *Wiseguy* movie script, the title of which, as I said, was changed to *GoodFellas* for the movie. Once again, Nick had saved my ass. The truth is, if it hadn't been for Ed McDonald and Nick Pileggi, I'd have been twenty years in the ground already. When I signed on the deal for *GoodFellas*, in 1989, Scorsese sent me a check, two weeks before principal photography, for $480,000. The Feds didn't even know it. They knew about it, but not the amount. Scorsese made sure I got that check privately—that was part of the deal. My lawyer Bob Simels got cock. I screwed him good on that one, and oh, did he get pissed. I also got fifteen percent of the net—money that my great-grandchildren will never see because, thanks to the accounting crooks, the movie is still in the red. Yeah, right. It's the Hollywood floating bottom line. They're so creative, those studio accountants. Even with the videos, DVDs, and TV rights they sold, I haven't seen another penny. Nothing. They're so despicable, those studios. The highest grossing movies are still in the red. They've got the best accountants in the world. What I say is, "I survived the mob. I survived the government. I'll never survive this lunatic town." A little piece of advice for you writers out there: if you're going to go to a studio, fuhgeddaboutit, don't go for that back-end point shit. Take the money up front or fuhgettaboutit. That's Hollywood.

Right in the middle of the movie work, Kelly gave birth to our son, Justin. Having my son was the most wonderful thing of my life. When he was born it was unbelievable. I was there for the birth. I have a much better relationship with him than my father had with me, but as I said, I don't blame my father for that. He was a victim of a lot of circumstances.

Just as we started gearing up to film *GoodFellas*, Jimmy Burke's fearsome daughter Kathy reared her ugly head. She tried to shake down DeNiro for $100 large to give him the right to use the name "Burke." We said, "Fuck her, we'll change the name." That's why the name is Jimmy Conway in the movie. Thank God this happened before they filmed all the Burke scenes. During this whole process, I really came to respect DeNiro. I was never much for celebrity worship, which is like a disease out here, but DeNiro was special. He was so intense about getting Jimmy Burke down right that he had me coaching him all the time. I was getting ten phone calls a day from DeNiro or Scorsese. My own phone bill was $4,000-plus a month, which Scorsese covered. And the calls came at all hours. When Kelly was in delivery, who should call me but Bobby DeNiro. You should have seen it, my girl is giving birth, and while she's yelling I'm trying to coach DeNiro, who's about to shoot a scene where somebody gets whacked. I'm telling Bobby how to pistol-whip a guy's head at the same time my new kid's head is popping out. You could say it ruined the moment.

Now Ray Liotta was a different matter. He didn't want me to influence his take on his performance, so we had little contact until after the film opened. He had his own way of doing things, probably the way he was taught acting or something, and I respect him for that. But Ray's a great guy, a great talent (he recently blew me away in *Narc*), and we remain good friends to this day.

I never went on location because I was still very low-profile at the time. They kept me in the wings. My contributions were all by phone. I didn't even get to go to the premiere; they gave me a private showing at the studio with ten or twelve of my family and friends. Besides, I was again having huge substance abuse problems. When the movie opened I was living on the ranch in Juniper Hills, California, but during the 1990 Academy Awards celebration, Kelly and I were both in treatment centers—she had started up again after Justin's birth. I was at St. John's in Burbank. I watched the Awards show—our film was up for over a half-dozen awards. I laughed when Joe Pesci won Best Supporting Actor for his toned-down (believe it or not) portrayal of Tommy DeSimone. At various other awards ceremonies the movie cleaned up: Best Film, Best Director, Best Actor, Supporting Actress—you name it. And the inspiration for the whole thing was reading about it all at St. John's Treatment Center. Here was this movie about me being this great party guy, and when the movie about me hits, I made none of the parties that go with all that movie business. But the limos came by the center and out came Bob DeNiro and Scorsese, and I had lunch with them. It was nice of them to make that gesture.

But my life in the Mob had made me famous. Kelly and I celebrated. We were flush. We rented a house in Valencia and went to Ventura to buy lots of antiques to furnish it. While we were there, we lunched on a great fish.

■　■　■

That year brought one more big surprise. Another interesting movie premiered, and there was no way on earth I would be invited to this opening: it was the movie by Nick's wife called *My Blue Heaven*. Even if I had been on a week-long coke binge, I couldn't have missed all the similarities to my own life. The lead character in Witness Protection, living in white-bread suburbia, took the new name Todd (I had taken Martin Todd Lewis). The story revolves around the relationship between Todd, terrifically played by Steve Martin, and his case officer, who was constantly bailing him out of trouble (just like me and Ed McDonald). There were constant references to Todd's inability to find good Italian groceries out west, like marinara and arugula (I was forever complaining about this.) But the biggest similarity was when Todd called his case officer to tell him had gotten married to a girl named Shaldene (my quickie wife was Sherry). And just like my real life, the agent tried to tell Todd he had committed bigamy, but Todd begged to differ, since he, like me, had used his new name. I tell you, if I didn't love Nick so much, I'd have sued Nora's ass.

■ ■ ■

The other major event was that my book royalty situation was about to get resolved. Since day one I had wanted to challenge the Son of Sam law, and luckily my publisher, Simon & Schuster, wanted to fight it, too. So we had this big, big, white-shoe legal outfit from Madison Avenue representing me and the publisher. They picked up all the lawyers' fees. The Academy of Acting and also the book publishers all kicked in. So they picked up the majority of the lawyer fees, almost a million dollars for just one case. I never even paid my share of the legal fees. They didn't want my money. By this time the legal crap had gone on for four years. Then just before Christmas 1991, the case was heard by the Supreme Court. I didn't go to the hearing or nothing. These guys are getting $500 an hour—what do I got to go there for? And guess what? We won a unanimous verdict: 8–0! They said the law was unconstitutional because I had never been convicted of anything. You see, I was never even arrested for the crimes that I admitted to. Never mind convicted—I was never even arrested.

Basically the court said it was okay to admit to a crime, thanks to the First Amendment, but if you were never convicted, thanks to the Witness Protection deal, you were free to sell your story. The judges were beautiful. And the publishers were ecstatic because it saved their asses by allowing them to make all kinds of deals with other people who were accused of crimes. Those people would never play along if they weren't going to get paid; same thing with Hollywood. So everybody was happy. Anyway, it was a big landmark case. Every state in the union had to redefine the Son of Sam law after that.

Then the money started rolling in big-time. It was almost as good as the days of the JFK cargo heists. When I finally won in court, I'd get royalty checks that the government would launder and pay me in cash. Sometimes I'd get $30,000 to $60,000 at once! They'd give it to me all in hundreds. Marshal Bob had to drive out to the house with my money. He's making what, sixty grand a year? Here he is handing me his salary four times over (and I'm not paying any taxes on it, either). When he gave it to me, I pulled the same shit I had done with the moron agent in Kentucky when I got my book money: I'd make him count it in front of me. "One . . . two. . . . " And when he finished, I'd make him count it again. "One . . . two. . . . " Looking back, their holding it those past four years was a good thing because I would have pissed it all away as I got it, twenty or thirty thousand at a time.

But I still went through it all, believe it or not. Simels took half of it right off the top. That was my deal with him for representing me all those years for free. Whenever I had gotten low on cash, and I couldn't get any from McDonald or my brother, I'd call Simels up. I'd sell him another two points of my rights for $10,000. Three points for whatever I could scrounge out of the guy. I had promised him twenty-five percent to represent Karen and me in the Nassau

County case, after she had gotten indicted. I put a shitload of it into CDs, to cover my taxes. I was always good with taxes because I knew that's how the Feds nailed so many bosses, not to mention my own brother, who thought they had covered their tracks.

The rest of it went to buy a ranch in Redmond. Also, by that time, I owed treatment centers hundreds of thousands of dollars, and I had to pay them. And I was still using, so a lot of it got pissed away on drugs. So, bottom line, over a half-million dollars went through my hands in a little over a year.

KELLY: When the movie went into production, it was a pretty good time. Everything seemed to be behind Marty for the first time. The rent was paid in advance for a year, the trials were over, and we had a beautiful little house. It was going well. And we were getting the calls every day from Robert DeNiro, and all that kind of stuff.

The next major thing that occurred for us, after all the movie hoopla, was we had to move. Henry got a couple of DUIs. He got two in one day. He got one, got out, came home, had a glass of wine, and was on his way to meet Bob Simels at the Beverly Hills Hotel and got another one. At the same time I had gotten two DUIs a week apart. The treatment center doesn't work until you're ready to have it work. That's the bottom line.

I also had my daughters, ages eleven and eight, from my first marriage down for the summer, and they were taken and my ex-husband had to come down and get them. We had to go through the court system for four months to get Justin back. They were taken because we were drunk, and because we were drunk in front of them. Then we went into treatment and got Justin back right away. That was just the end of the

Valencia place. We moved in with our sponsors and got Justin back. I got my girls back a bit later.

Toward the end, though, there was a call, while Justin was away during that four-month period, that we had to get out of the house. We had to get out of both houses. They called us and said, "It's time to go. You got to go." They had had a leak or something. They got that one on wiretap. That happened a lot. For the first ten years of our relationship, I would dread going over overpasses or anything because I thought somebody was going to shoot me in the back of the head. They were tracking him still, after all those years—the old guys from New York were after him. They weren't dead yet. Some were in prison, but I guess their brothers and their sons were pissed. And Jimmy Burke was still alive, and possibly barking orders from inside prison, for all I knew.

CHAPTER SIXTEEN

SOUTHERN CALIFORNIA

M oving to SoCal after *GoodFellas* changed everything. My marriage to Karen was finally over.
She had filed for divorce in 1990. It was hard,
but the distance made it easier. Kelly and our infant son,
Justin, came down and joined me, and we started our new
life together. We housesat at my brother's luxurious place
in Woodland Hills early in our relationship. The place was
like nothing I'd ever seen—we were relaxing in the Jacuzzi
in the master bedroom and eating outside on the patio.

We were celebrities in our own minds.

The only real drawback was the lack of good Italian food, which remained at the top of my list of necessities. Woodland Hills is located in what's known as "the Valley" and it was a schlep and a half to the nearest Italian deli. So I did my best with whatever was in arm's reach as far as ingredients went. There were a lot of "white folks" in the Valley and around that time, people were getting fed up with the typical foods—salads, Mexican, Chinese, and steakhouses. It was getting unoriginal, and the people in the Valley, as well as in LA, wanted to diversify with ethnic menus; Thai food, Moroccan "cuisine," and sushi bars were popping up as fast as Starbucks. Emeril Legassi "bammed" his way to the spotlight by topping pizzas with ham and goat cheese, fish and caviar. The "new" appetizer in a lot of homes was a few-thousand-year-old invention called "hummus." Screw that. I still needed my *Lobster Fra Diavolo* and *Pasta e Fagioli*.

Soon enough we made the move that millions of reinvented people had made before us—we relocated to Los Angeles. What a change. Los Angeles, the City of Angels. By the time Kelly and I got there, I felt as though I'd been saved by an angel. Considering my past life, I was amazed I had any angels left. LA was way different from anywhere I'd ever lived. It felt like Omaha because it's all spread out. But it's not like Omaha at all. In Omaha you can drive for miles and never see another person, just cows and sky. In LA you can drive forever and you're never out of the city—there's always more buildings, more shops, more people, and on and on.

■ ■ ■

So we were in a city, but it didn't feel like a city. There are only a couple of areas in LA with skyscrapers. Mostly it's one- and two-story buildings. There were tons of little bungalow houses with manicured lawns, and what they call "pod malls," or mini-malls, that have restaurants; Mom & Pop stores, 7-11s, and fast-food places were everywhere. And copy shops! There's a copy shop every couple of blocks. I couldn't figure it; how many copies do they need? Of what? (Scripts, of course.) And the LA *City Paper* contained wall-to-wall display ads for cosmetic surgery. I had never seen a population so unhappy with its appearance. Everybody in LA is into exercise. They're all trying to be younger than they are. It's the culture of "youth or death"—you're young and your skin is stretched tight and you look like you're twenty until you drop. Then people realize you were really ninety-five, although everyone thought you were forty or fifty, or they couldn't figure out what age you were. That is, everyone except the Hispanics, who ride the bus to work to clean or babysit for the youthful aging population. In which case, you look miserable and fifty when you're really only thirty. Back in Queens all we needed for acceptance was a shiny suit, a pinky ring, and a shitload of attitude. These people had it rough out here. If you don't look eighteen years old, you're history. My old world was starting to look good again.

■ ■ ■

Los Angelenos were a whole new breed of folks. The first day there, I saw an eighty-year-old woman in a turquoise jogging outfit. She was walking her Siamese cat on a leash, and the cat looked none too happy about it. At first I thought she was a nut. But she wasn't. I soon realized that a turquoise jogging outfit, something my mother or any woman in Kentucky or Seattle wouldn't have been caught dead in, was the norm. Some even wore baseball caps to complete their outfit. And cats on leashes? Well, I guess they need their exercise, too.

I was still in cahoots here and there with the FBI. There was a short break, but after I settled in LA, they tapped me to help snatch a wiseguy in Philadelphia who I used to know from my acquaintance with Paul Mazzei. The Feds assigned an Italian agent named Gary to link up with me, and after I started contributing, they sent him out more and more. He became the middleman between me and the Feds.

Gary was raised in the Bronx. He had a Bronx tale. I got to know him after a while, and he said when he first made it to LA in the early '80s, good Italian food was scarce. If you wanted spaghetti and meatballs, your cook for the night was Chef Boyardee. Ech. Los Angeles had Reagan's influence written all over it—like a real town from the Old West that coincidentally was the entertainment center of the world. It was sort of obnoxious, especially since so much of the country was just like the city in the '80s. It was like being stuck in limbo, and the "West" hadn't had much of a culinary revolution.

■ ■ ■

Gary and I would go together when the Feds would summon us to set up a "site meeting." The point of it was for me to speak to groups of agents and organized crime task forces about general and specific things. It got to be routine. After our first meeting at a site, we'd hang out for a couple of days, bullshitting and relaxing. We'd go and do whatever we wanted in town. Those FBI guys would just pick out a place to party. It didn't matter if we were in Montana or Wyoming, where the snow was on the ground and they'd ski, or in hot-as-balls Texas where they could golf. I had given skiing a shot in the army—it just wasn't for me. And I'd go bald from golf—either because the games would last forever or boredom would cause me to pull out all my hair. Wherever our site meeting was, I made sure there was a kitchen so I could keep active. I kept to the golden rule of cooking: use whatever you could that was fresh and cheap. In Arizona and Texas, it was beef central—I'd whip up some pan-fried steaks for steak pizzaiola for Gary and me and the agents who weren't hitting golf balls till midnight.

If I had half a brain, my life would have been smooth sailing from here on, what with all the second chances I'd been given. I had long ago figured that I had put the cat with nine lives to shame. But from time to time I would still revert back to my old addictions and bad behavior. That was the case in 1993 when I was arrested for slapping Kelly. I had gone to jail twice for smacking Kelly around. I had also violated parole by being drunk or using drugs, or something stupid.

By now I had gone through all the movie and book money. I was doing a bunch of other penny-ante jobs. I already had ten projects, like book and movie treatments, and so forth. These projects started about a year after *GoodFellas* came out. In all the press commotion, I had a meeting with a producer from *60 Minutes*, who introduced me to Peter Doyle, a screenwriter living in LA. The producer thought maybe we could collaborate on some writing projects. We met for drinks at Trader Vic's, sipping on those rum-based things that come with chunks of pineapple with little umbrellas stuck in them. My friendship with Peter and another very influential local businessman opened doors for me in the movie business—so much so that you wouldn't believe what I have in the works today.

■ ■ ■

Anyway, I found a carriage house apartment in Santa Monica for me and Kelly, and Saint Nick deposited money into my account and we moved in. I had this jerk-off parole officer at this time who'd show up every other day. They got this special high-security parole, and they could come any time, every day if they wanted. I think it's called, "Special Conditions" or "High-Profile." It was me and all the black gangsters—I was the only white guy on it except for the heads of the Aryan brotherhood. Now the parole officer allowed me and Kelly to live together in the apartment because Kelly was on parole also at the time. We're there about six, seven months; I started drinking, Kelly started drinking. We had fallen back off the wagon again when Kelly fell down in the parking lot around the corner from the apartment. She tripped over a speed bump and scratched up her knees and the bottoms of her hands. She came home and I bandaged her up and iced her down.

What happened next was that the parole officer, who was there the day before, came back to the apartment. By the time he got there, we were both drunk, and it was still early in the morning. So they cuffed me up for being drunk. They arrested me as Martin Lewis, aka Henry Hill. Anyway, now they saw Kelly all bandaged up and half-drunk. This parole jerk talked her into pressing charges against me for assault, again. Now there was a flight of concrete stairs going to the carriage house so he said, "What'd he do, push you down the stairs? Huh? Huh? Huh?" Anyway, they coerced her into giving them a statement because she was on parole and drunk. She was scared they were going to violate her rights. So she said anything they wanted her to say, and she gave a statement on tape recorder.

The cops came the next day and they told me I was being charged with a third assault on Kelly. I had figured I was in there just for being drunk, for a ninety-day dry-out. All of a sudden I was facing twenty years hard time. I asked the cop, "For what? What are you talking about, assault? What are you crazy?" He said, "Fuck you. You'll go to prison for the rest of your life." Here I was locked down, slammed down in Los Angeles. Now I'm fighting for my life. I can't believe this. They wouldn't even consider bail—when you're on parole and you violate it, you can't get out. Ten million, and you still can't get out. I had to fight a third-time assault, which meant three strikes and you're out, so I hired a lawyer for $20,000. Next I called up Scott, my local FBI friend. I couldn't believe what was happening.

Kelly sobered up the next day and we talked every twenty minutes on the phone. She said, "I don't remember what I said to them." I said, "They're charging me with my third assault on you." Then she gave a statement to the FBI and called the parole officer. "He didn't hit me," she said. "I fell down in a parking lot. We've got an investigator. We got witnesses." Anyway, push came to shove, back and forth between the lawyers and postponements, and I did eight or nine months for nothing. They wanted to give me a seven-year plea. My lawyer and soon-to-be federal prosecutor, Jim Henderson, knew the judge, a little black lady. Anyway, we made a deal. But I had to plea to some kind of stupid shit. I could've gone to bat and went to trial and gambled. I probably would have won—the FBI was in court every other time to bail me out. I had the LAPD in court before; I had the sheriffs in court. But this time I didn't feel like fighting. I think part of me knew I should go in the joint to dry out. So I went in again, and Kelly sobered up, and went to another treatment center right from there.

I'll be the first to admit that I've deserved the joint before—many times. But this last bust I didn't deserve. That guy just had a hard-on for me. He knew who I was. He got Henry Hill and he tried to get him good. He finally believed me in the end and wound up being my parole officer again for a minute before I got rid of him. But at first he actually believed that I beat Kelly up again. If you looked at my record, you would believe it, too. And seeing the two of us drunk, the way we acted, you could believe it.

I couldn't blame the guy, and we became friends after that; I was sober for about a year-and-a-half.

So now I was doing short time on this domestic thing, and right away I hooked up with the other busted Jews. In prison, the Jews are really tight, holding services every Friday and bagels and lox on Saturdays. We stuck together. I ran the Kosher kitchen in the federal prison. In fact, I started the Kosher kitchen. One thing about prison that most people aren't aware of is that they discriminate against Jews on the inside just like they do on the outside. Everybody messes with the Jews. But they didn't mess with me. There were some pretty tough Jews in prison, and you could make it okay as long as you stuck together. We protected the meek, because they were prey, especially in California. They've got the skinheads and all the anti-Semitic gangs, the same old bull that's been going on for thousands of years. Nothing's changed.

■ ■ ■

To be honest, the '90s are still a huge blur. I was arrested a number of times for drunkenness and domestic fights with Kelly. I had spent so much on drugs, booze, and lawyers over the years that by about 1999, everything was gone, including the ranch. I had nothing. Time to start over from scratch—again. All I can say is thank God for Nick Pileggi. He had me staying in a Santa Monica hotel on his dime. I found a local AA and started attending their seven A.M. meetings every day. By this time I had had enough. I was disgusted with what I had done with my life. I said, "Fuck it. I ain't drinking no more. This is it. Fuck this jail. Fuck this prison shit."

When I got out of the joint in 1999, I went into another halfway house where this woman would come up once a month and counsel us. She was a psychologist named Sable, a former heroin addict from New York who turned her life around. She worked for the foundation that helped support the place. Sable was really cool. She'd always be saying, "Henry, why don't you try something different this time? Maybe you'll stay out of prison." I said, "Leave me alone, I ain't gonna change, but I appreciate what you're trying to do." But she kept after me. She said, "Go over to this place. It's a brand new place, they just moved into this beautiful five-million-dollar building." I said, "Leave me the hell alone." Every month she used to come and try to talk me into it. But I didn't listen to her right away about this rehab place. I said, "I don't want no part of that. I'll be good on my own." Basically, I was trying to do it on my own. I was seeing Kelly at the time, and she was doing well and working.

Now, I was staying clean, but it was getting shakier and shakier every day. I was in and out of rehab and living by myself in this hotel high on Nick's dime, and Kelly was coming to see me—she had her own apartment. But I was trying hard, and attending AA meetings every day. At one meeting, I met and became friends with this tattoo artist named Gromet from Venice Beach. This guy had a purple Mohawk hairstyle, weighed about 200 pounds—built like a brick shithouse—and tattooed and pierced from head to toe. He had just finished doing ninety days in this rehab place—the same place that Sable had been telling me about.

One day Gromet said, "Henry, I got this place that I just got finished with. Why don't you come over there? It's better than the stinking hotel you live in. There's sober people around there. If you stay in your hotel, you're going to be smoking crack and drinking in a couple of weeks." He made a lot of sense to me. Gromet told me that they had just moved from downtown LA to this five-million-dollar gorgeous, two-building place that's better than Betty Ford. I was about a year sober, so I didn't need to go to primary care.

I asked, "Where's this place?"

"It's just a few blocks from here, down on Venice Boulevard."

Anyway, he talked me into taking a ride with him over to this place, so I got in the car with him and went down there. There was a bus stop right there on the corner. "This is pretty convenient," I thought. We hit the place, the old Cabrino Hotel, and I walked into these two beautiful buildings on Venice Boulevard and Helms, which wasn't far from Santa Monica. Not too shabby. I'd heard about this place for ten years. But then they had a little old beat-up building in downtown LA. But the new place turned out to be terrific. It's called Beit T'Shuvah, "The House of Return." It had a hundred people who lived there as in-patients, sixty residents in primary care, forty residents in sober living, and another forty residents in independent living. And there were some people there for five years.

I walked in and met two women who ran this place, Harriet Rossetto and Elaine Breslow. Elaine happens to be one of the richest women in Beverly Hills. Her husband Warren owns a whole marina. Beautiful people. And that's who built the two buildings and set up the whole place, with the Jewish Federation—they don't take state or government money. It's all supported by private donations. And the rabbi and these two broads run the place. The thing about recovery and treatment centers is that usually it's very regimented, but this place is not. They believe in a different kind of sobriety. And it works. Everything's done on an individual basis. They got the best psychiatrists in Beverly Hills, the best doctors. They donate their hours and time there. It's unbelievable. They raise three or four million every year at just one gala at the Beverly Hills Hotel. It's not a treatment center, it's a community.

They told me that they had had just completed this place. They asked me, "Are you Jewish?" I said, "Yeah. I was supposed come down and see you people when I got out but I didn't want to live in a halfway house some place that's fifty-something years old. I just didn't want to go through that stuff again." They said, "No, no. This is a different type of place. There's no set program here. Everybody is an individual and we treat everybody as such." In the recovery field you don't hear that often. With most of these shrinks, it's their way or the highway. Here, the only requirements for me were just to stay sober, sleep there at night, go to a certain number of meetings a week, and attend Shabbat, Friday night Jewish services. If you chose to, in the morning, you could go to Torah study, but that wasn't even mandatory. Normally at these places you've got to make appointments to go see a counselor, or stand outside by his door. But this place is unbelievable, the doors are always open. You can go at any time and talk to any one of them.

So I asked, "How much is it?"

"How much can you afford to pay?"

"I don't know, what do you charge? I've been sober a year."

"We charge eight-hundred for sober living. But whatever you can afford is alright. We'll take you even if you're broke."

The bottom line was they charged anywhere from $5,000 a month to $5 a month. The Jews take care of the Jews there. So they said, "You can rent a room, it's about $600 a month." I was paying like $1,500 a month at the stinking hotel. Here they let you pay when you're able. "When you get work, you pay us." You don't hear about things like this. I paid them the

$600 and started living there.

I had never seen a place like this. Everybody accepted you with open arms. I said to them, "I don't have a normal job. I'm a writer, I guess"—or whatever the hell I thought I was. Gromet didn't tell them I was Henry Hill—from the movie. Eventually, little by little, Gromet must've told a couple of people who I was because people started looking up to me.

They had delicious food at Beit T'Shuvah and I could eat there if I wanted to or I could take my lunch with me. It's an amazing place. I ended up staying there for two years. That's the first time that I stayed clean and sober.

After I'd been there a week, I heard that this rabbi was looking to meet me. Gromet told me, "Don't worry about him. He's a whacko, but he's a rabbi like you've never seen before. He's been to the same places we've been to. He's been to prison."

"A rabbi that's been to prison? What the hell kind of a rabbi is that?"

"He curses, too," said Gromet.

This Rabbi, Mark Borovitz, is now one of the directors and he has got some story, too. At this time, he was fifty or fifty-one years old and actually used to be a Jewish gangster in Cleveland, kiting checks, robbing people blind. He had a couple of used car lots. Typical stuff—he wasn't a Murder, Inc., dude. Actually, he did thirteen years in the joint. When he walked out of prison for the sixth or seventh time, he had to leave Cleveland because the boys chased him out of town. Anyway, he was asked to leave, politely, before they were going to whack him.

So he moved out here but he kept getting arrested even in California. Now, as I said, in California a Jew has got it tough in jail. It's not pretty. But Mark was a big, tough asshole with a loud mouth. So he survived. So he gets to walk out of this California prison on $50,000 bail because his family came to bail him out. But he said, "No, I'm finished with crime. I'm going to do these two or three years," or whatever it was. He decided he didn't want to be bailed out and told his father, "Send in the Torah, and some other Jewish books." He came from a religious family. His father was a rabbi there, and his brother was a rabbi. Anyway, he stayed in a California prison for a couple of years, and read all those books, finding the God of his understanding. He studied the Torah while he was in there and he was going to change his life for the better when he came out. He decided he was going to be a rabbi, which is amazing, because he'd had enough.

He got out and went to this little halfway house down in the shitty part of town—the Jewish halfway house that the Jewish Federation started because there was nothing for Jewish inmates. Well, this little halfway house is a broken-down little shack with the ceiling falling in on Lake Street and El Dorado in downtown LA. And there was this old, old lady, Harriet Rossetto, who used to volunteer to go to the jails and go through all the records of everyone who got arrested. And when she came across a Jewish name she'd circle it. She would send a rabbi in to see him and they would help him if they could; if the guy had no family, this or that, or if he had no lawyer.

After Mark was there a year, he fell in love with Harriett, who is ten years his senior. Now they had this little, broken-down house in downtown LA, but Rabbi Mark is a mover 'n' shaker. Fast forward twelve years, and they got this new place. Mark was still a gangster, but now he's a gangster for God. Anyway, I started going every morning to study the Torah and listen to him. I became very friendly with Rabbi Mark, and it was Rabbi Mark who convinced me that I had a soul.

I didn't have to stay there. Since I wasn't in primary treatment I was able to come and go. Usually it's a three-month, six-month, nine-month, year program—whatever you choose. A lot of people stay there to literally put their pasts behind them, so they're there years before they leave. But I had Kelly, and I had a whole different agenda. And I was older than the average kid there. But my entire circle of friends and family became that place and it still is to this day.

I used to live on the third floor in the second building, which was independent living. I had lived in sober-living for a couple of months and then I went up to independent living, where we had our own kitchen and our own private entrance. It was like a high-class hotel. We'd go downstairs and schmooze with the schmoolies—we called them—the kids that were just coming in. We'd tell them, "Stick around, don't run. This place can help you." You work with the others. That's part of AA. That's part of what keeps you sober, giving it away, because nobody can understand somebody unless they've been through it. I lived there for two years, became part of the place. It gave me a foundation, a support system like I never had before.

I met a lot of really nice people, but some of the men there were nuts, and the women were even nuttier. There were some beautiful women in that place. Three-quarters of the people there have trust funds. All addicts and alcoholics are crazy, but some of these guys had lost hundreds of millions of dollars. The only reason they're there is to get their credit cards back and then they get back into the mansions they got in Beverly Hills or Malibu. So that was who you were dealing with, but I liked them because they were nicer than the other addicts I was used to dealing with.

For the first year or so, Kelly had an apartment right down the street. On and off, I was there about three years. I didn't have a drink or smoke a joint—it was the longest I'd ever stayed sober in my entire life. Going to those meetings was the most remarkable thing I'd ever done. I learned a lot there. I learned that I was a decent person, no matter what I did in the past. I began to believe. It was a huge turning point for me. I still go there often.

CHAPTER SEVENTEEN

HOORAY FOR HOLLYWOOD

The next person who came into my life in a big way was Bob Pick, a fellow patient at the Malibu AA. I had seen him at a couple of meetings there. Then he went out again, on the run, and wound up as a client there. I hooked up with him again in Venice when I saw him all strung out at Beit T'Shuvah. We became friends. Bob used to come to my third-floor room a lot because it was quiet there. He'd come up there for the serenity. Then I started taking him out for coffee. I didn't know who this guy was. I offered him money a couple of times. "You need a couple of bucks?" He never took it, but I always offered. He used to come to my room when I had all these projects I was trying to develop.

Then he got out, and I found out he got back with his wife in Malibu. *A house in Malibu?* And that's all I knew about him. Then I heard that he had something to do with one of the studios and that he had a few dollars. But that was it. Everybody over there had money. It turned out that he owned a lot of the property that the studios are built on. In fact, he owned whole studios. It turned out he was also a lawyer and a former prosecutor, plus he owns a third of Hollywood. His father was one of three of the largest real estate owners in Hollywood. He owns the Sunset Hyatt and banks down by Hollywood and Vine.

At the time, movie producers had found me and were pulling me into all sorts of consultancy deals, options, what have you. By this time, my last major nemesis was gone— Jimmy Burke died in a Buffalo prison of lung cancer on April 13, 1996—so I was feeling more comfortable with the idea of being a public person. A lot of people still think I'm crazy for ever surfacing, and they might end up being right, but I had had enough of living in the shadows. If they get me, they get me.

Anyway, Bob saw me battling every day with these movie people and occasionally getting screwed out of different deals. Every day he'd tell me a little more about himself. So we started to pal around together. One day he told me, "If you had an office where people could come to, they would look at you a lot differently. If you had a production company, they would take you seriously."

"Well, how do I do that?" I asked.

"Get in the car," he said.

Then he set me up with a production office on Wilshire Boulevard. On the surface, this world seems about as far away from the gangster life as you can imagine. But the slime just below the surface is sickening. Wilshire is the hub for Hollywood super agencies, power brokers, and film producers. Now I became one of them, and I can tell you that they have more in common with the con artists of my youth than I ever thought possible. It recently occurred to me that my adventures on Pine Street, in Brooklyn, New York, prepared me nicely for swimming with the sharks on Wilshire. Of course, these guys have better offices than Paulie Vario's crew. We just closed our Wilshire office, but the company is still up and running. It was a bad location, but I went in there every day and worked and worked and worked. And we have some big deals, like on the Boston College fixes, and quite a few others.

■ ■ ■

They say you can't go home again, but I don't have to worry about that since my old life follows me wherever I go, especially here in *Silicone* Valley. Take, for instance, my first "power lunch." Like so much in my life, this happened by accident. I never wanted to be a "producer," unless by that one means producing the right outcome on a college basketball game, or a truckload of swag from Kennedy Airport. But I had some true stories I thought I could option just to pay my bills. Nonetheless, I was roped into attending a meeting at one of the top management agencies in Hollywood by a hustling new producer, whom I'll call Johnny, who had more interest in selling my stories than I did.

So there I was with one of the most powerful movie agents, listening to Johnny soften him up about my exploits in the Federal Witness Protection Program since *Wiseguy* hit in 1985. To my surprise, the agent seemed interested. He immediately phoned one of today's top young actors, a real heartthrob, to let him know he had just the right project for him. After hanging up, the super agent asked Johnny-the-producer if he could speak privately with me for a moment. Great, I think. He's worried I'll have someone clip him if I don't get a deal. I'll never live my reputation down—and just when I'm trying to go straight.

"So, Henry," the agent said when we get out on the smoking deck, "I got this little problem, and I was wondering if you could help me with it."

I soon learned an important lesson. You see, out here guys like me are heroes. I tell you, it's messed up. All the movie people want to shmooze the hoods, and all I want is their money. "Show me the money" was my motto long before *Jerry McGuire* was ever dreamed of. I've learned that ever since the days when Chicago's Johnny Rosselli palled around with Harry Cohn of Columbia Studios, and Bugsy Siegel partied with actor George Raft, the hoods (or former hoods, in my case) are like some prized piece of jewelry you parade around with at a party. To think I could have moved here thirty-five years ago and saved myself a lot of grief. Oh, well. Live and learn.

In any event, I helped out Mr. Super Agent. It seemed his niece was dating a made guy in Vegas, and the whole family was worked up about it. So I made a few calls. Nothing major. The guy was a harmless wannabe, which greatly relieved Mr. Super Agent's family. Bottom line: I got my second movie option after *GoodFellas*. And when I realized that producer Johnny, like most other producers, was nothing more than a fast-talking schlep, I decided anybody could do it, especially a guy who used to make his living as a con man in the big leagues.

As far as making "the Hollywood scene" goes, you might be surprised to know that I don't like to go out at night. When the sun sets, I like to be home. It was always with Kelly. We prefer each other's company to almost anybody else's. But if I do go out, I don't pay—ever. I haven't paid since GoodFellas. came out. I get house charges in every restaurant you can name. I don't need money in this town to live. It is unbelievable. That's the way they treat you in this town if you become a celebrity. It's pretty sick, actually— they treat these otherwise normal people like gods.

A lot of people hear me now on Howard Stern's radio show. I used to listen to him faithfully. In the early '90s he was talking about the movie and quoting it all the time, so I just called in. I met him and Robin and Jackie a bunch of times. I call in every now and then, too. I'm sort of a regular now. The trouble is, I usually call when I've fallen off the wagon and feeling like I want to talk to somebody.

I have made some good celebrity friends, but to me they're just friends. People like Bobby DeNiro, Ray Liotta, Melanie Griffith, Howard Stern, Anthony Hopkins, and a hundred others. I'm still amazed that all these people want to meet me. Some are close friends, but others just want to schmooze. I just want to make money.

■ ■ ■

The bosses still get in touch with me, but only to help them with movie deals. One wiseguy drove up from Palm Springs just to meet me. And the guy was a boss, an underboss. He wanted me to help him with a script he wanted to peddle. I gave him some leads and that was that. Still, a lot of people back east don't even know I live here, which is good. But no matter where I go, people out here recognize me, and it's starting to make me nervous—I still worry what Justin would do if something happened to me. So I'm moving out of state and I'll just commute to LA for all this deal-making bullshit. I'll sell my current house. I know a couple of people who want to buy it, and I don't want the responsibility because I lived hand-to-mouth too long. Everything was cash. People think I got valises buried, but they don't know. That's the way those people lived. First of all, I never thought I'd live to sixty. You never worried about money, it was always available to you.

■ ■ ■

In 2002, my divorce from Karen was finalized. She had put off finalizing it for twelve years—she just couldn't handle the thought of me marrying Kelly. She got half of everything, and she's entitled to it—for a lot of things that go way back and are still too personal to go into. Kelly and I got married a month later on the beach at Malibu at Bob Pick's place. It must have cost him $30,000. It was beautiful, with a big orchestra. But she had waited seventeen years, so she deserved it. I had put it off and told her for years I'd sign half of everything over to her, but I just didn't want to get remarried.

MY LIFE
TODAY

In 2003, I walked my daughter Gina down the aisle. She was a beautiful bride, the happiest girl you've ever seen. Now everyone is cool with me but my miserable in-laws. The last fifteen minutes of the reception they lit into me. First my father-in-law started with me. It was almost over, when he started telling me, "You owe me $3,000!" See, he was a shylock, and he was just doing his thing—collecting. He said, "Tomorrow's my birthday. You should pay me." I said, "How old are you gonna be?" "Eighty-six." I wrote him out a check for $86,000. "Now, I'm closed."

They're pissed because I finally divorced Karen in 2002, and they still want more out of me. Their cash cow is going away. As if they haven't gotten enough already. Number one, my sister-in-law got my $700,000 house for free. She's still got it. I gave my father-in-law a brand new Volvo when I went into the Program in 1980. I left the silk-screening business to my in-laws. But that's just the beginning. After the Estee Lauder score, every one of those jokers got bags of diamonds and shit. At the wedding I was pissed off that none of them gave my daughter any of the nice stones for a wedding gift. She got a nice karat, karat-and-a-half ring, but I had beautiful stones that they could've laid on my daughter. Instead they wore the diamonds to the wedding.

Plus, my mother-in-law took two new cars. I saved my mother-in-law and my sister-in-law from going to prison. They were co-conspirators. Believe me, I had no anger toward any of them. But now they act like lunatics. They want to give me more grief. Well, I took their daughter away so the hatred is there. You can never replace that, I guess. But the money and the jewels and this and that, and the house— they could have done a lot worse. And they're still bitching.

Karen's sister is the only one who doesn't give me any shit because I never went after the house. I have no animosity toward her for the house. She paid for my son's college. And if I'd have sold it back then I'd have just pissed away the money in a week. It was only worth—back then—maybe $150,000. I rebuilt the house from the top down.

■ ■ ■

It was sad to see Karen, poor thing. She's overweight and walks with a cane; she's got pain patches. She's got a business now, a cosmetic company she owns. She gets money from me whenever I get some. Security-wise, she's doing well, living under a new name. She called me up the day after the wedding, crying, "Stay a couple of days." I felt bad for her, but I didn't even go to the house, and she's got a beautiful home. I didn't go to nobody's house.

The kids are fine with me, but, naturally, they're closer to their mother. My sister, Elizabeth, the one who was a nun, left the nunnery after seven years. Now she is the head of the board of education in Queens. We keep in touch.

Besides the face-off with the in-laws, there was other bad news in 2003: my old girlfriend Linda died on February 28, 2003. The poor thing had cancer. I didn't even know she was sick. I had started calling her again because I wanted her to say something for this book, and I kept getting the answering machine. She wasn't picking up. I thought, "What the hell? Are you mad at me?" She wasn't calling back because she was in a big cancer hospital and she didn't want me to know. She died in three weeks. She had gotten married years ago, but it only lasted three months. I was blown away when I found out about her death. It was weirder because her phone was still on and you get her voice on the machine even though she's dead.

People are constantly asking me if I'm afraid that one of Paulie's or Jimmy's kids will come and get me—I'm not that hard to find these days. Believe it or not, even Paulie's family is friendlier to me than the in-laws. I still have some contact with Paulie's grandkids. They all got out of the business, even though they were all starving when the jig was up. Everything fell apart for them: the unions, the Kennedy Airport free lunch, the numbers, the shylocking. Don't get me wrong; they wouldn't invite me to dinner or anything, but they seem to understand what happened and why I had to do what I did back then. If they had wanted to be done with me, they would've done it a long time ago. But they seem to realize how it all got out of hand. And they've moved on. They inherited the classy side of Paulie, for sure.

As crazy as it sounds, there is one person who I'm a little bit worried about and that's Kathy Burke, Jimmy's daughter. In New York she's almost like a made guy now, and she's married to a made guy. But he's doing eighteen years, so they got their own problems. She's mad at me because of all the money I made from the book and movie.

■ ■ ■

The last few years I've been getting into painting a lot. The first time I ever picked up a brush was in a treatment center. They do it for therapy because it makes you use the other half of your brain—not the criminal half. In some ways, I'm a terrible artist. I mean, I can't even draw stick people. I can't. But I love to do watercolor. I can layer it. I guess you could call my stuff conceptual art. I draw targets and I throw ice picks at them until it sticks. Then I take the ice pick and sign it and glue it to the back of the canvas. And I counterfeit, I mean imitate, a lot of shit—if I see something, I can paint it. I did a painting of Kelly near the ocean recently, a watercolor. It looks just like her; she's at the beach with the waves coming in. I usually don't do people, but I took a shot at it and it came out really good.

My friends who frame my posters have a big art gallery in Venice, and occasionally they sell some of my small stuff there. It's just a framing place, but a huge store. The owner is a real nice guy—he loves me to death. I make posters and he laminates them and sells them for me. It's a little spare money. I hope to make some serious money on it this year. I know some of my stuff could fetch $2,500 easy. My name helps. I have another friend, an art dealer, who moved some of my paintings for four, five, or six hundred. I've been offered shows and everything in New York. But now I'm going to do it. I've got a ton of pieces, and I used to give them away. I might get an art Web site and post them there. I enjoy doing it and it relaxes me. It's one of the only things that relaxes me. You start to use the other half of your brain, and you completely forget about all your work and problems. I need outlets to keep me from backsliding.

I even started having fun with acting. Recently I worked on a neat short film by Bryon Schreckengost (produced by me and Bob Pick) called *Snowflakes of Gold*. We plan to enter it in Redford's Sundance Film Festival next year. I also had a role in a film starring the great actor Steven Bauer (of *Traffic* and *Scarface* fame, among others) called *Dave's Poolside Observations*. Usually those things are just for giggles, but I recently acted in a film that gave me nightmares. I was doing a freebie as a favor for students at the LA Film School. My role was that of an addict who gets killed at the end of the story. I had no idea that playing a dead guy would bring back so many bad memories of my past life. In a strange way, I am an emotional guy. That's the kind of experience that sends me into depression again and falling back off the wagon—just like remembering all this stuff to do this book. I tell you, this whole process has been more painful than I imagined. And Kelly sees the effect it has on me.

■ ■ ■

As far as my life with Kelly goes, I have to say that when I'm sober it's bliss, but I take one drink and it becomes hell. It goes from heaven to hell. I can't blame her when she gets mad at me because she's put up with my back-sliding too many times. It tough—she used to be my running partner for seventeen years. I kind of miss that. The co-dependency. And she was a hoot when we used to party together.

My drinking problem is a little better now. First of all, I have such responsibilities today, and I'm taking them on more and more. And with the movie business, I can't be drunk. Because it's not going to work. I'm going to blow great opportunities. Pileggi and his wife told me ten years ago, "Henry, you're a gold mine." But everybody tells me that. All the stupid time I spent in bars and jails for drunk driving and shit, I could've made tens of millions of dollars.

I'm still the most hyper person you've ever seen. From the adrenaline, sometimes I get so much energy it makes me nuts. I drive people crazy. I've been cutting down on caffeine, too. I like caffeine in the morning, but I'm cutting down. When I have too much, you can tell. My guy at Starbucks makes me a blend, half-and-half, because full octane Starbucks can be the death of you, especially those espressos with three shots—frappaccinos. Recently I was in a lot of pain, I couldn't sleep, and the caffeine and adrenaline in my body was making me nuts. I was so hyper, I moved all the shit from my office, all my files and stuff. Kelly thought I was high. She was accusing me of being high on cocaine or speed. That pisses me off even more, when people accuse me.

The other thing people always want to know is what I think about the gangster life I grew up in. Believe me, I have no illusions about that world, and I hope my story turns people away from that life, not toward it. The truth is most of those guys ended up broke in prison, and spending every last cent they made—millions and millions and millions— for lawyers and appeals. So they wound up with nothing anyway. I don't care how much money they made. And they had to work eight days a week to keep it going. Just look at Johnny Dio. He was a business genius who owned Mizraki Foods in Detroit and all those big food plants and dress factories all over the country. He always had these legitimate companies, but they were major companies. He could have had it all if he was totally legit, but he married into the Profacis, of the Queens mob. He first got in trouble because he threw acid in that writer's face, Victor Riesel. So the FBI and the state went after him with two barrels. They never gave up on him, and in 1970 they got him on fraud charges. He was supposed to get out in 1979, but he died a couple months before his release at sixty-five years old. He should have retired to Palm Beach like Joe Kennedy, but he wound up dying in the joint.

There's only one guy who I can think of who really kept any money: Carlo Gambino was the one who got away with it all. He was the real godfather of New York. He died of old age and I don't even think he ever got arrested. Ten thousand guys have tried it and one succeeded. Great odds. That's what it is. And you've got to have a brain. The only guys who succeeded in that business even for a few years were intelligent people. Burke was a fucking genius. Paulie wasn't, he was simple—traditional, old grease ball. But he was a maniac.

If you would talk to the guys, you would think that all of them had respect and all that—it was all bullshit. Even back in the '70s. It didn't matter how tough you were. How much money you could earn was the only qualification. It was like the NBA and the Masters.

Then there are the idiots who thought dealing drugs was the way up. They are the stupidest ones of all. Drugs will either control you for the rest of your life or kill you. Those are the only possibilities. Some choice. I can't count how many guys I've seen die from drugs. As for me, I was lucky, but they still can control me if I get lazy for one second. Recently, when I was in pain for a bad shoulder, I took some painkillers and opened up a huge can of worms. The next thing I knew I was waking up in a hospital with eight different drugs in my system—and I don't remember anything about where I got them. The doctors said to me, "We want your body for science." They don't believe how I've made it this far.

In the end, most of the hoods were jerks. They thought they could never be touched. And if they got touched, they thought they'd have a connection, an official on the take. The lawyers used to bullshit them and take their money. After Apalachin and Bobby Kennedy, you just knew the writing was on the wall, but these wiseguys were too dumb to read it. They were in denial. When they finally nailed Paulie, he must have felt like a complete idiot. All the time he thought he had been getting one over on the Feds by using a phone booth, they had been watching him like a hawk: they had compiled over 50,000 telephoto pictures, 26,000 feet of color film footage, and over a million feet of recording tape.

Joe Kennedy doublecrossed them all. Vario and the old bootleggers remembered Joe Kennedy. When he'd get hot, Paulie used to go on the lam to Florida and California. Then, he'd hop it up with the best of them, the Joe Kennedy types. That's the way it was back then. I remember as a kid at the cabstand, them telling stories of Havana and all the bootleggers who partied with them there. But when some of the bootleggers went legit, they turned on the rest like Paulie. When Joe put his son Bobby in the Justice Department, it was the beginning of the end for all the wiseguys. Although Bobby himself didn't really bag any of the big bosses, I have to give him credit. He got the ball rolling.

■ ■ ■

I still help out the government occasionally. It's not only teaching, which I do once or twice a year. There's Quantico, the FBI training center. They got agents coming from different branches, and they move them around within the

Bureau. They take these paramilitary guys and get them more well-rounded. I sort of help give them crash course in Organized Crime 101. They pay me a little bit. There's a new government program I'm involved with called Citizen's Academy. It's not widespread, but it's growing. They take people like politicians and do a month-long program, becoming like big brothers of the neighborhood, learning about what to keep an eye out for and when to look out for it. It's a one-month course and it culminates with a big dinner. I'm a guest speaker and I tell them what they should keep an eye out for in their area.

■ ■ ■

As I am finishing this book, I have just moved up to the mountains of the great northwest with Kelly and Justin, and enjoy fishing and painting. We live right on a river that you'd swear was the most gorgeous thing on earth, with trout practically jumping into your boat. I am so relieved to be away from all the temptations of Los Angeles. Maybe now I'll have a better chance at sobriety. But I have to be honest; I have a long way to go. I still fall off the wagon from time to time, and it is not pretty. As an addictive person, I know I'll be fighting this monkey for the rest of my life. And to be even more honest, I know that some of this comes from depression. I've done some terrible things in my life, some of which only God and my victims will ever know about. Living with these memories is a punishment that's far worse than being in the joint, believe me. It may not be that way for some hoods with no conscience, but my curse is that I have one. Anyway, enough whining.

So, I plan to visit Hollywood only as needed, because I still have my production company, with scripts coming in every day, six projects in development, and A-list celebrities (and wiseguy bosses from Chicago to Moscow wanting to peddle scripts) ringing my phone off the frigging hook. I'm even helping the kids of the marshals and FBI agents get acting gigs. The movie folks all want to know where I've been since I sent Paulie and fifty other top guys away in the '80s and then fell off the face of the earth: how I survived, whether Paulie's crew came close to hitting me, how *GoodFellas* came to be, and how on earth a Brooklyn hood ended up "doing lunch" in the City of Angels. I tell you, it's been a hell of a journey, and if I hadn't lived it myself, I never would believe it. I survived the Mob. I survived the government. Now I'm trying to survive booze and Hollywood. So there it is, warts and all. I hope you've been entertained for a few hours. The pleasure has been all mine.

Ciao for now.

INDEX

Academy of Acting, 226

Actors, 37, 108, 155, 156, 166, 226, 250, 251. *See also* DeNiro, Robert; Liotta, Ray; Pesci, Joe

Adrienne (sister of Hill, Karen), 111–12, 120

Agnew, Spiro, 74

Agro, Tommy, 60

Air France heist, 6, 50–52

Alcohol, Tobacco and Firearms (ATF), 27, 117–18

Alice (girlfriend of Germaine, Bobby), 108

Alor, Walter, 208, 210, 212, 213

Ambrosoli, Giorgio, 3, 193–94, 196, 197

Anders, Sherry, 3, 168, 170–75, 217–18, 226

Anthony, Val, 66

Apalachin Gangland Convention raid, 23, 260

Arico, Bill, 3, 88–89, 96, 115, 121, 178, 193–94, 200

    Estee Lauder heist and, 108–10

    murder of Ambrosoli, Giorgio, by, 196–97

ATF. *See* Alcohol, Tobacco and Firearms

Atlas, Ralph, 62–63, 76

Bachelors III, 73

Banana Split (horse of Hill, Gina), 144, 162

Basile, Phil, 53, 91, 130, 203

Batts, Billy, 4, 60–63, 89, 100, 195, 214

Bauer, Steven, 257

Bay of Pigs, 42

The Beatles, 46

Beit T'Shuvah ("The House of Return"), 240–45, 247

Berkowitz, David, 222

Bernstein, Carl, 155

Berti, Alberto, 202

"Big Soda," Nick, 76

The Blue Angel, 39

Bonanno family, 74, 85, 190, 194, 195, 196

Borovitz, Rabbi Mark, 3, 242–44

Boston College
 game fixing at, 5, 93–96, 99, 107, 151
 trial concerning, 157–59

Brasco, Donnie, 191

Breslin, Jimmy, 43–44, 154

Breslow, Elaine, 240

Brooks, Bob "Brooksy," 38–39

Brown, Donald (friend of Hill, Henry), 175–76

Brown, Wade, 87

Bruno (participant in murder of DeSimone, Tommy), 99

Bureau of Prisons, 215

Burke, Jimmy "The Gent," 5, 6, 10–11, 16, 19, 21, 27, 28, 29, 39, 40, 49, 52, 54, 59, 60, 75, 76, 88, 94, 97, 99, 105, 122, 124–26, 128, 136–37, 157–58, 169, 190, 191, 193, 215, 224, 229, 255, 259
 airport heists of, 46–48
 arrest of, 103–4
 cigarette scam of, 43
 control of Long Island/Queens by, 54
 death of, 248
 description of, 3–4
 Disney World takeover plans of, 82–83

drug use of, 119

heart of gold of, 44–45

imprisonment in Lewisburg of, 85

job scam trial of, 180–82

killing of Lufthansa crew by, 99–101

Lufthansa heist and, 98–99

murder of Batts, Billy, by, 61–63

murder trial of, 182

removal of bodies from Robert's Lounge by, 102

violent behavior of, 43–44, 123–24

Burke, Kathy, 105, 224, 256

Busch Gardens, 82

Cabrino Hotel, 240

Cafora, Joanna, 101

Cafora, Louis, 101

Capone, Al, 38, 78

Capp, John, 26

Carbone, Steve, 25

Carey, Governor Hugh, 27, 28, 151

Carson City, Nevada, 170

Castellano, Paul, 23, 99

Cennino, Larry, 87

Ciaccio, John, 82

Cincinnati, 141, 148–51, 156

Citizen's Academy, 261

City Paper, 233

Clemy (childhood friend of Hill, Henry), 32

Cohn, Harry, 250

Columbia Restaurant, 82

Columbia Studios, 250

Columbo family, 155, 214

Columbo, Joe, 39

Comfort, Bobby, 108

The Congress hotel, 198

"Conway, Jimmy," 224

The Copa, 32, 39, 61

Corcione, Alex "Bonesey," 61, 73, 75

Corio, Mike, 157–58

Corleone, Vito, 24

Covington, 141, 156

Cuban missile crisis, 42

Cuccia, Enrico, 195

Daily News, 44

D'Amato, Senator Alphonse, 53–54, 70, 181

DEA. *See* Drug Enforcement Agency

Dellacroce, Anielo "O'Neill," 100

DeNiro, Robert, 44, 224, 225, 228, 251

DeSimone, Cookie, 99

DeSimone, Phyllis, 40

DeSimone, Tommy "Two-Gun Tommy," 4, 16, 40, 45, 225

    death of, 99–101

    imprisonment of, 85–86

    murder of Foxy by, 84–85

    as participant in Air France heist, 51–52

Dio (Dioguardi), Johnny, 37, 67, 73, 85–87, 181, 258

Dio (Dioguardi), Tommy, 193

Diplomat Hotel, Florida, 74

District Attorney's offices, 27, 54, 97, 124

Doyle, Peter, 235

Drug Enforcement Agency (DEA), 214

Eaton, Richie, 182

Edwards, Parnell Steven "Stacks," 4, 99, 101, 145

El Toreador's, 172, 174, 210

Elaine's, 109

Elizabeth (sister of Hill, Henry), 255

Embassy Suites, 129, 141

Ephron, Nora, 155–56, 225–26, 258

Estee Lauder heist, 17, 20, 106, 114–15, 178, 254

    description of, 108–10

    disposal of jewels from, 110–15

Eubank, Weeb, 72

Fat Tony, 73

Federal Bureau of Investigation (FBI), 4, 6, 17, 20, 25, 26, 105–6, 158, 179, 197–98, 214, 233, 234, 259, 260–61, 262

Federal Transportation Bureau, 5, 25

Ferrara,Teresa, 101

Films, 39, 44, 100, 108, 140, 144, 155, 156, 166, 174, 178, 224, 250, 257.

    See also The Godfather;

    GoodFellas; My Blue Heaven

Fish, Steve, 111–13

Fisher, Artie, 57

Flash (horse of Hill, Greg), 144, 149

Florida, 25, 42, 102

Fort Bragg, 42

Foxy, 4, 99, 100

    murder of, 84–85

Frail, Len, 167–69, 170

Franceze, Michael, 155, 214–15

Frankel, Max, 202

Franklin National Bank scam, 195–97, 222

Fratianno, Jimmy "The Weasel," 26

Fuggo, Sally, 74

Gallo, Joey, 60, 61

Gambino, Carlo, 38, 45, 60, 259

Gambino family, 23, 39, 47, 54, 60, 73, 85, 89, 100, 190–91, 194, 195, 196, 202, 207, 214, 215

Gambino, Manny, 60, 89

Gary (Italian Fed), 234

Geffken's Bar, 47

Genovese family, 85

Geraldo, 162

Germaine, Bobby, 4, 18, 111, 115–16, 190, 191

Estee Lauder heist and, 108–11

Germaine, Bobby Jr., 121, 124, 125

Gloria (horse trainer), 179–80

The Godfather, 39, 40

GoodFellas, 7, 9, 10, 11, 14, 40, 44, 100, 155, 156, 172, 206, 216, 223, 224, 225, 231, 235, 250, 251, 262

Gotti, John "The Dapper Don/The Teflon Don," 4, 37, 47, 84, 85–86, 120, 158, 172

murder of DeSimone, Tommy, by, 99–101

Gribbs, Carmine, 56, 67, 73

Gromet (tattoo artist), 239–40, 242

Guevara, Ed, 4–5, 20, 25, 26, 118

Hampshire House hotel, 108

The Hamptons, 10, 22, 24–25, 104, 106

Henderson, Jim, 237

Henry Hill Savings & Loan, 52

Hernandez-Leon, Juan Tirso, 208, 210

Hill, Carmella (mother), 29–30

Hill, Gina (daughter), 5, 13, 21, 22, 25, 55, 141, 165–67, 187, 207, 218, 255

departure from Nebraska, 135–37

marriage of, 253, 254

in Witness Protection Program in Kentucky, 144–45, 148

in Witness Protection Program in Nebraska, 129–34

Hill, Greg (son), 5, 13, 21, 22, 25, 55, 141, 165–67, 187, 207, 218, 255

in Cincinnati, 150

departure from Nebraska, 135–37

in Witness Protection Program in Kentucky, 144–45, 148

in Witness Protection Program in Nebraska, 129–34

Hill, Henry

acting roles of, 257

advance from GoodFellas to, 223

advances for Wiseguy to, 175

Air France heist by, 50–52

airport heists of, 46–48

in alcohol treatment center, 237

alcohol use by, 236, 257–58, 261–62

alcoholism of, 12, 168

alias Haines, Peter, of, 106, 131

alias Lewis, Martin Todd, of, 144, 160, 168

army service of, 41–43

arrest for drug dealing of, 211–12

arrests for domestic violence of, 235, 236

arson of Oceanside nightclub by, 130

art by, 256–57

bet collecting of, 33

birth of, 29

breakup with Rotondi, Linda, of, 84

caffeine use by, 258

Catholic upbringing of, 41

childhood of, 29–30

cigarette scam of, 43, 45, 58–59, 128

in Cincinnati, 148–51

circumcision of, 58

as coach for *GoodFellas*, 224

conversion to Judaism of, 58

cooking skills of, 20, 22–23, 42, 131, 146, 161, 178, 234

courtship of Hill, Karen Friedman, by, 56–57

departure from Nebraska, 135–37

Disney World takeover plans by, 81–83

divorce from Hill, Karen Friedman, of, 231, 252, 254

drug dealing of, 10, 74, 91, 95, 121, 175–76, 190–93, 208–9

drug use of, 10, 11, 19–20, 24, 25, 74, 122, 132, 142, 158–59, 160, 180–81, 192–93, 206, 225

DUIs of, 160, 228

dyslexia/ADHD of, 12, 31, 40

early mob days of, 36

early relationship with Hill, Kelly Alor, of, 182–87

eating habits of, 23–24

education in prison of, 86

experiences in Milan of, 198–99, 201

on FBI payroll, 162

fencing stolen goods by, 52–53

fights with Hill, Kelly Alor, by, 238

financing of in-laws by, 253–54

first arrest of, 36

fixing of Boston College basketball games by, 93–96, 99, 107

gambling of, 73–78, 147

gunrunning by, 96–97, 107, 193

with Hill, Kelly Alor, in Monte Rio, 204–7

as Hollywood celebrity, 251–52

Hollywood production company of, 261–62

horse-drawn carriage business of, 148–50, 156

house of, raided by Feds, 117–18

imprisonment of, for extortion, 83–91

income after Son of Sam reversal of, 227–28

at the Independence racetrack, 146–47

jewelry stolen from, 114

and Jews in prison, 238

Laborer's Union, work in, 33

leaving of Hill, Karen Friedman, 206–7

life with Hill, Kelly Alor, today, 257–58

loansharking of, 56

marriage as Lewis, Marty, to Anders, Sherry, by, 170–75

marriage to Hill, Karen Friedman, 57–58

marriage to Hill, Kelly Alor of, 252

narcotics arrest of, 16

numbers racket of, 77–78

in Pasadena halfway house, 215, 221

on ranch in Redmond, 177–79

with Redmond brothers Jim, Bob, and Rich, 168–69

reflections on wiseguy lifestyle by, 258–60

relationship with Rotondi, Linda, of, 66–73

removal of children from, 228–29

robbery of jewelry store by, 115–16

short biography of, 9–11

"site meetings" with FBI of, 234

southern California cities lived in by, 219

start of Anders, Sherry, relationship by, 168, 170, 172

teaching/counseling work of, 11, 260–61

testimony against Burke, Jimmy, by, 103–4

testimony against Sindona, Michele, by, 199, 201–2

testimony at Boston College game fixing trial by, 157–59

testimony at job scam trial of Burke, Jimmy, and Vario, Paulie, 180–82

T-shirt company of, 78–79

U.S. mail truck heists, 48–49

Wilshire Boulevard production office of, 248

Witness Protection Program, entrance into, by, 9, 13–14, 15–21, 93–94, 106, 127–28

Witness Protection Program, exit from, by, 161–62, 175, 179

in Witness Protection Program in Kentucky, 137–49

in Witness Protection Program in Nebraska, 128–34

writing *Wiseguy* with Nick Pileggi, 153–56

Hill, Henry (father), 29–31, 89–90

Hill, Joe (brother), 21, 105, 175–76, 216

Hill, Judy (sister-in-law), 78

Hill, Justin (son), 5, 216, 223–24, 225, 231, 252, 261

Hill, Karen Friedman (wife), 5, 6, 7, 13, 21, 22, 25, 68, 69, 75, 82, 83, 89,

90–91, 98, 104, 106, 109, 111, 113, 118, 120, 121, 124, 165–68, 170–72, 181, 182, 203, 205, 207, 211, 212–14, 216, 218

as caretaker for Middleton, C.P., 177–79

as co-conspirator, 17, 18–19

as cosmetologist, 176–77

courtship by Hill, Henry, of, 56–57

departure from Nebraska of, 135–37

and DeSimone, Tommy, 99, 101

divorce from Hill, Henry, of, 231, 252

drug use of, 208

end of relationship with Hill, Henry, of, 186–87

Fish, Steve, and, 111–13

in home of Anders, Sherry, 174

as horse breeder with Gloria, 179–80

life today of, 254–55

marriage to Hill, Henry, of, 56–57

relationship with Hill, Kelly Alor, of, 208–9

as witness in trial of Anders, Sherry, 218

Witness Protection Program, entrance into by, 17–19

in Witness Protection Program in Kentucky, 141–45, 148

in Witness Protection Program in Nebraska, 129–34

Hill, Kelly Alor (Kelly Norblatt) (wife), 5, 69, 203, 221, 223, 224, 227, 231, 232, 235, 238, 239, 244, 245, 261 in alcohol treatment center, 237

alcohol use by, 236

attempted rape of, 211

daughters Rochelle/Shannon of, 183

drug use of, 225

DUIs of, 228

early relationship with Hill, Henry, of, 182–87

with Hill, Henry, aka Lewis, Marty, 216–19

with Hill, Henry, in Monte Rio, 204–7

marriage to Alor, Walter, by, 208, 210

marriage to Hill, Henry, by, 252

removal of children from, 228–29

statement against Hill, Henry, by, 236

visits to Hill, Henry, in jail of, 212

Hill, Moe (father's stepfather), 90

Holiday Inn, Rockville, 67, 69

Hollywood, 11, 227, 248, 249

accountants in, 223

Idlewyld Airport. *See* Kennedy Airport

Independence, Kentucky, 141, 148, 156

Internal Revenue Service (IRS), 58–59

Island Park, New York, 35

Jewish Federation, 240, 243

JFK. *See* Kennedy Airport

Johnson's Boatyard, 36

Juniper Hills, California, 100, 225

Kennedy Airport, heists/extortion of, 45–48, 107, 154, 182, 204, 249, 255

Kennedy Airport Racketeering trial (KENRAC), 7, 203–4, 214

Kennedy, Bobby, 260

Kennedy, Joe, 259, 260

Kenney, John, 195

Kentucky, 10, 165, 227, 233

departure by Hill family from, 162–63

Korda, Michael, 153–54

Krugman, Marty, 5, 16, 17, 98, 99, 101, 123–24, 145, 193

Kuhn, Rick, 5, 94–96, 159

Laborer's Union, 33

Lanso, Ed, 114

Las Vegas, 65, 97, 250

The Latin Quarter, 39

Legassi, Emeril, 232

Lewisburg Federal Prison, 4, 6, 85, 95, 139, 194, 203

Lexington, Kentucky, 137, 141, 154

Lexington penitentiary, 138–39

LiCastri, Paolo, 101

Liotta, Ray, 224, 251

Long Island, 54, 191

Lopez, Louie, 82–83

Los Angeles, 11, 261

description of, 232–34

Los Angeles film school, 257

Lucchese family, 4, 28, 47, 73, 81, 83, 95, 100, 117, 123, 194, 207, 215

Lucchese FBI squad, 25–26, 27

Lucchese, Gaetano "Tommy," 5, 12, 16, 33, 34, 35, 37, 56, 59, 67, 72, 78, 90–91

imprisonment of, 86–88

murder of Batts, Billy, by, 61–63

Luciano, Lucky, 38

Lucille (sister of Hill, Henry), 161

Lufthansa Heist, 3, 4, 5, 6, 12, 16, 17, 19, 21, 88, 94, 107, 111, 119, 120, 122, 125, 190, 192, 193
    description of, 97–99
    photos shown to Hill's of murdered crew from, 117–20

Mackel, Thomas, 54

Magic Mountain, 100

Malibu Alcoholics Anonymous program, 6

Manhattan, 26, 54, 73, 107, 114

Manhattan Correctional Center (MCC), 17, 84, 122, 200

Mann, Danny, 121–22

Manri, "Joe Buddha," 101

Manzo, Frank "The Wop," 56

Marie (sister of Hill, Henry), 161

Marshal Al. *See* McNeil, Al

Marshall Bob, 166, 227

Maxwell Plum's, 83

Mazzei, Paul, 6, 121, 191, 192, 234
    fixing of Boston College basketball games by, 94–97

MCC. *See* Manhattan Correctional Center

McDonald, Ed, 6, 21, 22, 26, 27, 28, 103–4, 106, 122, 127, 140–41, 151–52, 157–58, 170, 201, 205, 214–15, 222, 223, 226, 227
    debriefing of Hill, Henry, by, 93–98
    placing Hills in Witness Protection, 16–19

McMahon, Robert "Frenchy," 6, 50–51, 101, 190

McNeil, Al, 6, 21, 106, 138–41, 143, 162–63, 166, 198

Miami, 102, 128

Michael's Steakhouse, 66, 67, 72

Microsoft, 168, 216

Middleton, C.P., 6, 177–79

Milan, Italy, 190, 198

Mizraki Foods, in Detroit, 258

Monte Rio, California, 204–7, 208

Monteleone, Tom, 101

Mulligan, Huey, 44

Murder, Incorporated, 29, 33, 37, 243

Mussolini, Benito, 194

Mustache Petes, 35

My Blue Heaven, 155, 225–26

1969 Super Bowl, 73–75

Nalo, Sammy "The Arab," 108–10, 115–17

Namath, Joe, 66, 71–75, 150

Nassau County, 120, 121, 227–28

Nassau County jail, 105, 122

New York, 10, 23, 42, 128, 129, 132, 137, 139, 142, 145, 154, 156, 157, 159, 160, 165, 169, 180, 198, 203, 222, 229, 256

New York Magazine, 153, 154, 173

New York Times, 204

Newman, Al, 85

Norblatt, Kelly. *See* Hill, Kelly Alor

North Carolina, 57, 122, 128, 181

O'Connor, arrest of Sammy Nalo by, 116–17

Oddo, Richie, 118–19

Omaha, Nebraska, 10, 128–34, 155, 232

Otto, Steven, 35

p2 (secret right-wing group), 197, 202

Patriarca family, 87

Paulie (horse of Hill, Kelly Alor), 184

Penny (friend of Hill, Kelly Alor), 183

Penny (horse of Hill, Kelly Alor), 184

Pepe (jeweler), 110–11

Perla, Rocco, 95, 159

Perla, Tony, 94–95, 159

Perry, Rich, 159

Pesci, Joe, 144, 225

Pick, Bob, 6, 247–49, 252, 257

PickHill productions, 6

Pierre Hotel, 114

Pierre Hotel heist, 108

Pileggi, Nicholas, 7, 159, 160, 169, 170–71, 173, 179, 204, 205, 206, 215, 221, 222, 223, 235, 238, 239, 258
   writing *Wiseguy* with Henry Hill, 153–56

Pittsburgh, 6, 95, 96, 117, 121, 191, 192

Pizza Connection, 16, 190, 195

Polici, Sal "Sally Umbatz," 100–101

Pope John Paul I, 195

Profaci family, 259

Purple Gang from Harlem, 190, 191

Q-Motor-Inn, 83

Quantico, 260

Queen City Trolley, 149

Queens, 54, 160, 191, 233, 255

Quivers, Robin, 251

Redmond, Washington, 10, 167, 172, 173, 183, 203, 228

Regency hotel, 108

Rich (friend of Hill, Henry), 180

Riesel, Victor, 259

Riggiero, Angelo, 85

Riker's Island, 59

Robert's Lounge, 43, 47, 82, 193
   arrest of Hill, Henry, at, 82–84
   bodies buried in, 102

Rockville Centre, 20, 95, 113

Ronsisvalle, Luigi, 195

Roosevelt Raceway, 150

Rosado, Casey, 46, 75, 82–83, 91, 110

Rose (girlfriend of Hill, Henry), 141–42, 149–50

Rose, Pete, 150–51

Rosie (girlfriend of Batts, Billy), 61

Rossano, Joey, 105

Rosselli, Johnny, 250

Rossetto, Harriet, 240, 243

Rotondi, Linda, 7, 72, 82, 84, 98, 104–5, 113–14, 120, 142, 159, 170, 255
   relationship with Hill, Henry, of, 66–73

60 Minutes, 235

Sable (psychologist), 238–39

Salerno, Tony, 73

Santos, Jimmy, 52

Savino, John, 105

Schreckengost, Bryon, 257

Scorsese, Martin, 10, 39, 206, 223, 224, 225

Seattle, Washington, 165–67, 169, 170, 175, 179, 198, 206–7, 233

Sepe, Angelo, 88, 101

Sergio-Borgo, Fernando, 210, 214

Shapiro, Dana, 56

Shea Stadium, 73, 74

Sheepshead Bay, 36

Sherman, Richard, 215

Sherwood Diner, 125

Sicilian Rule, 13

Sicily, 23, 190

Siegel, Bugsy, 250

Simels, Bob, 151, 205, 222, 223, 227, 228

Simon & Schuster, 151, 153, 172, 226

Sindona, Michele, 194–202, 198, 222

    Ambrosoli, Giorgio, murder and,
        196–97

    death of, 202

    Franklin National Bank scam and,
        195–97

    laundering of drug money by, 194–95

    Milan trial of, 196–202

    trial of, 196–202

    Vatican Bank money laundering and,
        194–96

Slagel, Jim, 168

Son of Sam law, 204, 222, 226–27

South Ozone Park, 43

Sparks Steak House, 23–24

Sports Illustrated article, 151–52, 156–57,
    160

Spritzer & Fuhrman, 115

St. John's Treatment Center, 225

Stella (sister of Hill, Henry), 161

Stern, Howard, 251

Suffolk County, 104

The Suite, 5, 43, 59–62, 83, 100, 105

Sundance Film Festival, 257

Sunset Hyatt, 248

Suvino, John, 52

Sweeney, Jim, 96, 157, 159

Sweeney, Tom, 26, 118

Tampa, 82

Teeballs, Tommy, 73

Tempo Dance City, 59

Terminal Island, 213–14

The Godfather, 24, 37

Tony Ducks, 56, 67

Trader Vic's, 235

Trafficante, Santo, 82

TransWorld Airlines, 46–47

Treaty for Mutual Assistance on Criminal
    Matters, 196

Trilateral Commission, 205

Tub's, 186

TWA. *See* TransWorld Airlines

U.S. Attorney's Offices, 102, 104, 106,
    131, 151, 158, 159

U.S. Treasury Department, 197

Vaghera Super Prison, 202

Vance, Jack, 7, 148–49, 156, 160, 180

Vancouver, 154, 169

Vario, Lenny, 7, 32, 45, 56, 72, 73, 75, 123,
    181, 193

Vario, Paul Jr., 7, 56, 181

Vario, Paul "Paulie" Sr., 5, 7, 10, 12, 13, 16,
    17, 19, 21, 28, 29, 32, 33, 40, 41, 43, 45,
    47, 53, 56, 59, 60, 61, 73, 75, 79, 81, 89,
    91, 97, 105, 111, 119, 122, 123, 125,
    126, 128, 160, 169, 192, 193, 204, 214,
    217, 223, 255, 256, 259, 260, 262

    cheating of, by Hill, Henry, 49

    control of bookmakers by, 76–77

    control of Brooklyn/Bronx/
        Manhattan/Staten Island by, 54

    death of, 215

    DeSimone, Tommy, murder and,
        99–100

    Disney World takeover plans by,
        82–83

drinking habits of, 39

imprisonment in Lewisburg of,
85–88

job scam trial of, 180–82

as mentor to Hill, Henry, 37–39

possessions of, 34–36

Hill-Rotondi affair and, 69–70

rise to mob boss of, 33–34

Vario, Peter, 7, 66–68, 69, 99, 181, 190, 192

Vario, Phyllis, 39

Vario, Tuddy, 8, 32, 33, 43, 45, 179

Vatican Bank

laundering of drug money through,
194–95

scandals of, 3, 190, 196, 202

Venetucci, Robert, 88–89, 194

Veralynn (roommate of Rotondi, Linda),
66–72

Veterans Administration, 86

Villa Capra, 56–57

Virginia City, Nevada, 170, 173

Washburn Alley, 87

Werner, Lou, 98, 102, 125–26

Whalen, Judge Francis, 215

Wiseguy, 7, 10, 14, 204, 217, 223, 250

writing of, 153–56

Wiseguy lifestyle

boats and, 36

bootlegging in, 34–35

drug dealing in, 259

end results of, 258–60

first impressions of, 31–32

food and, 22–23

get-rich-quick schemes of, 38

women in, 40

Witness Protection Program, Federal. *See*

also Hill, Gina; Hill, Greg; Hill,
Henry; Hill, Karen Friedman

monthly allowance in, 175

operation of, 135–37

rules of, 106, 160–61

Workshop Tavern, 168